WITHDRAWN

The Railroad in American Art

The MIT Press
Cambridge, Massachusetts
London, England

The Railroad in American Art

Representations of Technological Change

Edited by Susan Danly and Leo Marx

This book was set in Bodoni Book and Frutiger
by Graphic Composition, Inc.
and printed and bound by Toppan Printing Company
in Japan.

Library of Congress Cataloging-in-Publication Data

The Railroad in American Art.

Includes index.
1. Railroads in art. 2. Art, American. 3. Art, Modern—
19th century—United States. 4. Art, Modern—20th century—United States. I. Danly, Susan. II. Marx, Leo, 1919–

N8237.8.R3R34 1987   760'.04496251 86–21037
ISBN 0-262-23126-3

Contents

Preface

This book has its origin in an exhibition and symposium, *The Railroad in the American Landscape: 1850–1950*, held at the Wellesley College Museum in April 1981. The range and quality of the paintings, prints, and photographs displayed there surprised many people. To be sure, anyone familiar with American art might have expected to see George Inness's *The Lackawanna Valley* and one or two other well-known works, but few were prepared for what they saw. Gathered in one place were dozens of arresting images of the railroad composed in a variety of media by a remarkably large number of the nation's most gifted artists. The result was as impressive as it was unexpected, and it provoked many intriguing questions: How shall we account for the remarkably strong hold of the railroad image on the imagination of American artists? To what extent did the patronage of railroad companies influence the number, character, and quality of these works? To what degree was the fascination with the railroad attributable to its novelty? its visual properties? its social and economic significance? How did individual artists incorporate the image of the new machine into the established iconographic language of landscape painting? With these and other questions in mind, the editors of the present volume, who organized the Wellesley exhibition, decided to undertake a more thorough exploration of the subject.

The essays fall into two groups. The opening and closing chapters are comprehensive in scope; the others are case studies aimed at providing the reader with a more detailed analysis of the work of individual artists. The introductory essay surveys railroad imagery in paintings, prints, photographs, and book and magazine illustrations produced over the last hundred and fifty years and focuses on the interchange between the fine and popular arts and the way it reveals the shared cultural values—the ideologies—embodied in railroad imagery. For many American artists the image of the railroad expressed the promise and the danger of technology in modern industrial society.

Each of the case studies deals with a specific aspect of railroad imagery in the visual arts. In his essay on Asher B. Durand's painting *Progress*, Kenneth Maddox examines the artist's use of commercial bank note engravings to show the penetration of railroad imagery into the collective consciousness of Americans. In Durand's landscape, the fragility of the wilderness in the face of economic development is expressed by the confrontation between the Native Americans and the railroad. These seemingly small compositional elements loom large in the interpretation of this idealized Hudson River school scene.

George Inness's *The Lackawanna Valley* is perhaps the best known of all railroad landscape paintings of the nineteenth century. Despite much scholarly discussion, it still occupies a somewhat enigmatic place in Inness's career. Nicolai Cikovsky, Jr., examines the commissioning of the painting by the Delaware, Lackawanna, and Western Railroad and its relationship to other Inness landscapes painted along the railroad's route. He demonstrates that the subject of these works, as well as changes in painting style, signaled a new "modern" sensibility for Inness.

Beginning in the 1860s, photography played an increasingly important role in documenting the spread of railroads across the American landscape. Andrew Joseph Russell's album *The Great West Illustrated* was the direct result of railroad patronage of the visual arts, and Susan Danly's essay argues that it exemplifies the merging of the commercial goals of the Union Pacific Railroad with the photographer's aesthetic concerns. Such railroad advertisements greatly enlarged the audience for railroad imagery, and the sheer number and visual force of these photographic images affected other art forms as well.

The architectural work of H. H. Richardson for the Ames family, Boston backers of the Union Pacific Railroad, is well known. In the Ames gatehouse in North Easton, Massachusetts, Richardson demonstrated his consciousness of geological forms by using uncut boulders and bold massing. Less familiar, however, are the specific sources for Richardson's monument to the family's enterprise located on the route of the Union Pacific near Laramie, Wyoming. James O'Gorman's essay on Richardson examines this "man-made mountain" as an expression of the contemporary fascination with geology, spurred by the construction of the transcontinental railroad and its photographic advertisements.

At the turn of the century, as the process of urbanization accelerated, artists became interested in views of the railroad as part of the cityscape rather than of the landscape. In his study of modernist painters, Dominic Ricciotti shows that the urban train, subway, and elevated represented the dynamic force of modern life and were key elements in an ever-changing technological world.

In contrast, Charles Sheeler's Precisionist factoryscapes present a more ordered, static view of the railroad-in-the-landscape. His commitment to photography and advertising art certainly accorded with his positive attitude toward the railroad, a point made clear in Susan Fillin-Yeh's essay on *Rolling Power*, Sheeler's painting of locomotive wheels. Her analysis of *Fortune* magazine's commission and publication of the painting, as well as its relationship to contemporary photography, underscores the dual nature of this memorable image as fine art and as commercial advertisement.

Taken together, the essays in this volume stress the broader social and cultural implications of railroad imagery. For one artist in particular, however, the railroad was a direct expression of deep personal concerns. Throughout his career, Edward Hopper produced railroad images in drawings, prints, and paintings, and Gail Levin shows how an essentially public image penetrated the psyche of the artist and intermingled with his aesthetic vision.

The concluding essay by Leo Marx argues that the unusual resonance of these railroad-in-the-landscape images derives from a multifaceted event (arguably the most important in modern history)—the emergence of a new kind of society whose distinctive form of power is science-based technology. The railroad was one of the decisive innovations of industrial capitalism; and almost immediately after it appeared on the national scene in 1830, it took a firm grip on the imagination of many of the nation's leading artists. Following the iconological model of Erwin Panofsky, Marx suggests that the "something else" behind the manifest subject of the railroad-in-the-landscape was

the profound ambivalence with which American artists contemplated the transformation of a predominantly rural and agricultural society into one that is
predominantly urban and industrial.

Although the essays that follow do not cover all
aspects of this complex subject, they explore many
of the major questions raised by the treatment of the
railroad in the visual arts. American artists recognized this new instrument of power as an embodiment of certain decisive issues in our culture, and
their work remains an invaluable resource in our
continuing effort to come to terms with the hope and
fear surrounding the advance of technology.

Acknowledgments

The varied artistic response to the railroad in American culture demands a wide variety of scholarly approaches. This volume therefore reflects the collaborative efforts of many people. We wish to thank each of the contributors for their work and support. We are most grateful to the Museum and the Department of Art at Wellesley College, where the ideas behind this book first took shape. Eugenia Parry Janis generously shared her knowledge of the history of photography and Ann Gabhart provided the resources of the museum for the exhibition and symposium that preceded this publication. The National Endowment for the Humanities gave additional financial support for those activities.

Kermit Champa and Catherine Zerner of the Department of Art at Brown University and Joel Snyder of the University of Chicago were very supportive of Susan Danly's dissertation research and continued work on A. J. Russell and Alexander Gardner. The staff of the paintings department at the Museum of Fine Arts, Boston, especially Theodore Stebbins and Judith Hoos Fox, lent their curatorial skills and good humor during all phases of this project. Brita Mack at the Huntington Library provided valuable assistance with photographs, as well as her critical assessment of the manuscript. T. J. Clark, Henry May, Michael Smith, G. R. Stange, and Anne Wagner read drafts of Leo Marx's essay, and Debbi Edelstein, our editor, provided the finishing touches. This book would never have been published without the efforts and the constant encouragement of Laurence Cohen.

We would also like to acknowledge the help of numerous institutions who aided in our research and gathering of photographs for illustrations: The Boston Public Library, The Library of Congress, The Maryland Historical Society, The Museum of Modern Art, The National Gallery of Art, Washington, D.C., The New York Public Library, The Union Pacific Historical Museum, The Smithsonian Institution, The Beinecke Rare Book and Manuscript Library, and The Yale University Art Gallery.

Susan Danly and Leo Marx

Introduction

Susan Danly

It is fitting that the first significant appearance of the railroad in American painting of the nineteenth century occurs in the work of Thomas Cole, the founder of American landscape art. Cole had a profoundly ambivalent attitude toward the growth of industry in the United States, and his early attempt to integrate the image of the railroad into a view of his most private retreat in the Catskills suggests the increasing importance of the growth of industry as an iconographic theme. In two paintings of Catskill Creek (figures 1, 2), one done before the arrival of the railroad and the second after, we see the transformation of the forest to domesticated farmland during the late 1830s. An "iron horse" in the middle distance of the 1843 view replaces the wild horses in the 1836 one. In the foreground of the later version the advances of civilization are observed by a figure who surveys a landscape of farms, houses, and fields where there once were wildflowers and forests. Barbara Novak has noted the subtle alterations of the composition in these two works, especially the elimination of trees and the emphasis on horizontality in the later version, which suggest that Cole gradually moved away from idealized toward more realistic landscape imagery during the 1840s.[1] But what is most important for this discussion is that Cole has added the foreground figure with the axe, aligned directly above the train—hallmarks of the changes in the American landscape during this period.

There is little in these two works to suggest that Cole regretted the transformation from wilderness to pastoral. He recognized nature's constant flux and saw that man's constructions could be harmoniously accommodated within the pictorial landscape. In his work of the 1840s, he often depicted a settled landscape, dotted with farm houses, log cabins, and mills—scenes that show man living in unison with nature. In such a world the railroad posed no threat. It was only where, as in the *Course of Empire* series, man-made structures threatened to overwhelm those of nature that Cole suggests the human race has overstepped its bounds.

Cole's introduction of the figure with the axe was readily appropriated as a standard composition element in many other Hudson River school railroad landscapes.[2] In Thomas Doughty's *A View of Swampscott, Massachusetts* (figure 3), a similar figure in the foreground contemplates a panoramic view of the picturesque coastal farms north of Boston. The tiny train in this painting is all but hidden in a grove of trees, yet the viewer's eye is inevitably drawn to it, as the engine forms the apex of the recessional triangle in the center of the composition. Spatially, the

Susan Danly

1
Thomas Cole, *View on the Catskill, Early Autumn,* 1837. Oil on canvas, 39 × 63 in. The Metropolitan Museum of Art. Gift in memory of Jonathan Sturges by his children, 1895.

2
Thomas Cole, *River in the Catskills*, 1843.
Oil on canvas, 28¼ × 41½ in. Museum of
Fine Arts, Boston. M. and M. Karolik
Collection.

3
Thomas Doughty, *A View of Swampscott,
Massachusetts*, 1847. Oil on canvas,
32³/₁₆ × 48¼ in. Worcester Art Museum.

train mediates between the wilderness of the huntsman in the foreground and the cultivated farmland in the distance. Doughty's ability to suggest the compatibility of these two worlds, of nature and technology, surely must have appealed to his patron's aesthetic and commercial sensibilities.

Doughty's painting was purchased by Charles Stetson, a prominent art collector and proprietor of one of New York's leading hotels, Astor House. Stetson's hotel advertised its advantageous rail connections to resort areas, and he was often a guest of the promoter of the Eastern Railroad, depicted in Doughty's painting. The Eastern Railroad was the impetus for the development of Boston's North Shore during the 1840s from an area of small fishing villages into a summer resort area for wealthy urbanites. Describing the picturesque sites along the route of the railroad, the *Boston Times* reported in 1847 that the train "gives a glorious ride of nine miles, with a sea view all the way on one side and groves and highly cultivated farms all about."[3]

The easy coexistence of wilderness, farmland, and railroad in these paintings becomes an overt ideological statement in the work of Asher B. Durand, especially in his painting *Progress* (figure 43). Here the entire history of the development of the East Coast by white settlers unfolds before the eyes of three Native Americans. From their craggy vantage point in the foreground,[4] these Indians observe the "progress" of nineteenth-century transportation from horse-drawn wagon to canal boat to railroad. Although Durand himself often traveled by train in search of picturesque landscapes, he bitterly regretted the advent of the railroad near his own summer residence on the Hudson River.[5]

Other prominent landscape painters had less difficulty assimilating the railroad into their art and daily lives. John Kensett, for example, included a diminutive train, marked by a puff of smoke, in his 1857 painting *Hudson River Scene* (Metropolitan Museum of Art). Like Durand, his work celebrates the wilderness of the Hudson River Valley, but it also recognizes the river as an important locus of commercial activity. Taken together, the substantial railroad investments he made between 1848 and 1872 and the patronage of Charles Gould, treasurer of the Ohio and Mississippi Railroad, who bought several of the artist's works in the 1850s, help to explain Kensett's favorable view of the relationship of the railroad to the landscape.[6]

Kensett was also treated to a promotional tour through what is now West Virginia sponsored by the Baltimore and Ohio Railroad in 1858. The B & O was the first American railroad to promote its commercial interests through the visual arts, and during the 1850s it published illustrated travel guides, organized tours, and publicized the scenic attractions of its route. In the wake of a financial crisis in 1857, the railroad called upon William Prescott Smith, who had organized other tours,[7] to take charge of the "aesthetic and social department" of an artists' excursion, while Charles Gould selected a group of artists, including Kensett, Louis Lang, Louis K. Minot, Thomas P. Rossiter, and James Suydam, to join the tour. These artists were encouraged to examine not only "the magnificent scenery" along the route, but also the "notable productions of human science and labor." Urging American artists to reject "ancient gods of the Mouldy Past," the B & O called for them to concentrate on the achievements of a modern technological society:

Write, paint, sketch and chisel that when, ten and thrice ten, hundreds of years are gone, and when our fires are quenched, our iron bodies heaps of rust, the noble archways that have born us over rivers and mountain gorges shall have crumbled into ruin [perhaps some winged creature from some other sphere] finding a mossy stone with the letters "B.O.R.R." may know they stand for the "Baltimore and Ohio Railroad," the grandest and most renowned work of its age.[8]

To facilitate the mission, the B & O turned a special railroad car into a photography studio so that the travelers could make "the beautiful scenery of the road known to the general public."

An account of the artists' excursion in *Harper's Monthly* noted that this kind of advertising was a truly American phenomenon and was the first instance of a railroad, "the embodiment of utilitarianism," embracing the arts. The author of the article, D. H. Strother, one of the artists on the trip (figure 4), heralded this new relationship:

Latterly, steam and the fine arts have scraped acquaintance, the real and the ideal have smoked pipes together. The iron horse and Pegasus have trotted side by side, puffing in unison, like a well-trained pair. What will be the result of this conjunction Heaven knows. We believe it marks the commencement of a new era of human progress.[9]

His language acknowledges the contradictory cultural meanings attached to the railroad—the coexistence of real and ideal, the material and the ideological. At mid-century, the construction of the American railroads was idealized as a manifestation of the technological "progress" of capitalism. Through patronage of the arts, railroad companies sought to elevate the train's image from that of a utilitarian invention to a symbol of America's potential for economic growth.

The artists compared the wilderness of the Alleghenies to the picturesque landscapes of European

4
David Hunter Strother ("Porte Crayon"), Title page of "Artist's excursion over the Baltimore and Ohio Rail Road," in *Harper's New Monthly Magazine* XIX, 1859. Wood engraving, 6 × 4 in. Wellesley College Library.

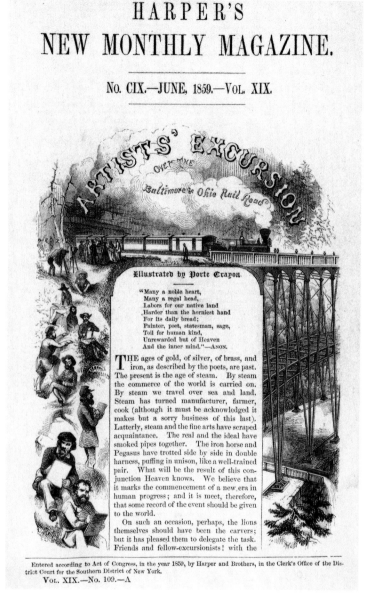

Old Master painters Claude Lorrain, Jacob van
Ruysdael, and Salvator Rosa. At Harper's Ferry Kensett pointed to a particularly picturesque view of the
surrounding mountains; and on a more rugged
stretch of the journey, other artists admired the spectacular vistas afforded from railroad trestles. In a
rare photograph from the tour, an excursionist ges-
tures toward the train on the Tray Run Viaduct over
the Cheat River Gorge (figure 5). One of the more
exhilarating experiences of the trip was a ride on the
cow-catcher in front of the locomotive as the train
passed over the summit of the Alleghenies; the event
was recorded by camera (figure 6) and recounted in
both *Harper's* and *The Crayon*. Clearly delighted by
the entire trip, at the end of their journey the artists
resolved:

That this important link in the great American central route is eminently worthy of the patronage of the
American people, and that the wonderful beauty,
picturesqueness and grandeur of its scenery, as well
as the perfect construction, equipment and management of the railroad, offer attractions to the traveller
not surpassed in the United States. [10]

At a reunion in New York a year later, several artists presented the railroad with oil sketches made on
the excursion. Thomas Prichard Rossiter's painting

5
Anonymous, *Tray Run Viaduct over the
Cheat River,* 1858. Albumen print photo-
graph. The Maryland Historical Society.

7

6
Anonymous, *Beyond Piedmont, near Oakland,* 1858. Albumen print photograph. The Maryland Historical Society.

Opening of the Wilderness (figure 7) was most likely a result of this trip.[11] Some scholars see in it a portent of the negative aspects of the incursion of the railroad into the wilderness. However, in light of the artist's enthusiastic endorsement of the B & O excursion, it seems unlikely that Rossiter intended any criticism. Indeed, the railroad had selected similar machine shops and round houses for a travel guide illustration of Piedmont, West Virginia, a site the guide stated "presented a very neat as well as imposing picture."[12] Furthermore, the dark clouds and dramatically lit sky in the painting are also found in popular prints of the period. Fanny Palmer, in a Currier & Ives colored lithograph *The "Lightning Express" Trains* (figure 8) shows a similar scene, with engines spewing smoke into a luminous nocturnal sky.

The romanticized attitude toward the railroad was also conveyed by the general "machine aesthetic" of the period. Along with names like Lightning, Rocket, and Cyclone, engines were dubbed Ajax, Hercules, Jupiter, and Hannibal—mythological heroes associated with power and speed. Steam engines were brightly decorated with landscape scenes on their headlamps and coal cars (figure 9). In addition, artists often were hired to paint scenes on the interior of passenger coaches to remind travelers of the scenery passed en route.[13]

7
Thomas Prichard Rossiter, *Opening of the Wilderness*, c. 1858. Oil on canvas, 17¾ × 32½ in. Museum of Fine Arts, Boston. M. and M. Karolik Collection.

8
Fanny Frances Palmer, *The "Lightning Express" Trains,* 1863. Colored lithograph, published by Currier & Ives, 17½ × 22⅝ in. Yale University Art Gallery. Mabel Brady Garvan Collection.

9
Jonathan Ord, *Baldwin Locomotive—The
"Tiger,"* c. 1856. Chromolithograph,
21½ × 37 in. The Old Print Shop Inc.,
Kenneth M. Newman.

In 1869 Jasper Cropsey decorated an engine for the Brooks Locomotive Works, "with oil paintings on every spot where they could be placed."[14] The artist associated the picturesque landscape and leisure travel by rail even more directly in his *Mount Chocorua and the Railroad Train, New Hampshire* (Department of the Interior, Washington, D.C.). His association of landscape and railroad extended to his architectural pursuits as well. Cropsey's designs for passenger stations on the Gilbert Avenue Elevated Railroad in New York combined the latest building techniques in cast and wrought iron with decorative details such as finials, peaked roofs, and curvilinear flower motifs—forms drawn from the picturesque aesthetic.

Cropsey also juxtaposed the natural and manmade worlds in one of his best-known paintings, *The Starrucca Viaduct* (figure 10), a view of the most famous bridge on the route of the New York and Erie Railroad. The viaduct appears in Cropsey's sketches of 1853 and continued as an important motif in his work until the end of the century.[15] Referred to as the "Eighth Wonder of the World" by its nineteenth-century admirers, the Starrucca Viaduct, with its gracefully curving arches, recalls the engineering feats of ancient Rome. With the diminutive train and bridge as the central focus of the composition, Cropsey utilizes a standard Hudson River school formula

11

10
Jasper Francis Cropsey, *Starrucca Viaduct,*
Pennsylvania, 1865. Oil on canvas,
22⅜ × 36⅜ in. The Toledo Museum of Art.
Gift of Florence Scott Libbey.

in the overall structure of the painting: *repoussoir* trees at the sides; figures on a rocky outcropping in the foreground; and a placid body of water and mountains in the distance. The railroad thus appears in an idealized setting, suggesting the easy assimilation of new technological forms into the aesthetic mode of the picturesque.

In George Inness's famous *Lackawanna Valley* (figure 11; reproduced in color in figure 58), the image of the train is poised between an idealized pastoral world and the reality of the changing American landscape. The artist has combined a rather formulaic Hudson River school foreground with a more topographical rendering of the growing industrial town of Scranton, Pennsylvania. Although art historians differ in their interpretations of this enigmatic work, clearly the painting points toward the impending transformation of America from a rural to an industrial society. Where Cole had drawn attention to the change from wilderness to pastoral landscape, Inness shows the next step in the nation's development: the countryside in the process of becoming the cityscape. As in Durand's *Progress*, Cole and Inness provide us with a new form of history painting. Rather than presenting a momentous historical event or allegory, these artists selected landscapes rich in ideological import. For most nineteenth-century painters

and their patrons, the changes wrought by the railroad represented the inevitable results of industrial progress. That Inness could view the railroad as compatible with the landscape is stated even more overtly in one of his *Delaware Water Gap* paintings (figure 12), in which cattle graze peacefully beside the tracks and a rainbow arches overhead. In this work the train becomes the symbolic pot of gold.

Photography also played a critical role in the dissemination of railroad imagery in America. Among the earliest landscape views taken with the new negative processes were scenes along the routes of eastern railroads. Indeed, nineteenth-century photographers often drew analogies between their new art form and the railroad as symbols of the new technological age. When Albert Southworth, the famed Boston daguerreotypist, addressed members of the National Photographic Association, he used an elaborate metaphor to compare photography and the railroad:

Observation is the locomotive to be attached to the train of thought and engineered under your own conductorship; the power which turns the revolving wheels must be created from your own store, your freight is to be truth, and knowledge and wisdom.[16]

Both photographers and painters selected picturesque views of the landscape, but painters tended to include the railroad as a small compositional detail,

fully integrated into the overall format of their landscapes, while photographers more often monumentalized railroad structures and emphasized innovative building techniques rather than the natural world.

They were also interested in detailed studies of new industrial forms: suspension bridges, railroad tracks, and steam engines. One of the first bridges to attract the attention of photographers was John Roebling's suspension bridge at Niagara Falls, completed in 1855. A vital link of the New York Central, the bridge connected New York with the growing cities of the Midwest and soon began to rival Niagara Falls as a tourist attraction. As early as 1856 Southworth and Hawes produced both daguerreotype and stereo views of the bridge, and the Langenheim Brothers of Philadelphia included views of the monumental entrance to the bridge in their series *Photographic Views at Home and Abroad*.[17] William England's view taken in 1859 (figure 13) is typical of these early photographic studies. He concentrated on the structural aspects of the bridge, clearly showing the guy wires, suspension cables, and the two-tiered construction that accommodated horse and buggy traffic as well as the train. Although the bridge dominates the foreground in England's photograph,

11
George Inness, *The Lackawanna Valley*, c.
1855. Oil on canvas, 33⅞ × 50¼ in. National Gallery of Art, Washington. Gift of
Mrs. Huttleston Rogers, 1945.

12
George Inness, *Delaware Water Gap,* 1861.
Oil on canvas, 36 × 50⅛ in. The Metropolitan Museum of Art. Morris K. Jessup Fund,
1932.

15

13
William England, *Niagara Suspension Bridge,* 1859. Albumen print photograph, 9½ × 11½ in. The Museum of Modern Art, New York.

the dramatic waterfall is still visible in the distance. Here the new technological sublime literally frames the natural sublime.

In nineteenth-century America a pervasive belief in Manifest Destiny tended to conceal the contradictions between the need for economic growth and an aesthetic desire to preserve the natural landscape. These contradictions are nowhere more apparent than in the paintings, prints, and photographs of the western landscape produced between 1865 and 1900. Images of the railroad as the symbol of economic expansionism and man's technological triumph over nature were produced alongside grandiose landscape paintings that presented the geological monuments of the West as the ultimate expressions of divine creative power.

In 1865 the western territories constituted a vast repository of natural resources waiting to be tapped by industry, science, and the arts. Albert Richardson, a New York *Tribune* correspondent and author of a popular travel book, *Beyond the Mississippi* (figure 14), described the allure of the West:

Its mines, forest and prairies await the capitalist. Its dusky races, earth monuments and ancient cities importune the antiquarian. Its cataracts, canyons and crests woo the painter. Its mountains, minerals and stupendous vegetable productions challenge the naturalist.[18]

14
Thomas Nast, Title page of *Beyond the Mississippi* by Albert D. Richardson, 1867. Wood engraving, 6¼ × 4 in. Wellesley College Library.

Construction of a transcontinental railroad was widely regarded as the key to the development of this potential wealth. Thus images of the railroad in the western landscape can be seen as direct expressions of the ideology of Manifest Destiny. In landscapes of the Hudson River school, the railroad makes a gradual and incidental incursion into a pastoral setting, but in images of the western landscape, the train dramatically divides the undeveloped wilderness from the civilized world. In Fanny Palmer's print *Across the Continent. "Westward the Course of Empire"* (figure 15) and Andrew Melrose's painting *Westward the Star of Empire Takes Its Way* (figure 16), the train is the obvious harbinger of the "progress of Civilization."[19] It cuts a path through a prairie landscape, setting a man-made world on one side of the tracks and nature on the other. Furthermore, in the Melrose painting it is the train that illuminates the natural world, spotlighting the flora and fauna of a fast-disappearing wilderness.

Perhaps the most dramatic confrontation brought about by the incursion of the railroad into the West was between the white settlers and the Native American populations. This is clearly suggested in Palmer's print, where the smoke from the train literally obscures the Indians' view of the wilderness. The displacement of the Indian by the railroad quickly became a major motif in both the visual arts and travel writing about the West. For example, George Pine's book *Beyond the West* of 1871 concluded that the Indian must conform to white culture or be annihilated, and the frontispiece shows an Indian and a white settler standing side by side as a train passes.[20] From 1865 railroad companies were actively involved in the process of treaty negotiations with Indian tribes whose lands were appropriated for railroad rights-of-way. When the government failed to meet its treaty obligations and peaceful negotiations failed, the railroad companies called for military action. Theodore Kaufmann's painting *Railway Train Attacked by Indians* (figure 17) provides a melodramatic image of the Plains Indians' response to the railroad, and numerous reports of such attacks filled the travel literature of the period.[21] Kaufmann uses a low vantage point, receding railway tracks, and the portrait-like rendering of the Indians' faces to enhance the theatricality of his scene.

Curiously, Thomas Nast relied on almost identical compositional elements to satirize the futility of such attacks in a cartoon, "All Hail and Farewell to the Pacific Railway" (figure 18), published in *Harper's Weekly* just two years later. In his cartoon, the Indian bears the features of Wendell Phillips, a radical politician of the period who supported the rights of Native Americans against the railroad companies.

15
Fanny Frances Palmer, *Across the Continent.
"Westward the Course of Empire Takes Its
Way,"* 1868. Colored lithograph, published
by Currier & Ives, 17¾ × 27¼ in. Museum
of the City of New York. Harry T. Peters
Collection.

16
Andrew Melrose, *Westward the Star of Empire Takes Its Way—Near Council Bluffs, Iowa*, c. 1865. Oil on canvas, 25¼ × 46 in. E. W. Judson, New York.

17
Theodore Kaufmann, *Railway Train Attacked by Indians,* 1867. Oil on canvas, 36¼ × 56¼ in. The John F. Eulich Collection, Dallas, Texas.

Critical of the monopolistic practices of the Union Pacific, Phillips lauded such Indian raids:

The telegraph tells us the Indians have begun to tear up the rails, to shoot passengers and conductors of this road. We see great good in this. At last the poor victim has found the vulnerable spot in his tyrant.[22]

Nast's cartoon ridicules such ideas and depicts as useless both Phillips's attempts to prevent railroad monopolies and the Indians' efforts to stop the expansion of the railroad and the accompanying destruction of their hunting grounds and religious sites.

The disastrous impact of the railroad on the indigenous populations of the West was apparent as early as 1867, when J. C. Browne, a prominent Philadelphia photographer, noted:

The rail is driving the [buffalo] rapidly away, for the locomotive roars louder and runs faster than he; and the Indians on the prairies share his disgust, and will go with him to distant feeding grounds, whenever this "warpath" as they call it, is completed.[23]

Browne, like many painters and popular printmakers, felt the urgency of this historical moment because of the changes that were about to overtake what remained of the American wilderness. Landscape photographers were among the first artists to record these changes, and they were hired to do so,

in many instances, by the railroads. Browne's travels in the West were reported in the pages of *The Philadelphia Photographer*, which also carried articles on the railroad photographs of John Carbutt, Charles R. Savage, Alexander Gardner and A. J. Russell. These photographers produced not only small stereographic views, but also large albums, which because of their size and picturesque compositions began to supplant lithography as the medium best suited for travel imagery.

Alexander Gardner's album *Across the Continent on the Kansas Pacific Railroad* included over a hundred views taken on a proposed route along the thirty-fifth parallel from Kansas to California. Built along the flatter terrain and lower mountain passes of New Mexico and Arizona, this route was to compete with the Union Pacific's route through the Rocky Mountains to the north. In order to convince the government and potential investors of the feasibility of this route, Gardner's photographs emphasized the flat landscape, location of rich mineral deposits, and the pacification of the Native American populations.[24]

"ALL HAIL AND FAREWELL TO THE PACIFIC RAILROAD."

18
Thomas Nast, "All Hail and Farewell to the Pacific Railroad," from *Harper's Weekly* XII, July 10, 1869. Wood engraving, 14 × 9⅛ in. Brown University, John Hay Library.

In a photograph of construction workers on the Kansas plains, for example, Gardner showed how easy it was to lay rails on such flat terrain, which required little grading or tunneling (figure 19). A contemporary travel guide describes a similar scene in language that reveals the ideology of Gardner's image:

We found the workmen, with the regularity of machinery, dropping each rail in its place, spiking it down, and seizing another. Behind them, the locomotive, before the tie layers; beyond these the graders; and still further, in the mountain recesses, the engineers. It was civilization pressing forward—the Conquest of Nature moving toward the Pacific.[25]

Gardner's title for this photograph, *Westward the Course of Empire*, clearly demonstrates that he too believed in the expansionist ideology of the period.

Another photograph from this series, *View near Fort Harker* (figure 20), presents a landscape that is formally defined by the presence of the railroad. Tiny human figures dot the flat terrain, giving a sense of perspective, both in a literal and a metaphorical sense. Their scale underscores the vast expanse of the prairie, and yet somehow the horizontal reach of the newly constructed railroad trestle manages to bridge the gap between land and sky, valley and hill.

19
Alexander Gardner, *Westward the Course of Empire, Laying Track 300 Miles West of the Missouri River*, 1867. Albumen print photograph, 5¹⁵⁄₁₆ × 8 in. Boston Public Library, Print Department.

20
Alexander Gardner, *View near Fort Harker*, 1868. Albumen print photograph, 5⅞ × 8 in. Boston Public Library, Print Department.

Gardner, ever conscious of the importance of the railroad, carefully constructs his composition so that the train, silhouetted against the empty sky, divides the rock-strewn scrubland from the cloudless space above. The spareness of his image echoes the barrenness of the plains.

A primary interest in landscape links Gardner's photography with that of Andrew Joseph Russell. Russell's album *The Great West Illustrated* includes several scenes of railroad construction, but his principal subject is the western landscape itself, represented by panoramic vistas, geological forms, and burgeoning towns. His is a landscape clearly positioned within the context of historical change, both natural and man-made. These photographs often reveal interesting visual parallels between the natural and man-made environments. For example, in his view of the Union Pacific at Green River (figure 21), the shape of the monumental rock formation in the distance is echoed in the foundations of a trestle bridge in the foreground. The train in the middle distance provided access to the wilderness and visual analogies to its natural forms. This particular

21
Andrew Joseph Russell, *Temporary and Permanent Bridges and Citadel Rock, Green River,* 1868. Albumen print photograph, 8⅝ × 11½ in. Yale University, Beinecke Rare Book and Manuscript Library.

association of structures at Green River was also noted in one of the most popular travel books of the period, *Picturesque America:*

And all through this region fantastic forms abound everywhere, the architect of nature exhibited in sport. An eastern journalist— a traveller here in the first days of the Pacific Railway—has best enumerated the varied shapes. All about one lie "long troughs, as of departed rivers; long level embankments, as of railroad tracks or endless fortifications."[26]

The landscape painter Thomas Moran was also fascinated by this site. He first discovered it while on a railroad tour he took to make sketches for Appleton's, a leading publisher of travel guides. He included a diminutive train in an early watercolor, *Cliffs, Green River, Utah* (figure 22), and continued to paint watercolors and oil paintings of the Green River cliffs into the twentieth century.[27] Moran also produced views along the route of the Denver and Rio Grande Railroad for Ernst Ingersoll's guide to the Rocky Mountains, *Crest of the Continent*, published in 1885. He was often accompanied on these rail excursions by his long-time friend the photographer William Henry Jackson, and the two men collaborated on the selection of vantage points for their compositions (figures 23, 24).[28]

22
Thomas Moran, *Cliffs, Green River, Utah*, 1872. Watercolor, 6¼ × 12 in. Museum of Fine Arts, Boston. M. and M. Karolik Collection.

23
William Henry Jackson, *Toltec Gorge and Tunnel*, c. 1887. Albumen print photograph, 21³⁄₁₆ × 16³⁄₁₆ in. Boston Public Library, Print Department.

24
Thomas Moran, *Toltec Gorge and Eva Cliff
from the West,* 1892. Watercolor,
12½ × 9⁹⁄₁₆ in. Courtesy of Cooper-Hewitt
Museum, Smithsonian Institution/Art
Resource, New York.

Albert Bierstadt, perhaps the best known of the western landscape painters, shared with Moran and Jackson a keen interest in railroads. During the 1870s as a guest of Collis P. Huntington, a director of the Central Pacific, Bierstadt traveled by rail to the Sierra Nevada, where he sketched the scenery for some of his most dramatic landscapes. In 1871 he participated in a much-publicized tour on the Union Pacific organized for the Grand Duke Alexis of Russia. The high point of this trip was a buffalo hunt from the train, organized by Bierstadt. His complicity in killing buffalo for sport is bound to strike us as ironic, since in his paintings the artist implies it was the Native Americans who were responsible for the demise of this once abundant animal (figure 25). Indians hunted buffalo for sustenance, while the railroads encouraged professional hunters and sportsmen to kill for profit or amusement, and they often left meat to rot beside the tracks (figure 26). As a result, during just a few years in the 1870s almost the entire buffalo population of the prairies was destroyed, and rations of beef were passed out on the reservations. But Bierstadt's romantic fiction of the Indian as hunter endured.

Bierstadt's most direct patronage from the railroad came in 1871, when he was commissioned by Huntington to paint a landscape along the route of the Central Pacific.[29] He chose a view of Donner Lake in the Sierra Nevada, perhaps because the site was so well known in western lore. In 1846 a wagon train was trapped in the mountain pass by an early snowstorm. By the end of the winter, the starving pioneers were reduced to cannibalism, and their gruesome fate was often recounted in railroad travel guides:

As we look down from the beautiful cars, with every want supplied and every wish anticipated upon that historical and picturesque spot in the summer, where those poor immigrants suffered all that humanity could suffer, and died in such a heart-sickening way, we could not release ourselves from the sad impression which this most terrible item in the history of those times made upon the mind.[30]

To avoid a similar fate for its passengers, the Central Pacific had constructed miles of snowsheds, and the long, wooden structures are clearly visible in Bierstadt's view of the pass (figure 27). In a summer scene with the luminous lake in the distance and storm-blasted tree trunks and tall pines in the foreground, Bierstadt has gathered the stock details of romantic landscape painting. The extent to which he idealized the scene can be assessed by a comparison

25
Albert Bierstadt, *The Last of the Buffalo,* 1888. Oil on canvas, 71¼ × 119¼ in. The Corcoran Gallery of Art. Gift of Mrs. Albert Bierstadt, 1909.

27

26
Ernest Griset, "Slaughter of Buffalo on the Kansas Pacific Railroad," from *The Plains of the Great West* by Richard Irving Dodge, 1877. Wood engraving, 4⅜ × 6½ in. Brown University, John Hay Library.

27
Albert Bierstadt, *Donner Lake from the Summit*, 1873. Oil on canvas, 72 × 120 in. The New-York Historical Society, New York City.

29

with a Russell photograph taken just a few years earlier, in which the site appears as a barren, rocky outcropping, with few picturesque trees or verdant slopes (figure 28).

Bierstadt was not the only painter who counted railroad magnates among his important patrons. Thomas Moran sold several watercolors to Jay Cooke, the owner of the Northern Pacific Railroad. One of his most ambitious paintings, *The Mountain of the Holy Cross* of 1875, was purchased by Dr. William A. Bell of the Denver and Rio Grande Railroad. Bell, an amateur photographer and explorer, had served as member of the Kansas Pacific Survey of 1868, as had Alexander Gardner.[31] Presumably he viewed Moran's work as validating the morality of westward expansion, especially since it aggrandized the landscapes along the train's route. Capitalists like Huntington and Bell sponsored such images because they merged the aesthetics of tourism with the ideology of economic expansionism.

While railroads were constructed for commercial purposes, they soon came to rely on tourism for an important source of revenue. Railroad patronage of photographers and painters helped advertise the aesthetic pleasures of travel, and the reproduction of their work in the popular journals of the period brought images of the grandiose scenery of the West

28
Andrew Joseph Russell, *Snow Sheds of the C.P.R.R. and Donner Lake,* 1869. Albumen print photograph, 8⅝ × 11½ in. Yale University, Beinecke Rare Book and Manuscript Library.

to an even larger audience. Although excursions had become commonplace for investors, politicians, and artists during the 1850s and 1860s, it was not until after the Civil War, when the Pullman Palace Car Company introduced the sleeping car, that luxurious accommodations became available to a wider tourist trade.[32] Travelers could experience the sublime landscape they had previously known only in art, and Disturnell's 1872 travel guide *Across the Continent and Around the World* made the aesthetic function of train travel explicit by claiming that the route of the Denver and the Rio Grande "present[ed] a scene of fascination worthy of the pencil of a Bierstadt or a Church."[33] To capitalize on that notion, the railroads advertised the train window as the frame of nature (figure 29).

The aesthetics of train travel were much discussed in the popular journals of the late nineteenth century. The wealthy publisher Frank Leslie gave extensive coverage in his weekly newspaper to a transcontinental rail tour he made in 1877. Leslie and his wife, several friends, and reporters and illustrators for the paper traveled from New York to San Francisco. The journey lasted five months and produced enough material for articles that appeared in *Leslie's Illustrated Newspaper* over the next two years.[34] Illustrated with wood engravings after sketches and photographs made on the tour, the articles described in detail the pleasures of rail travel for the rich: the luxury of the Pullman cars, gourmet food prepared by a private chef, and the attractions of the passing scenery. The excursionists experienced "the grandeur and savage freedom" of the prairies from the observation platform of the railroad car:

The long, parallel lines of smooth shiny rail and the diminishing ranks of telegraph poles, stretching away as we sit on the rear platform, are wonderfully important and suggest features of the scene.[35]

Photography was the principal medium through which the aesthetics of travel developed, both as advertisements and as travelers' personal mementos. As Susan Sontag has noted, the taking and collecting of travel photographs is the tourist's way of "certifying experience,"[36] and they justify the journey and provide an instantaneous memory of its events. Train travel itself becomes an aesthetic experience, a search for picturesque views to record with the camera. At the turn of the century the experience of the photograph as mediator between the real world and the viewer began to influence modernist art. Traveling by train to a Photo-Secession exhibition in Pittsburgh in 1904, an art critic for the influential

29
Rand McNally & Company, *The Great Rock Island Route*, 1889. Chromolithograph, 22¼ × 14½ in. The Henry E. Huntington Library and Art Gallery.

magazine *Camera Work* compared the view from his Pullman car window to the work of contemporary modern photographers:

I pulled up the blind and looked into the night. Ah the deceitfulness of this world! I beheld so many Post and Eickemeyer winter scenes that shivering I fell asleep . . . In the morning, I could hardly trust my eyes when I beheld one "Hand of Man" after another coming toward me down the track. The audacity of the Pennsylvania Railroad to plagiarize this idea. [37]

The "Hand of Man" referred to here is a photograph made by Alfred Stieglitz and published in *Camera Work* in 1902 (figure 30). As editor and publisher of this avant-garde art journal, Stieglitz urged painters and photographers alike to seek out subjects that truly represented a modern urban society. Describing the visual impact of Stieglitz's photograph, the German art critic Ernst Juhl wrote: "Who could have imagined before seeing the 'Hand of Man' that so prosaically realistic a scene as a railroad depot could be invested with so much poetic feeling." [38]

The poetic modernism of Stieglitz's image is Janus-like, combining elements from nineteenth-century railroad images with more modernist formal concerns such as tonalism and abstract compositional structure. His choice of vantage point, focusing on the train as it bears down the track toward the

30
Alfred Stieglitz, *The Hand of Man*, 1902. Photogravure, 6⁵⁄₁₆ × 8½ in. Wellesley College Art Library.

front plane of the image, is not unique. Both William Henry Jackson and William Rau had used similar compositions in their decidedly commercial railroad photographs. Stieglitz, however, evokes a greater poetic mood in his work through photogravure, a printing technique that enhanced the tonal qualities inherent in the smoke-filled train yard.

In an important essay entitled "A Plea for the Picturesqueness of New York," written in 1900, the critic Sadakichi Hartmann underscored the dramatic shift in American art at the beginning of the twentieth century. There was a growing interest in urban subject matter. Picturesqueness was no longer a pictorial quality limited to pastoral scenes; it could also be found in the cityscape. And, according to Hartmann, among the most picturesque urban sites was the elevated railroad:

For many years I have made it my business to find all the various picturesque effects New York is capable of—effects which the eye has not yet got used to, not discovered and applied in painting and literature, but which nevertheless exist. Have you ever watched a dawn on the platform of an elevated railroad station when the first rays of sun lay glittering on the rails? [39]

Hartmann particularly admired Stieglitz's *Hand of Man* for its "feeling of mystery." While he acknowledged that the photographer had manipulated the lighting effects in the foreground, this image re-

mained essentially "a straightforward depiction of the pictorial beauties of life and nature." [40] Commending Stieglitz for his rejection of the painterly excess of the Photo-Secessionists, Hartmann saw this photograph as evidence of a return to the documentary tradition of the nineteenth century. For Hartmann, modernist photography was the result of both new subject and new style: "Scenes of traffic or crowds in the street, in a public building, or on a seashore, dock, canal, bridge and tunnel, steam engines and trolley, will throw up new problems." [41]

That the railroad could generate new formal concerns in painting as well as photography is evident in works by members of the Stieglitz circle. The sensation of speed and distortion of form experienced in train travel are reflected in an early work by Georgia O'Keeffe, *Train at Night in the Desert*, a watercolor she exhibited at Stieglitz's 291 Gallery in 1917 (figure 31). The abstracted landscape experienced while on a swiftly moving train is also apparent in Arthur Dove's *Fields of Grain as Seen from the Train* (figure 32). His association of modernism and the railroad is also suggested in his title for an essay on abstract painting, "The 20th Century Limited or The Train Left Without Them." [42] For Dove, abstract art, like the fast train, was a mark of a modern technological age. Those who dismissed either were out of step with the times.

31
Georgia O'Keefe, *Train at Night in the Desert*, 1916. Watercolor, 12 × 8⅞ in. Collection, The Museum of Modern Art, New York. Acquired with matching funds from the Committee on Drawings and The National Endowment for the Arts.

32
Arthur Dove, *Fields of Grain as Seen from Train*, 1931. Oil on canvas, 24 × 34⅛ in. Albright-Knox Art Gallery, Buffalo, New York. Gift of Seymour H. Knox, 1958.

Images of the train, however, were more prevalent in the work of representational painters in the early decades of the twentieth century. The members of the Ashcan school, who, as Hartmann observed, "believe[d] in the poetical and pictorial significance of the 'Elevated' and the skyscraper,"[43] deliberately sought out scenes of industrial drabness and even ugliness. But their predilection for tonal harmony and rapid, spontaneous brushwork rendered the gray skies, hazy smoke, and grimy snows of the urban landscape as beautiful passages of paint. Although not as concerned with abstraction as the members of the Stieglitz group, these artists shared their fascination with the railroad as a picturesque element in the cityscape.

In George Bellows's *Rain on the River* (figure 33), the drabness of the industrial landscape is belied by an aesthetic of texture and color. The subject was first suggested by Hartmann:

A picture genuinely American in spirit is afforded by Riverside Park. Old towering trees stretch their branches toward the Hudson. Almost touching their trunks the trains on the railroad brush by. On the water, heavily loaded canal boats pass slowly and now and then a white river steamboat glides by majestically, while clouds change the chiaroscuro effects at every gust.[44]

Bellows exploits the pictorial qualities of the billowing white smoke of the railroad and the austere, rain-slicked ledges of Riverside Park. He melds nature and industry together with tonal harmonies and sensuous brushwork that yields a unified painterly surface. Other Ashcan artists selected similar distant and elevated vantage points that obscured the grimier details of urban railroad yards. In *Roundhouses at Highbridge* (figure 34), for example, George Luks transformed a scene of industrial pollution into a wonderfully painted canvas of pink and gray plumes of smoke. The combination of impressionist technique and railroad imagery is perhaps derived from the work of Monet and Pissarro, but contemporary American critics saw these paintings as a commitment to the development of a truly American subject matter.

New York City at night was an especially important subject for American painters. The elevated railroad traversing the darkened city had particular appeal, as Hartmann's evocative description makes clear:

A train passes by, like a fantastic fire-worm from some fantastic fairyland, crawling in mid-air. A little locomotive emits a cloud of smoke, and suddenly the commonplace and yet so mystic scene changes into a tumult of color, red and saffron, changing every moment into an unsteady gray and blue.[45]

While nocturnal railroad scenes were common in nineteenth-century American art, they were set primarily in wilderness landscapes. With the work of John Sloan, the cityscape became the new emblem of modernity. This is particularly true of his depiction of the elevated in *The City from Greenwich Village* (figure 35), a painting he felt represented "the beauty of the older city . . . giving way to the chopped out towers of modern New York."[46] Sloan also incorporated the elevated into several paintings made between 1908 and 1928, in which the bustle of urban street life is framed quite literally by the iron gridwork of the elevated tracks.[47] In Sloan's work people as well as architecture were defined by their relationship to the railroad.

Sloan's busy, animated street scenes suggest the vitality of urban life, but other artists of the period used the railroad to focus on more equivocal aspects of modern life. The feelings of mystery, emptiness, and dislocation evoked in Charles Burchfield's watercolors of train yards convey the sense of alienation so prevalent in modern industrial society. *Gates Down* (figure 36) depicts a mood rather than a specific locale. With a palette of bruised purples, swirls of black smoke, and spots of bright color, Burchfield renders the dynamic forms of a rushing train and the

33
George Bellows, *Rain on the River,* 1908. Oil on canvas, 32³⁄₁₆ × 38³⁄₁₆ in. Museum of Art, Rhode Island School of Design. Jesse Metcalf Fund.

34
George Luks, *Roundhouses at Highbridge,* 1909–10. Oil on canvas, 30³⁄₈ × 36¹⁄₈ in. Munson-Williams-Proctor Institute, Utica, New York.

37

35
John Sloan, *The City from Greenwich Village,* 1922. Oil on canvas, 26 × 33¾ in.
National Gallery of Art, Washington.
Gift of Helen Farr Sloan, 1970.

sounds of a clanging crossing-gate bell. The allure of such industrial subjects drew him from his small Ohio hometown to the freight yards of Buffalo. Deriving unexpected aesthetic pleasure from the smoke and smell of this dirty manufacturing town, Burchfield explained that "the soot-and-smoke blackened surfaces, the coal-dust filmed earth, the gleaming rails, the sturdy, grim men, and even the bitter, acrid odor of the hot, grey-violet smoke was far from disagreeable."[48]

Burchfield's fascination with the industrial environment made his work useful to capitalist promotional interests. Commissioned by *Fortune* magazine in 1930 to illustrate an article entitled "Vanishing Backyards," Burchfield produced a series of watercolors of what has been called the metropolitan corridor, the landscape surrounding urban railroad tracks.[49] Much like Burchfield himself, *Fortune*'s writer expressed perverse satisfaction with this industrial wasteland:

It is smelly, but it is also exuberant and vigorous to strew the country with things worn out and left over. Every garbage dump, every row of ramshackle houses lining the railroad track, is evidence of our boundless wealth. This is space that we do not need.[50]

36
Charles Burchfield, *Gates Down*, 1920.
Gouache and watercolor, 18¹/₁₆ × 23¹⁵/₁₆ in.
Museum of Art, Rhode Island School of
Design. Gift of Mrs. Una Hunt Drage.

Burchfield's interest in urban subjects eventually waned, and in the later part of his career, he had an increasingly subjective, expressionistic vision of nature. It was as if his attempt to resolve the tension between aesthetic beauty and industrial ugliness was no longer feasible.

This same dilemma confronted many other American artists during the 1930s, and they gradually lost interest in the railroad as an element of the picturesque cityscape. During the Depression years, artists could no longer ignore the destructive forces of industrialization. Sprawling factories and railroad yards were increasingly concentrated in urban areas. Small town depots were abandoned, and the empty railroad track became the emblem of modern life—of alienation and loss, as in the haunting works of Edward Hopper.

Photographers hired by the Farm Security Administration to document the social upheaval of the Depression often used the metaphor of the empty track to suggest the passage of time. Walker Evans's photograph of the depot in Edwards, Mississippi, graphically demonstrates the demise of small, rural towns (figure 37). Evans realized that the railroad itself was fast becoming part of America's past. In a series of portfolios published by *Fortune*, he traced the slow decline of the steam engine. With such

37
Walker Evans, *Edwards, Mississippi*, 1936.
Silver print photograph, 7¹⁵⁄₁₆ × 9¹⁵⁄₁₆ in.
Library of Congress. Estate of Walker Evans.

40

titles as *Before They Disappear, The Last of Railroad Steam,* and *People and Places in Trouble,* Evans drew attention to the outmoded technology and transformed the railroad from an emblem of progress to one of decline. Evans's nostalgia is most evident in his portfolio *Along the Right of Way* from 1950. In a sequence of landscape views taken from a moving train, Evans hoped to "flush the mind with images of enchantment that a child feels with train trips."[51] The photographer's attempt to recapture the aesthetic pleasures of train travel had become a journey in America's outgrown past. Modern factories are set beside abandoned mills and empty boxcars are juxtaposed with working-class clapboard houses.

America's foremost history painter at mid-century, Thomas Hart Benton, drew on traditional railroad imagery even more consciously. He described the importance of the railroad in American life:

For the nomadic urges of our western people, the prime symbol of the adventurous life has for years been the railroad train. . . . With the coming of the automobile the railroad is losing its high place, but during my boyhood it was the prime space cutter and therefore the great symbol of change.[52]

In his mural decoration for the Indiana pavilion at the Century of Progress Exposition of 1933, the railroad appears as the symbol of industrial progress and western expansionism in the past but, significantly, not in the present. Benton had a profound distrust of his own "machine age" and sought a return to the values of a pastoral life:

America had been made by the "operations of people" who as civilization and technology advanced became increasingly separated from the benefits thereof. I would go on in my history of the frontiers, where the people controlled the operations, to the labor lines of the machine age where they decidedly do not.[53]

Benton's nostalgic view of the railroad is best seen in his painting and print *Wreck of the Ol '97* (figure 38). Drawing on the subject of a traditional folk song, Benton evokes the thrill of speed and the sensation of sounds uniquely associated with the railroad. But it is an old-fashioned steam engine, not a modern streamlined train, that fueled Benton's imagination:

To this day I cannot face an oncoming steam train without having itchy thrills run up and down my backbone. The automobile and the airplane have not been able to take away from its old moving power as an assaulter of space and time. Its whistle is the most nostalgic sound to my ear.[54]

Benton's nostalgia came just at the moment when the streamlining movement in industrial design seemed to promise new life to the railroad. To revitalize a sagging passenger business, in the 1930s railroad companies hired a number of prominent designers to glamorize train travel as a modern, leisure activity.[55] While some trains were rebuilt entirely with new diesel engines, others merely received a sleek aluminum shell over their older, less efficient steam-driven engines. These refurbished trains were meant to suggest aerodynamic efficiency and futuristic elegance. Henry Dreyfuss's designs for the famous Twentieth Century Limited encompassed the exterior of the engine as well as the furniture, glassware, and dishes (figure 39). In 1939 *Design* magazine lauded Dreyfuss's new train as the "start (of) another era of progress in railroad transportation," thus reiterating the nineteenth-century ideology of industrial progress.[56]

The American artist who perhaps most eloquently expressed this continuing belief in industrial progress was Charles Sheeler. His painting *Rolling Power* (figure 109) is the artist's most direct link with the streamlining movement, but his sense of the pervasiveness of an industrial aesthetic is represented more fully in the factoryscapes he painted for the Ford Motor Company at their River Rouge Plant. In 1927, as part of an advertising campaign initiated by Edsel Ford, Sheeler was hired to photograph Ford's

38
Thomas Hart Benton, *Wreck of the Ol' 97*,
1944. Lithograph, 10¼ × 15 in. The New
Britain Museum of American Art. William
Brooks Fund.

huge manufacturing complex just outside Detroit.[57] These photographs in turn inspired three of Sheeler's best-known paintings: *American Landscape* (1930; figure 107), *Classic Landscape* (1931; figure 118) and *City Interior* (1936; Worcester Art Museum). In each of these Precisionist scenes, the artist stresses the sharp geometry and abstract patternings of a man-made environment. The railroad figures as the central motif in each work, around which the spatial organization and composition are ordered. In *Classic Landscape*, for example, the track serves as a perspectival device in a way that is reminiscent of the photographs of A. J. Russell or William Henry Jackson.

The use of the railroad as an abstract shape resonant with meaning is still a striking aspect of American art, even in the post–World War II era of modernism. For Franz Kline especially, the train remained an image of dynamic force. In his youth, he loved the sights and sounds of the railroad, and his landscape paintings of the 1940s were scenes of the Pennsylvania countryside dotted with railroad bridges and trains. Kline was particularly attracted to the site of the Delaware Water Gap, where George Inness had painted railroad landscapes almost a century before. Two of Kline's most important Abstract

39
Henry Dreyfuss, *Observation Lounge* (Twentieth Century Limited), 1938. Gouache, 15 × 20 in. Albany Institute of History and Art.

Expressionist works of the 1950s were named after famous engines, *Chief* (figure 40) and *Cardinal*. Kline returned to train imagery for the title of a late work, *Caboose* (1962). Through these titles, he gave contextual definition to his powerful, broad strokes of black paint and the monumentality of his abstract shapes.

Modern abstract sculptors have also drawn inspiration from train travel. David Smith's *Hudson River Landscape* (figure 41) resulted from a number of trips he took along the banks of the Hudson River. It was the sensation of train travel that defined for him the meaning of the piece:

[A] recent work called "Hudson River Landscape" started from drawings made on a train between Albany and Poughkeepsie, a synthesis of drawings made from ten trips going and coming over this seventy-five mile stretch. . . . Your response may not travel down the Hudson, but it may travel on any river or on a higher plane. [58]

At first glance, the abstract forms of the minimalist sculptor Carl Andre bear no obvious relation to the railroad. But Andre, who at one time was a brakeman and conductor on the Pennsylvania Railroad, acknowledged that the emphasis on horizontality and recession in his work derived from his perception of railroad tracks viewed from the train. [59]

40
Franz Kline, *Chief*, 1950. Oil on canvas,
58⅜ × 61½ in. Collection,
The Museum of Modern Art, New York.
Gift of Mr. and Mrs. David M. Solinger.

41
David Smith, *Hudson River Landscape*,
1951. Welded steel, 49½ × 75 × 16¾ in.
Whitney Museum of American Art. Pur-
chase. Acq. 54.14. Photo: Geoffrey
Clements.

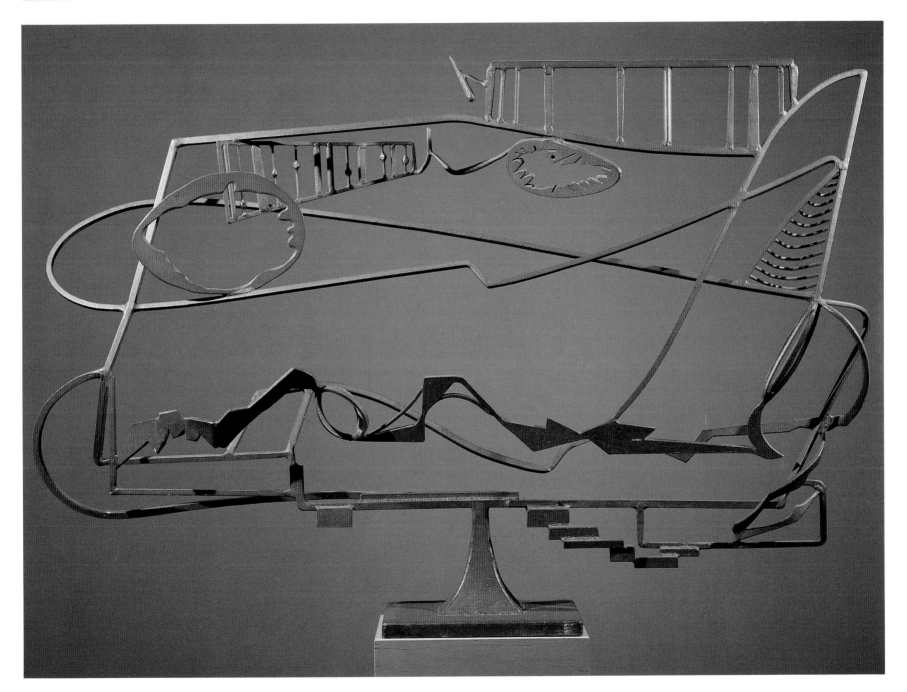

In the photorealist paintings of John Baeder, the railroad has lost its original function. The streamlined train in *Pullman* (figure 42), for example, has been transformed into a modest roadside diner; it has become a permanent fixture of the American landscape. In describing his own childhood attachment to the railroad, Baeder reminds us of those nineteenth-century travelers who first saw the vastness of the landscape through the train window:

The window was a frame, and I was able to get my full share of visuals. . . . I cherished looking out of the window at all those small-town backsides—the angle of vision gave me some sense of power and freedom—new found values.[60]

"Power and freedom" were associated with the railroad from its first appearance in the landscape. They were values based on a belief in technological progress under capitalism—an ideology that found broad expression in American art, both figural and abstract. In recent decades, with the demise of rail travel, the image of the railroad has lent itself to evocations of the past. It expresses a sentimental longing for an era when technology and the land seemed to coexist in a harmonic balance—with the train window serving as a frame for the landscape and the land representing the natural resources necessary to build and sustain industrial growth. But the negative aspects of the railroad—the destruction of Native American peoples and the spread of social and environmental problems created by industrial growth—have also found visual expression; and precisely because it raises issues so vital to both our economic growth and cultural consciousness, the railroad has remained a powerful image.

42
John Baeder, *Pullman*, 1974. Oil on canvas, 60 × 72 in. O. K. Harris Works of Art, New York.

47

Notes

1

Barbara Novak, *Nature and Culture* (New York: Oxford University Press, 1980), 162–163.

2

For a discussion of these iconographic elements in American landscape painting, see Nicolai Cikovsky, Jr., " 'Ravages of the Axe': The Meaning of the Tree Stump in Nineteenth-Century American Art," *Art Bulletin* 61 (December 1979): 611–626.

3

Joseph Garland, *Boston's North Shore* (Boston: Little, Brown, 1978), 84–89.

4

For a discussion of George Caleb Bingham's use of similar compositional formulas, see Henry Adams, "A New Interpretation of Bingham's 'Fur Traders Descending the Missouri,' " *Art Bulletin* 65 (December 1983): 675–680.

5

Kenneth W. Maddox, "The Railroad in the Eastern Landscape: 1850–1900," in *The Railroad in the American Landscape: 1850–1950*, ed. Susan Danly Walther (Wellesley, MA: Wellesley College Museum, 1981), 23.

6

Ibid., 29 and 75.

7

Smith was also the author of *The Book of the Great Railway Celebrations of 1857* (New York: D. Appleton), 1858.

8

[D. H. Strother], "Artists' Excursion over the Baltimore and Ohio Rail Road," *Harper's New Monthly Magazine* 19 (June 1859): 5.

9

Ibid., 2.

10

[John Durand], "An Excursion on the Baltimore and Ohio Railroad," *Crayon* 5 (July 1858): 208.

11

Kensett, Suydam, Hicks, Lang, and Mignot also produced sketches for Smith. For a further discussion of this trip see Maddox, 84–85 and cat. no. 13.

12

Eli Bowen, *Rambles in the Path of Steam* (Philadelphia: Bennett and Smith, 1855), 309.

13

John White, *The American Railroad Passenger Car* (Baltimore: Johns Hopkins University Press, 1978), 432–434.

14

Maddox, 88.

15

For a discussion of the various versions of the Starrucca Viaduct, see William B. Talbot, *Jasper Cropsey, 1823–1900* (Washington, D.C.: National Collection of Fine Arts, 1970), 90–92.

16

"Address to NPA delivered June, 1870 by Albert Southworth," *The Philadelphia Photographer* 8 (1871): 322.

17

For a discussion of the Niagara Falls daguerreotypes, see Robert Sobiezsek and Odette Appel, *The Spirit of Fact: The Daguerreotypes of Southworth and Hawes, 1842–1862* (Boston: Godine, 1976), nos. 96–97. The Langenheim salt prints of Niagara were included in the exhibition catalogue *Image of America, Early Photography, 1839–1900* (Washington, D.C.: Library of Congress, 1957), 26–27.

18

Albert D. Richardson, *Beyond the Mississippi* (Hartford: American Publishing Company, 1867), i.

19

The phrase "Westward the Course of Empire" derives from a poem by the eighteenth-century cleric and philosopher Bishop George Berkeley. See his "Verses by the Author on the Prospect of Planting Arts and Learning in America" in *The Works of George Berkeley, Bishop of Cloyne*, ed. A. A. Luce and T. E. Jessop (London: Thos. Nelson and Son, 1955), 369–373. The phrase was further popularized in the nineteenth century in Emanuel Leutze's murals for the United States Capitol, which depict the history of westward expansion from Old Testament figures to Daniel Boone.

20

George Pine, *Beyond the West* (Utica: T. J. Griffiths, 1871), 256.

21

For a discussion of the Native American resistance to railroad construction, see Dee Brown, *Hear That Lonesome Whistle Blow* (New York: Holt, Rinehart and Winston, 1977), 81–85.

22

Wendell Phillips, *Harper's Weekly* 12 (July 10, 1869): 436.

23

John C. Browne, "A Photographer among the Prairie Dogs and Buffaloes," *The Philadelphia Photographer* 4 (1867): 206.

24

For a discussion of the relationship between the railroad and the development of landscape photography, see Susan Danly Walther, "The Landscape Photographs of Alexander Gardner and Andrew Joseph Russell" (Ph.D. dissertation, Department of Art, Brown University, 1983).

25

Richardson, 567.

26

E. L. Burlingame, "The Plains and the Sierras," in *Picturesque America*, ed. William Cullen Bryant (New York: D. Appleton and Co., 1874), II, 174. The eastern journalist quoted here was Albert D. Richardson.

27

Carol Clark, *Thomas Moran, Watercolors of the American West* (Fort Worth: Amon Carter Museum, 1980), nos. 260–291.

28

See Beaumont Newhall and Diana E. Edkins, *William Henry Jackson* (Fort Worth: Amon Carter Museum, 1974), 138; and Elizabeth Lindquist-Cox, *The Influence of Photography on American Landscape Painters* (New York: Garland Press, 1977), 132–150.

29

Gordon Hendricks, *Albert Bierstadt* (New York: Abrams, 1973), 220–228.

30

Pine, 385.

31

He wrote of his experiences in William A. Bell, *New Tracks in North America*, 2 vols. (London: Chapman and Hall, 1869).

32

See, for example, Charles Nordhoff, "California," *Harper's New Monthly Magazine* 42 (May 1872): 865–881. For a pictorial history of the railroad car, see Lucius Beebe, *Mr. Pullman's Elegant Palace Cars* (Garden City, NY: Doubleday, 1961); for a more scholarly study on the history of design, White, 65.

33

Across the Continent and Around the World (Philadelphia: Disturnell, 1872), 100.

34

For reprints of the 1877 excursion articles, see Richard Reinhardt, *Out West On the Overland Train* (Palo Alto: American West Publishing, 1977).

35

Ibid., 46.

36

Susan Sontag, *On Photography* (New York: Dell, 1977), 9.

37

"Pilgrimage to the Secession Shrine at Pittsburg," *Camera Work* 2 (1904): 54.

38

Ernst Juhl, "The Jubilee Exhibition at the Hamburg Art Galleries," *Camera Work* 5 (1904): 48.

39

Sadakichi Hartmann, "A Plea for the Picturesqueness of New York," in *The Valiant Knights of Daguerre*, ed. Harry Lawton and George Knox (Berkeley: University of California Press, 1978), 57.

40

Hartmann, "A Plea for Straight Photography," in Lawton and Knox, 111.

41

Hartmann, "On the Possibilities of New Laws of Composition," in Lawton and Knox, 130.

42

Reprinted in Barbara Haskell, *Arthur Dove* (San Francisco Museum of Modern Art, 1974), appendix.

43

Hartmann, "Studio Talk," *International Studio* 30 (December 1906): 183.

44

Hartmann, "A Plea for Picturesqueness," 59.

45

Ibid.

46

Quoted in David Scott, "The City from Greenwich Village," *Studies in the History of Art* (Washington, D.C.: National Gallery of Art, 1972), 106.

47

See, for example, *Sixth Avenue and Thirtieth Street*, 1907 (Private Collection Philadelphia) and *Six O'Clock, Winter*, 1912 (Phillips Collection, Washington, D.C.).

48

Quoted from Burchfield's journal, November 9, 1917, in Matthew Baigell, *Charles Burchfield* (New York: Watson-Guptill, 1976), 117.

49

For a comprehensive study of the emergence of the railroad as a distinct urban environment, see John Stilgoe, *The Metropolitan Corridor* (New Haven: Yale University Press, 1983).

50

"Vanishing Backyards," *Fortune* 1 (May 1930): 77–81.

51

Walker Evans, "Along the Right of Way," *Fortune* 42 (September 1950): 106–113.

52

Thomas Hart Benton, *An Artist in America*, 3rd ed. (Columbia: University of Missouri Press, 1968), 70–71.

53

Benton, "American Regionalism: A Personal History of the Movement," *An American in Art* (Lawrence: University of Kansas Press, 1969), 149.

54

Benton, *An Artist in America*, 71.

55

See Donald J. Bush, *The Streamlined Decade* (New York: Braziller, 1975) and Jeffrey Meickle, *The Twentieth Century Limited: Industrial Design in America, 1925–1939* (Philadelphia: Temple University Press, 1979). The latter work in particular discusses the relationship of the railroad to this industrial aesthetic.

56

Walther, *The Railroad in the American Landscape*, 126.

57

The Rouge: The Image of Industry in the Art of Charles Sheeler and Diego Rivera (Detroit: Detroit Institute of Arts, 1978).

58

David Smith, *David Smith by David Smith* (New York: Thames and Hudson, 1968), 71.

59

Jeanne Siegel, "Carl Andre—Artworker," *Studio International* 180 (November 1970): 178.

60

John Baeder, *Diners* (New York: Abrams, 1978), 9.

1

Asher B. Durand's *Progress:* The Advance of Civilization and the Vanishing American

Kenneth W. Maddox

In a captious review, the editor of *Putnam's New Monthly Magazine* denounced the entries in the 1853 exhibition of the National Academy of Design. Walking through the Academy's galleries, the reviewer did not experience the enthusiasm he felt one should expect from "high art." Instead, the paintings produced the contrary effect: "Everything in the New World appears to be progressive; but the art which, by common consent, is called 'fine.' "[1] This, he conceded, was in the nature of things. The men of wealth who built the Erie Railroad at a cost of thirty million dollars and engaged in other great undertakings for the public good, he wrote, may well be forgiven for not giving us a gallery of paintings:

They might as well have attempted to build a pyramid in the style of King Cheops. Picture galleries, pyramids, and railroads, were never intended for the same people and the same century. If we have one we must forego the other, and we are sensible of our good fortune in living in an age which gives the preference to railroads.[2]

The sentiment was common to the age. In 1848 Ralph Waldo Emerson recorded in his journal that "the Railroad is that work of art which agitates & drives mad the whole people; as music, sculpture, & picture have done on their great days respectively."[3] But unlike the *Putnam* reviewer, Emerson did not condone the replacement of art by the machine; for

in the same year he also noted, "Nature uniformly does one thing at a time: if she will have a perfect hand, she makes head & feet pay for it. So now, as she is making railroad & telegraph ages, she starves the . . . *spirituel,* to stuff the *materiel & industriel.*"[4]

One of the faults the *Putnam* editor found with the Academy's exhibition was the repetitious nature of the entries, and he especially took to task Asher B. Durand's compositions: "There is still the 'Landscape—Durand.' The same birch tree, the same yellow sky, the same amiable cattle, the same mild trees and quiet water. What a mild, quiet, and amiable world is this to Durand!"[5] Given the progressive inclinations of the reviewer, it is strange that he failed to mention a painting that was atypical for Durand—a large canvas entitled *Landscape, Progress* (figure 43). With the two trees silhouetted against the sky the most prominent element of the composition, the painting at first appears to repeat Durand's familiar landscape motifs and to duplicate many of the Claudian features found in *View towards Hudson Valley* (1851, Wadsworth Atheneum), which was painted two years earlier and may have been included in the same exhibition.[6] But the amiable cattle which so dismayed the *Putnam* critic are not conspicuously evident in *Progress,* a composition with clearly defined polarities. On the left, Indians

Kenneth W. Maddox

43
Asher B. Durand, *Progress,* 1853. Oil on
canvas, 48 × 72 in. The Warner Collection,
Gulf States Paper Corporation, Tuscaloosa,
Alabama.

stand on a precipice strewn with the remnants of storm-blasted trees and gaze at the landscape below. On the right, the wilderness gives way to a pastoral scene, suggestive of the Hudson River Valley, filled with commercial activity. In the distance a diminutive train makes its way across a viaduct along the shores of the river.

The scene fulfills the warning issued six years before by the *Literary World*. It cautioned:

The axe of civilization is busy with our old forests, and artisan ingenuity is fast sweeping away the relics of our national infancy. What were once the wild and picturesque haunts of the Red Man, and where the wild deer roamed in freedom, are becoming the abodes of commerce and the seats of manufactures.[7]

The display of industry in *Progress* violates Durand's own dictum that a landscape "will be great in proportion as it declares the glory of God, by a representation of his works, and not of the works of man."[8]

Instead, Durand has created a visual metaphor of America based not only upon nature, but also upon the symbols of industrial growth and power. It is significant that when John Durand described the painting in his biography of his father, he omitted all reference to the Indians and wilderness and stated only that it was "a large landscape composition,

painted for Mr. Charles Gould, showing on American soil the use of canal, steamboat, and railway, and that of the telegraph, then recently perfected."[9] Durand's historical landscape lifted to high art a theme found in such popular imagery as Terence Kennedy's *Political Banner* (figure 44). In Kennedy's painting a screaming eagle, perched on a limb above the emblem of the United States, is surrounded by sailing ships, steam vessels, grazing livestock, agricultural and industrial implements, a canal, and the railroad, which appears in the forested landscape. The banner, proclaiming Whig support for commerce and illustrating Henry Clay's "American System," leaves little doubt that an agrarian nation was now defining itself in terms of technology.[10]

Although Durand's *Progress* was commissioned by Charles Gould, who at the time was a broker and who later would become treasurer of the Ohio and Mississippi Railroad,[11] there is no evidence that Gould influenced Durand's choice of theme. In the same year that he commissioned Durand's painting, Gould purchased a scene of the White Mountains from John F. Kensett, described as "simply a wild scene in nature, showing no traces of civilization—a bold mountain sketch," for the generous price of $750.[12] Moreover, an exchange of letters between Durand and Gould concerning *Progress* reveals Gould's subservient attitude toward the painter and

indicates that he had little control over the commission, which had caused a strained relationship between the two men. On April 19, 1853, Gould wrote to Durand:

My Dear Sir

I do not know what is etiquette in the premises and shall be pardoned if an error be made. I have not had the opportunity to see it, but Mr. Kensitt [*sic*] informs me that your picture for me is finished and is in the Gallery.

Whenever you desire the payment please inform me what is the amount.

Yours very truly
Chas. Gould[13]

Durand must have been offended by the note, for the next day Gould wrote the following letter:

My Dear Sir

A lame hand compels me to write by an amanuensis, hence my note was more formal than if I had written it myself; as I generally give the *idea* and let the words be the writer's. I am exceedingly sorry that you suppose I intended to be *chilling* or cold even in the slightest degree. I meant to say only that whenever it was desired by you I would be most happy to pay the amount which is your due; and wanted to say it in a courteous way. I did not know the ordinary mode of making payments under such circumstances, as I never had a picture sent to the Gallery before having it in my house.

I was sorry not to get an invitation; but said to Mrs. Gould that I presumed a card was addressed to me and not duly delivered.

44
Terence Kennedy, *Political Banner,* c. 1839.
Oil on wood, 65 in. diameter. New York
State Historical Association, Cooperstown.

Be assured I entreat you that no act of mine shall
ever interrupt the kind feelings which I trust exist
between us—and believe me.

Very sincerely
Your friend
Chas Gould[14]

Two years later an invitation from Durand to Gould to
view Emanuel Leutze's *The Embarkation of Columbus on His Last Voyage of Discovery* indicates that
any breach had probably healed.[15]

Although the *Putnam* critic ignored Durand's
Progress in his review of the Academy's exhibition,
the painting, which was given the most prominent
position in the main room of the exhibition galleries
(figure 45), was extolled by other critics. The reviewer for *The Knickerbocker* boldly declared, "We
observe a higher degree of perfection than this fine
artist has ever previously attained. It is purely
AMERICAN. It tells an American story out of American facts, portrayed with true American feeling, by
a devoted and earnest student of Nature."[16]

The painting proclaimed the advancement of civilization, but as Durand's contemporaries realized, it
also contrasted "the ruggedness of primeval nature
with the culture and forces of our present civilization."[17] In 1856 *The Crayon*, which felt that the Indian had not received justice in American art, urged

the artists to record his features before the red man passed from the face of the earth. The influential art periodical may have been recalling Durand's *Progress* when it observed that "setting aside all the Indian history of the West, how much there is that is romantic, peculiar, and picturesque in his struggles with civilization in our own section of country."[18] It is in this conflict between wilderness and industrial progress that the "purely AMERICAN" quality of Durand's theme is found.

Durand certainly felt some sympathy for the plight of the Native American driven from the wilderness. Only a few years earlier he had also suffered from the invading forces of progress when he was forced from his home along the Hudson River by the Erie Railroad, which was building a branch line to Newburgh. Although he had considered making this retreat his permanent residence, the banks of a stream meandering through his property were wanted for the railroad. As his son relates, "The ground was turned up; fever-and-ague made its appearance, drove him from his summer retreat, and obliged him to resume his annual search for the picturesque in the undisturbed wilderness."[19]

The conflict in *Progress* between nature and civilization appeared earlier in Thomas Cole's *The Oxbow* (1836, The Metropolitan Museum of Art). Cole's canvas is also divided with the wilderness on the left and the cultivated landscape on the right, but it is the painter himself, not Indians, who watches the inexorable advance of civilization. In Cole's list of subjects for pictures, there is a projected series that closely anticipates Durand's theme. It is described as "The Past & The Present—this might be American scenery—a scene in its primeval wildness—with Indians—the same under the hand of civilization," although he added, "but better illustration would perhaps be a Temple or city of ancient Greece or Italy in its glory—sacrifices & processions. The same in a state of ruins. Perhaps Paestum would do—the American might be past, present & future."[20] Cole's *Past* and *Present*, which were executed for P. G. Stuyvesant in 1838, forgo both classical and American settings in favor of the more romantic medieval mode. His series for Luman Reed, *Course of Empire* (1836, The New-York Historical Society), which depicts the rise and decline of a civilization, could easily have been interpreted by Cole's contemporaries as a thinly veiled allegory of the past, present, and possible future of America.

While there is little evidence to suggest that *Progress* reflects the pessimism of a cyclical view of history, a sense of decline and destruction informs the very picture that purports to celebrate progress. As one reviewer wistfully noted:

At the right of the picture are seen the various improvements of the age—the telegraph—railroad—canal—manufactory—steamship, &c &c. At the left, the wild Indian is seen taking a last look at the land of his fathers, and for the last time treading those mountain glades, so beautiful in their wild scenery, but so soon to change and disappear before the white man's resistless march of improvement.[21]

Durand's canvas reversed the stock romantic nineteenth-century images of the philosopher on a hillside meditating upon the ruins of the civilization below, as found in such influential works as C. F. Volney's *Les Ruines, ou Méditations sur les révolutions des Empires*[22] (figure 46). It is nature and the children of nature who now face annihilation, not civilization. Trees, not columns, lie in fragments upon the land. This reversal of values was noticed by Captain Frederick Marryat, the popular English novelist, when he recorded his impressions of a journey along the Erie Canal in 1837:

Extremes meet: as I look down . . . upon the giants of the forest, which had for so many centuries reared their heads undisturbed, but now lay prostrate before civilization, the same feelings were conjured up in my mind as when I have, in my wanderings, surveyed such fragments of dismembered empires as the ruins of Carthage or of Rome. There the reign of Art was over, and Nature had resumed her sway—here Nature was deposed, and about to resign her throne to the usurper Art.[23]

Here, said I, here once flourished an opulent city, here was the seat of a powerful empire .   *Ch. II.*

46
Frontispiece engraving from *A New Translation of Volney's Ruins,* 1802. The New York Public Library, Rare Book Division. Astor, Lenox and Tilden Foundations.

Deposed as well were the Indians, and with their destruction grew the idea of the noble savage.[24] During the first half of the nineteenth century, the tragedy of the dying Indian, which has been termed "the cult of the vanishing American" by G. Harrison Orians, became an important theme in American culture. Established with the poems of Philip Freneau in the 1780s, the lament over the passing of the Indian became especially prevalent following the publication in 1826 of James Fenimore Cooper's *The Last of the Mohicans*.[25] One of the earliest manifestations of the theme in the visual arts is in John Gadsby Chapman's painting *The First Ship*, which was exhibited at the National Academy of Design in 1837.[26] This canvas is now lost, but an engraving of a similar painting (figure 47) was published in the gift book *The Token and Atlantic Souvenir* in 1842. In Chapman's image the savage watches the first approach of western civilization, unaware that the event signals the beginning of his own destruction. As the text accompanying the engraving states:

Here we see the "seminal principle" of a series of struggles, unparalleled for the fierceness of the passions involved in them; . . . the gradual decay and extinction of a most marked race, the slow retreat of the wigwam and the tomahawk, and the onward progress of the axe and the log cabin. There is no more saddening chapter in the world's history, than that which records the fate of the Indian race.[27]

47
Anonymous, engraving after John Gadsby Chapman, *The First Ship*, published in *The Token and Atlantic Souvenir*, Boston, 1842. The New York Public Library, General Research Division. Astor, Lenox and Tilden Foundations.

Durand obviously was inspired by Chapman's painting when he took up Cooper's subject for his landscape *The Indian Vespers, Last of the Mohicans* (figure 48). As in Chapman's image, a lone figure of an Indian with raised right hand stands on a promontory beneath the protective boughs of a tree and surveys the horizon. Durand returned to the same composition in *Progress*, only there the river valley is filled with the teeming activity of the white settler.

By 1853, when Durand painted *Progress*, the European-inspired idea of the noble savage had given way to the antiprimitivistic "idea of savagism" in which both the defects and the virtues of the Indian were considered to reflect his state in nature. As Alexis de Tocqueville had observed, the extinction of the Indian was as inevitable as the advance of the white man:

Their implacable prejudices, their uncontrolled passions, their vices, and still more, perhaps, their savage virtues, consigned them to inevitable destruction. . . . They seem to have been placed by Providence amid the riches of the New World only to enjoy them for a season; they were there merely to wait till others came. Those coasts, so admirably adapted for commerce and industry; those wide and deep rivers; . . . the whole continent, in short, seemed prepared to be the abode of a great nation yet unborn.[28]

The savage, weighed in terms of civilized society, was found wanting, and the Indian—like the wilderness—was to yield to progress; the mandate of the settler to conquer the land necessitated the destruction of everything alien to civilization. When William Gilpin proclaimed in 1846 that "the *untransacted* destiny of the American people is to subdue the continent—to rush over this vast field to the Pacific Ocean," he also made clear that the savage, who stood as an obstacle to advancement, was faced with the alternatives of becoming civilized or being destroyed. "The American realizes," Gilpin stated, "that 'Progress is God.' "[29]

The theme was given official governmental sanction. In the same year that Durand painted *Progress*, Thomas Crawford's *The Progress of Civilization* was commissioned for the east pediment of the United States Capitol (figure 49). Crawford's composition, which was also called *the Past and Present of America*, shows both the beneficial effects of civilization and the extinction of the Indian.[30] It follows the ideas suggested by Captain Montgomery C. Meigs, who was the officer in charge of the extension of the Capitol building: "In our history of the struggle between civilized man and the savage, between the cultivated and the wild nature are certainly to be found themes worthy of the artist and capable of appealing to the feelings of all classes."[31] The central

female figure of America divides the two groups of the pediment: on one side are personifications of the military, commerce, education, and industry; on the other, the most prominent figures are those of the settler clearing his land and the dying Indian chief seated on his grave, a figure also carved separately by Crawford. The stoical despair of this majestic figure, Henry T. Tuckerman remarked, adequately and eloquently symbolizes "the destruction of a Race, and marks the advent of civilization on this continent."[32]

Crawford's theme echoes that of Horatio Greenough's *The Rescue*, which was begun in 1838 but not installed in the East Portico of the Capitol until 1853, one year after the sculptor's death (figure 50). The composition, which shows the struggle between the Indian and the frontiersman, was said by Greenough to depict "the peril of the American wilderness, the ferocity of our Indians, the superiority of the white-man, and why and how civilization crowded the Indian from his soil."[33] William Cullen Bryant, whose poetry expresses a sincere empathy for the Indian, noticed the wider implications of the struggle depicted in Greenough's statue when he visited the sculptor's studio in Florence in 1845. "Besides the particular incident represented by the group," Bryant reported without editorial comment in his *Letters of a Traveller*, "it may pass for an image of the aboriginal

48
Asher B. Durand, *The Indian Vespers, Last of the Mohicans*, 1847. The White House Collection. © The White House Historical Association. Photo: National Geographic Society.

49
Thomas Crawford, *The Progress of Civilization*, 1854–56. Pediment, East Front, Senate Wing, United States Capitol, Washington, D.C.

50
Horatio Greenough, *The Rescue*, 1838–51. United States Capitol, Washington, D.C.

race of America overpowered and rendered helpless by the civilized race."[34] America was poised for an outburst of western expansion, and most accounts describing Greenough's statue expressed little sympathy for the native American. Upon seeing the statue, an American engraver traveling in Italy extolled with imperialistic rhetoric the preeminence of the white man:

The thought embodied in the action of the group, and immediately communicated to every spectator, is the natural and necessary superiority of the Anglo-Saxon to the Indian. It typifies the settlement of the American continent, and the respective destinies of the two races who here come into collision. You see the exposure and suffering of the female emigrant—the ferocious and destructive instinct of the savage, and his easy subjugation under the superior manhood of the new colonist. . . . He whose destiny is to convert forests into cities; who conquers only to liberate, enlighten, and elevate; who presents himself alike at the defiles of lonely wildernesses and the gates of degraded nations, as the representative and legate of laws, and polity, and morals; he, the type of your own glorious nation, stands before you.[35]

Durand's *Progress* was the first major American painting to illustrate "the settlement of the American continent, and the respective destinies of the two races who here come into collision." But the theme—known as "The Advance of Civilization"—of the savage watching the approach of the white settler had been popular since the 1840s.[36] As early as

1844 the subject was used for the frontispiece of S. G. Goodrich's *A Pictorial History of the United States*, and variations on the theme appeared in his almost endless series of children's textbooks during the next quarter of the century (figure 51). The Advance of Civilization motif was also widely incorporated in contemporary bank note engravings, some of which predate Durand's canvas.[37] In one engraving the space is reduced telescopically so that the savage, rather than viewing the distant threat of civilization, directly confronts the various components of urban activity, thus graphically illustrating the collision of the destinies of two races (figure 52). After the Civil War the scenario was expanded to include the conquering of the West. It was used as the frontispiece engraving for *Harper's Weekly* from 1870 to 1889 and as the cover of *Frank Leslie's Historical Register of the Centennial* in 1876. Various versions of the theme appeared in the paintings of a number of lesser-known artists during this time.[38]

Durand was a bank note engraver from 1824 to 1834, and it is in his own studies for engravings that we find the seminal development of the concept for *Progress*. Most scholars have credited Durand with creating the standard for bank note design, and his engravings were extensively imitated by others.[39]

Ninety of Durand's original drawings in India ink and sepia for bank note engravings are preserved in the New York Public Library. Describing them, Durand's son wrote that one "cannot but regret that delicate art of this description should have been bestowed on productions of so little account," but he recognized that "they were remunerative, and may be considered in the same light as the fine art of old times bestowed on the decoration of armour, jewelry, and ecclesiastical utensils."[40]

Many of Durand's early designs depict the railroad, a motif that became increasingly popular with bank note engravers as the century progressed. Two drawings of railroad cuts show the use of horse-drawn cars and must be listed among the earliest images of the railroad in America (figure 53). A depiction of an early train in profile was subsequently incorporated in a vignette showing the allegorical figure of Industry surrounded by his attributes and a design of Archimedes lifting the world with a lever.[41] In a later vignette of Jupiter being carried on the back of an eagle, probably taken from an engraving of Raphael's *The Vision of Ezekial*, Durand added a train and ship in the distance (figure 54).[42]

Several of Durand's designs depict on an emblematic level the confrontation of the Indian and the

51
Frontispiece engraving, "An American Indian Contemplating the Progress of Civilization," in Samuel G. Goodrich, *A Pictorial History of the United States of America* (Philadelphia: Sorin & Ball, 1844). The New York Public Library, General Research Division. Astor, Lenox and Tilden Foundations.

FRONTISPIECE.

An American Indian contemplating the progress of civilization.

52
Bank note engraving. American Bank Note
Company. The New York Public Library,
Prints Division. Astor, Lenox and Tilden
Foundations.

53
Asher B. Durand, *Railway Cut.* Drawing for
a bank note engraving, from *Vignettes.* The
New York Public Library, Prints Division.
Astor, Lenox and Tilden Foundations.

54
Asher B. Durand, *Jupiter with Putti Being
Borne on the Back of an Eagle.* 1840. Draw-
ing for a bank note engraving, from
Vignettes. The New York Public Library,
Prints Division. Astor, Lenox and Tilden
Foundations.

white man found in *Progress*. In one of these vignettes, two seated figures flank a shield surmounted by an eagle (figure 55). The shield is inscribed with the coat of arms of the municipality of New York, which depicts the alternating figures of a beaver and flour barrel placed between the saltirewise sails of a windmill. The motif is an adaptation of the seal, which was adopted by the city in 1686, showing its coat of arms inscribed on a shield supported by the standing figures of a sailor and an Indian (figure 56).[43] In his design Durand has changed the positions of the figures to correspond to geographic reality. The Indian is seated on a hill on the western side of the shield and has a forest of pine at his back. On the right, the sailor has been transformed into the archetypal American whose characteristics would become identified with Brother Jonathan and Uncle Sam. He wears a top hat and vest and points in an easterly direction to a ship, signifying his point of origin. A quadrant rests by his side, and an anchor, which also serves as a symbol of hope, is by his feet.[44] As in Chapman's *The First Ship*, the Indian is gazing upon the forces that will eventually annihilate his people. In variations of the design by Durand, the superior power of western civilization becomes explicit as the stalwart figure of the colonist holds his

55

Asher B. Durand, *Indian and Colonial Figure Flanking Shield.* Drawing for a bank note engraving, from *Vignettes.* The New York Public Library, Prints Division. Astor, Lenox and Tilden Foundations.

quadrant and is seated on a cannon. Yet it is in a later bank note—not done by Durand—that the theme reaches its dramatic conclusion (figure 57).[45] The dispossessed Indian surveys a manufacturing city of billowing smokestacks. Beside him, a windmill, decrepit and unused, stands in disrepair. The sails of the windmill, a symbol of power on New York's seal, have become as impotent and as anachronistic to an industrialized America as the Indian.

As a youthful engraver for a mercantile community, Durand seemed to embrace the nationalistic impulses proclaiming the superiority of the white man over the savage and the inevitability of the advancement of civilization over the wilderness. But as a mature landscape artist, Durand would have been acutely aware, as Cole was before him, of the need to preserve the undefiled purity of a God-given wilderness. Durand's sympathy may not have been totally on the side of progress when he painted his canvas in 1853; yet at mid-century the nation, which in a delicate balancing act had been able to deify both nature and progress, was confident of its "manifest destiny."[46] As Tocqueville perceptively noted, it was the exciting prospect of the new, not the destruction of the old, that permeated the minds of most Americans:

An ancient people, the first and legitimate master of the American continent, is vanishing daily like the snow in sunshine, and disappearing from view over the land. In the same spots and in its place another race is increasing at a rate that is even more astonishing. It fells the forests and drains the marshes; lakes as large as seas and huge rivers resist its triumphant march in vain. The wilds become villages, and the villages towns. The American, the daily witness of such wonders, does not see anything astonishing in all this. This incredible destruction, this even more surprising growth, seems to him the usual progress of things in this world. He gets accustomed to it as to the unalterable order of nature.[47]

Despite whatever empathy he might have had for the vanishing American and whatever reservations he might have held concerning the transformation of the land, Durand undoubtedly shared this belief in the spirit of progress. Based on images already widespread in the popular arts, *Progress* heralds with an obvious parade of symbols the inevitable advance of white man's civilization. It was the "unalterable order of nature." Although Durand is now remembered for his images of the wilderness, his painting *Progress* reveals, as Emerson and the editor of *Putnam's* observed, that it was the age of the railroad.

56
Seal of the City of New York. Museum of the City of New York.

57
Bank note engraving. United States Engraving and Printing Bureau. The New York Public Library, Prints Division. Astor, Lenox and Tilden Foundations.

Notes

Much of the material for this essay has been taken from my dissertation, in progress under the direction of Professor Barbara Novak, Columbia University. I am extremely grateful for her encouragement and support. Research was made possible by a generous grant from the Rockefeller Foundation. Earlier versions of the essay were delivered at the Goodson Symposium on American Art at the Whitney Museum of American Art in April 1980 and at the Symposium on the Railroad in the American Landscape at the Jewett Arts Center, Wellesley College, in May 1981. Portions of the essay also appear in the catalogue, *The Railroad in the American Landscape: 1850–1900* (Wellesley, MA: The Wellesley College Museum, 1981).

1
"Editorial Notes—Fine Arts," *Putnam's New Monthly Magazine* I (June 1853): 700.

2
Ibid., 702.

3
The Journals and Miscellaneous Notebooks of Ralph Waldo Emerson, ed. William H. Gilman et al., 14 vols. to date (Cambridge: The Belknap Press of Harvard University, 1960–) X, 353.

4
Ibid., XI, 13.

5
"Editorial Notes," 701.

6

See *The Hudson River School: 19th Century American Landscapes in the Wadsworth Atheneum* (Hartford, CN: Wadsworth Atheneum, 1976), 57.

7

"The Fine Arts: Exhibition at the National Academy," *The Literary World*, May 15, 1847, p. 348.

8

Asher B. Durand, "Letters on Landscape Painting" *The Crayon* I (January 31, 1855): 66.

9

John Durand, *The Life and Times of A. B. Durand* (New York: Charles Scribner's Sons, 1894; reprint, New York: Kennedy Graphics, Inc., Da Capo Press, 1970), 175.

10

For Kennedy's painting, see Agnes Halsey Jones, *Rediscovered Painters of Upstate New York, 1700–1875* (Utica, NY: Winchester Printing for Munson-Williams-Proctor Institute, 1958), 57–58. Whig banners painted by George Caleb Bingham in 1844 displayed similar themes. See E. Maurice Bloch, *George Caleb Bingham: The Evolution of an Artist*, 2 vols. (Berkeley: University of California Press, 1967), I, 73–77.

11

For Gould's role in the 1858 artists' excursion on the Baltimore and Ohio Railway, see my essay "The Railroad in the Eastern Landscape: 1850–1900" in *The Railroad in the American Landscape: 1850–1950*, 26–33.

12

The Illustrated News II (July 2, 1853), 16. Gould's purchase accounted for almost half of Kensett's receipts from his paintings sold that year. The highest price that Kensett's paintings usually commanded at the time was $200–300. See Kensett Papers, Archives of American Art, Reel N68–85, Frame 475.

13

Letter from Charles Gould to Asher B. Durand, April 19, 1853, manuscript, New York Public Library.

14

Letter from Charles Gould to Asher B. Durand, April 20, 1853, manuscript, New York Public Library.

15

In a note from Charles Gould to Asher B. Durand, November 10, 1855, manuscript, New York Public Library, Gould accepted Durand's invitation to view Leutze's work. Gould most likely either purchased that painting or a later version, for *Departure of Columbus from Palos in 1492* (1855) is listed in the American Art Associates, Sale of Charles Gould Estate, October 22, 1932. See Barbara S. Groseclose, *Emanuel Leutze, 1816–1868: Freedom is Our Only King* (Washington, D.C.: National Collection of Fine Arts, Smithsonian Institution, 1975), 87, no. 69.

16

"Exhibition of the National Academy of Design," *The Knickerbocker* XLII (July 1853): 95.

17

"The Fine Arts: The Exhibition of the Academy," *The Literary World* XII (April 30, 1853): 358.

18

"The Indians in American Art," *The Crayon* III (January 1856): 28.

19

Durand, 184–185.

20

"Appendix II: Thomas Cole's List 'Subjects for Pictures,' " in "Studies on Thomas Cole, An American Romanticist," *Annual II* [Baltimore: The Baltimore Museum of Art, 1967], 92, no. 90.

21

The Illustrated News I (April 30, 1853): 280.

22

Published in 1791, the first English translation appeared in London in 1795. A Philadelphia edition was published as early as 1799. During the nineteenth century Volney's work went through many editions, most of which contained a frontispiece showing a meditating philosopher on a hillside overlooking ruins. For Volney's possible influence on Thomas Cole, see E. P. Richardson, *Painting in America: From 1502 to the Present* (New York: Thomas Y. Crowell Company, 1956), 167.

23

Captain Frederick Marryat, *Diary in America*, ed. Jules Zanger (1839; reprint, Bloomington: Indiana University Press, 1960), 107.

24

For European concepts of the noble savage, see Hoxie Neale Fairchild, *The Noble Savage: A Study in Romantic Naturalism* (New York: Columbia University Press, 1928); Ruthven Todd, "The Imaginary Indian in Europe," *Art in America* LX (July–August 1972): 40–47.

25

G. Harrison Orians, *The Cult of the Vanishing American: A Century View, 1834–1934* (Toledo: The H. J. Chittenden Company, 1934). While Orians felt that in literature the theme quickly exhausted itself for want of variety, in the fine arts the Indian was frequently shown as the sole survivor of his tribe. Thomas Cole's *Indian Family* (ca. 1836, University of Kansas) may be the "Last Indian—dead hemlock" listed in Cole's "Subjects for Pictures," 90, no. 82. A. D. O. Browere's *The Lone Indian* (1839) and James Henry Beard's *The Last of the Red Man* (1847) were shown at the National Academy of Design. The *Cosmopolitan Art Journal* II (September 1858): 209, reported that Jesse Talbot had finished a finely conceived work called the *Indian's Last Gaze*. In 1866 Hiram Powers began work on his statue *The Last of the Tribes*, which shows an Indian girl fleeing before civilization. In a letter to Sidney Brooks, Powers wrote, "Cooper has written *The Last of the Mohicans* on paper. I shall have written, in my feeble way, the last of all the tribes in marble." See Donald Martin Reynolds, "Hiram Powers and His Ideal Sculpture" (Ph.D. dissertation, Columbia University, 1975), 205.

26

See Ellwood Parry, *The Image of the Indian and the Black Man in American Art, 1590–1900* (New York: George Braziller, 1974), 75–77.

27

The Token and Atlantic Souvenir (Boston: David H. Williams, 1842), 299.

28

Alexis de Tocqueville, *Democracy in America*, The Henry Reeve Text as revised by Francis Bowen, ed. Phillips Bradley, 2 vols. (1840; reprint, New York: Vintage Books, 1945), I, 26. See also Roy Harvey Pearce, *The Savages of America: A Study of the Indian and the Idea of Civilization*, rev. ed. (Baltimore: The John Hopkins Press, 1965) and Robert F. Berkhofer, Jr., *The White Man's Indian: Images of the American Indian from Columbus to the Present* (New York: Alfred A. Knopf, 1978).

29

William Gilpin, *Mission of the North American People* (Philadelphia: J. B. Lippincott & Co., 1873), 124 and 99.

30

See Lorado Taft, *The History of American Sculpture* (New York: The Macmillan Company, 1917), 80–85.

31

Quoted in Robert L. Gale, *Thomas Crawford: American Sculptor* (University of Pittsburgh Press, 1964), 109.

32

Henry T. Tuckerman, *Book of the Artists* (New York, G. P. Putnam & Son, 1867), 310.

33

Letter from E. G. Loring to Senator James Pearce, July (?) 1858, quoted by Pearce, 243.

34

William Cullen Bryant, *Letters of a Traveller* (New York: George P. Putnam, 1851), 236.

35

American Art-Union *Bulletin* (September 1851): 97, quoting the *Home Journal*.

36

This was the title used for William Rickarby Miller's engraving of Durand's painting. The engraving first appeared in *The Illustrated News* I (April 30, 1853): 281. In December 1853, *The Illustrated News* merged with *Gleason's Pictorial* [later *Ballou's Pictorial Drawing-Room Companion*], which republished the engraving in vol. VIII (April 7, 1855): 221.

37

While the exact dating of specific bank note vignettes is difficult, D. C. Wismer, *New York Descriptive List of Obsolete Paper Money* (Federalsburg, MD: The J. W. Stowell Printing Company, 1931) includes several descriptions of notes issued before 1853 with this motif. *Hodges' New Bank Note Safe-Guard; Giving Fac-Simile Descriptions of Upwards of Ten Thousand Bank Notes Embracing Every Genuine Note Issued in the United States & Canada* (New York: J. Tyler Hodges, Banker, 1859) indicates that by 1859 the theme had become ubiquitous.

38

For example, both Samuel Seymour's *Indians, Salmon Falls* (n.d.) and O. Rodier's *View of Ottawa, Illinois, from Starved Rock* (1876), which is a mirror image of Seymour's composition, incorporate elements found in Durand's painting.

39

See, for example, Charles Henry Hart, *Catalogue of the Engraved Work of Asher B. Durand* (New York: Grolier Club, 1895), 8–9; Alice Newlin, "Asher B. Durand, American Engraver," *The Metropolitan Museum of Art Bulletin*, n.s. I (January 1943): 168. For a more recent discussion of Durand's engravings, see Wayne Craven, "Asher B. Durand's Career as an Engraver," *The American Art Journal* III (Spring 1971): 39–57; Barbara Gallati, "Asher B. Durand as Engraver" in *Asher B. Durand: An Engraver's and a Farmer's Art* (Yonkers, NY: The Hudson River Museum, 1983), 14–17.

40

Durand, 72.

41

In the engraving (Grolier Club, no. 206), the locomotive has been replaced by a ship. While the Archimedes design is not listed in the Grolier Club catalogue, it is described by Durand, 71.

42

This is pointed out by David B. Lawall, *A. B. Durand, 1796–1886* (Montclair, NJ: Montclair Art Museum, 1971), 46. The religious content of Raphael's image has been transformed, however, to the classical theme of the apotheosis. Durand's drawing was engraved (Grolier Club, no. 209) with the ship and train omitted.

43

For a detailed description of the seal, see John B. Pine, *Seal and Flag of the City of New York* (New York: G. P. Putnam's Sons, 1915), 36–51.

44

See Lawall, 54–55. The anchor as symbol of hope was frequently used in bank note engraving and was also used by Durand in his painting *The Morning of Life* (1840, National Academy of Design).

45

For the incorporation of this vignette as part of the design for the stock certificates issued by the Centennial Corporation, ca. 1874–75, see Parry, 129–131.

46

In Durand's *Indian Rescue* (1846, The Anschutz Collection) there is little that is noble in the savages who hold hostage the white women about to be freed by the cunning of the white man. Durand's painting is a passive portrayal of Greenough's fervent declaration of white supremacy.

47

Alexis de Tocqueville, "A Fortnight in the Wilds," in *Journey to America*, ed. J. P. Mayer (New Haven: Yale University Press, 1960), 329.

2

George Inness's
The Lackawanna Valley:
"Type of the Modern"

Nicolai Cikovsky, Jr.

The Lackawanna Valley (figure 58) is now one of George Inness's most admired paintings, both in its own right and because it is probably the most famous and important image of the railroad in nineteenth-century American art. No other is as richly meaningful, as intelligent, and as fine in quality, and no discussion of the railroad in American art is possible or complete without it. For that reason, and because, despite its fame and many attempts to explain it, it remains an enigmatic painting, this is a fitting time and place to summarize what we know and are able to say about it.

The Lackawanna Valley was not always admired. Its origins were humble, and most of its early history was passed in obscurity and neglect. Nevertheless, more is known about *The Lackawanna Valley* than about any of Inness's other paintings, but that is not a great deal. We do not know exactly when it was painted or why, its early history, or, least of all, exactly what the painting meant to Inness and to his contemporaries. We do not even know its title; *The Lackawanna Valley* is a modern invention.

Much of what we know, or think we know, about the painting derives from three texts, given here in their entirety.

The earliest text is part of an interview Inness gave to a reporter from the *New York Herald* who visited his studio in 1893 or 1894 (the interview was published in 1894 as an obituary article):

Here . . . is a picture I made of Scranton, Pa., done for the Delaware and Lackawanna Company, when they built the road. They paid me $75 for it. Two years ago, when I was in Mexico city, I picked it up in an old curiosity shop. You see I had to show the double tracks and the round house, whether they were in perspective or not. But there is considerable power of painting in it, and the distance is excellent.[1]

Inness's son, George, Jr., embellished the story in his "official" biography of his father, published in 1917, and included a letter from his father to his mother:

Scranton, Sept., 1855

My dearest wife:

Above all things in the world I would love to see you. I have to think of you the more that I am in trouble. I left my baggage at St. John's and walked to Stroudsburg. The scamp never sent it. I left for Scranton with the promise from the stage proprietor that it should be sent to me the next day. It has not come, and I shall now be at expense to get it. I had to buy a shirt and other things, so that my money is almost gone. Send me ten dollars. I fear I shall need it. You will have to wait until I can send you money or until I return. There is no other way.

I kiss you a thousand times, my Love, and will hasten to you as soon as possible. Kiss my little ones for me. I will write you a long letter soon.

Your affectionate husband,
GEORGE INNESS

Nicolai Cikovsky, Jr.

58
George Inness, *The Lackawanna Valley.* Oil
on canvas, 33⅞ × 50¼ in. National
Gallery of Art, Washington. Gift of
Mrs. Huttleston Rogers, 1945.

This trip to Scranton was made in the pot-boiling days of his career, and was for the purpose of making a painting of the first roundhouse on the D.L.& W Railroad, which was to be used for advertising.

There was in reality only one track at the time running into the roundhouse, but the president of the road insisted on having four or five painted in, easing his conscience by explaining that the road would eventually have them.

Pop protested, but the president was adamant, and there was a family to support, so the tracks were painted in.

In the busy years which followed, the picture was virtually forgotten until thirty years or more afterward, when my mother and father were in the City of Mexico, they discovered the old canvas in a junk-shop. The shopkeeper knew nothing of its origin or who painted it, and explained that he had bought it with a job lot of office furnishings, and would be glad to sell it cheap. So my father purchased it for old time's sake. As he walked out of the shop he said, "Do you remember, Lizzie, how mad I was because they made me paint the name on the engine?"[2]

The third text, published in 1911, was written by Elliott Daingerfield, who knew Inness in the last years of his life and on that basis constituted himself the chief authority on Inness in the years after the artist's death:

. . . we see him speedily producing those remarkable transcripts of American scenery which first drew attention to his name. Wide reaches of field and meadow, the business of harvest, grazing cattle—the rush of trains, flowing streams under broadly-lit skies—all typical American scenes. . . .

He told me of doing a set of these pictures for the Erie Railroad [he meant D.L.& W.] people about the time that road was finished, which were to be used in advertising. Many years later he found one of these huge canvases in a dim little shop in Mexico City, which he gleefully bought for a few Mexican dollars.[3]

The earliest text, the interview with Inness, is the one from which all the others in some way descend. It tells where the picture was painted, for what occasion and for whom, what Inness was paid for it, and what the commission required him to do. It also tells of the circumstances of its rediscovery. Inness was speaking from memory of events that took place about forty years earlier, but everything he said is either verifiable or inherently plausible. The painting unquestionably depicts Scranton, Pennsylvania, and the facilities—particularly the roundhouse, tracks, and equipment—of the Delaware, Lackawanna, and Western railroad. It matches an 1859 photograph of the site (figure 59) and the wood car bears the railroad's initials on its side. The price Inness was paid, seventy-five dollars, though less than he had been asking and getting for his paintings, was not impossibly low.[4] Inness implied that he was required to distort perspective in order to show the tracks and roundhouse clearly. It does appear, by comparing the painting to the photograph, that the

roundhouse has been enlarged and that it and the tracks are seen from a slightly elevated point of view, as though to make them more prominent and their configuration more schematically precise and legible. The oddest part of the story is Inness's discovery of the painting in a curiosity shop in Mexico City. In the interview, Inness said he found the painting two years earlier. Though published in 1894, the interview probably took place in 1893, which would mean that he found the painting in 1891. In that year he visited California, and in February spent about two weeks in San Diego, just across the border from Mexico.[5] What is remarkable about the story, therefore, is not that the painting was found in Mexico City (or, perhaps, in some other city in Mexico), but how it got there. That we do not know.[6]

What in George, Jr.'s later retelling of the story came, secondhand and colorfully embellished, from the *New York Herald* interview, and what, if anything, came directly from his father or mother is not certain, though a great deal of the material in his biography comes from public sources rather than family lore. What he says of the number of tracks is surely wrong; in the painting, only one track runs into the roundhouse, not four or five (though others become sidings). But on other points he may be correct. The painting, as he said (perhaps on Daingerfield's authority), could have been used for

59
Anonymous, *Scranton, Pennsylvania, 1859, and Its Forefathers.* Photograph. Library of Congress.

advertising, though not perhaps in the way he meant. It is just as likely, however, that it was intended to hang in the company's offices to commemorate or document the founding of the railroad rather than to advertise it publicly. That would more satisfactorily account for its reappearance among a job lot of office furniture. And Inness may have been made to paint the company's initials on the train; they do seem to have been applied (to the wood car, however, not the engine) as an afterthought and without proper calculation of the space needed to hold them.

The most important piece of evidence that only George, Jr.'s text supplies—or has been taken to supply—is the painting's date. *The Lackawanna Valley* itself is not dated. On the basis of the 1855 letter that George, Jr. reprinted, and apparently on that basis alone, its date is always and without question given as 1855. But in the letter itself there is no mention of the painting nor any indication that the trip to Scranton was undertaken for the purpose of working on it. Only Inness's son connects the letter and its date with the painting. He may have known about that connection, but the text of the letter offers no compelling reason to make it.

The Lackawanna Valley was probably painted in 1856 or 1857. The D.L.& W. Railroad was founded in the early 1850s, and the painting was almost certainly commissioned to reflect that occasion. The most concrete evidence for a date later than 1855 is the fact that the roundhouse—the painting's most conspicuous and important part, a structure in which the railroad took considerable pride and which, as we have seen, Inness seems to have enlarged to enhance its prominence—was not completed until 1856.[7] The painting, therefore, could not plausibly have been painted earlier,[8] and it is not unlikely that it might have been painted, or finished, even later. A preparatory study, squared for enlargement,[9] suggests a process of careful deliberation behind the painting that could have taken many months (figure 60).

If *The Lackawanna Valley* was painted in 1856 or 1857, some previously unconsidered thematic and pictorial relationships arise. Daingerfield's text describes the most interesting of them. He reports that Inness told him he painted a *set* of paintings for the railroad that were to be used for advertising. And in an oblique, somewhat confused way he suggests what might have comprised the set. Though Daingerfield claims to be speaking in general terms of Inness's early work—of "typical American scenes" depicting "wide reaches of field and meadow, the business of the harvest, grazing cattle—the rush of trains, flowing streams under broadly lit skies"—it is possible to read his words as a description of two specific paintings, both entitled *Delaware Water Gap* and both now dated 1857 (figures 61, 62).[10] He conflates the two paintings in his description, but there is no mistaking them; no other works of that time correspond as closely to his description as these two Water Gap paintings.

To be sure, Daingerfield's account is neither entirely clear nor accurate in every point. But it states plainly enough that Inness painted a set of paintings, of which the painting found in Mexico, *The Lackawanna Valley*, was one. And the construction of his text can only imply that the two Delaware Water Gap paintings were the others. As long as *The Lackawanna Valley* was thought to be firmly dated 1855, a relationship to paintings dated 1857 was not considered—which is perhaps why, apart from its evident confusion, Daingerfield's text has never entered the discussion of *The Lackawanna Valley*. But if *The Lackawanna Valley* is released from that date, the relationship becomes both possible and plausible.

Two things in particular make it so. One is that the three paintings are similar in size: *The Lackawanna Valley* measures 34 by 50 inches, both of the Delaware Water Gap paintings measure 32 by 52 inches.

60
George Inness, *The Lackawanna Valley.*
Wash drawing, 12½ × 18½ in. Christie's,
New York.

The second is that they are compatible in subject: *The Lackawanna Valley* depicts the first roundhouse of the D.L.& W. and the railroad's yard in Scranton; the Delaware Water Gap was the route of the D.L.& W., and both Water Gap paintings depict the railroad passing through it.

The relationship is not without difficulties. The paintings differ in size, in style, and in their histories. The difference in size may suggest how the set developed. *The Lackawanna Valley* is two inches taller and two inches narrower than the other paintings. It is probably the earliest of the three, and its subject has historical precedence, since it depicts the railroad's founding while the others depict its later development and expansion. It is, therefore, thematically their generative center, while visually its squarer format would fittingly serve as the central panel in a triptych (figure 63). The paintings need not have hung as a group, of course, yet they fit together pleasingly: the rivers in the Water Gap paintings form inverted parentheses visually responsive to each other and centripetally framing the central panel, while the curve of the river in what is here proposed as the right-hand panel almost exactly echoes the curve of the railroad in *The Lackawanna Valley.*

61
George Inness, *Delaware Water Gap,* 1857.
Oil on canvas, 32 × 52 in. James Maroney,
New York.

62
George Inness, *Delaware Water Gap*, 1857.
Oil on canvas, 32 × 52 in. The Montclair
Art Museum. Gift of Mrs. F. Herman Fayen.

63
Reconstruction: *Water Gap/Lackawanna Valley/Water Gap*.

One of the most diffficult things to account for, if we are to think of them as a set, is the stylistic difference between *The Lackawanna Valley* and the two Water Gap paintings. In *The Lackawanna Valley* the handling is broader, more painterly, and the contrasts of value and hue are more emphatic than in the other two, which are painted with a delicacy of color and a meticulous, controlled handling and attention to detail. If the paintings are a set, there was at some point and for some reason a sudden change in Inness's style.

Inness was profoundly affected by the landscapes of the French Barbizon School, which he encountered on a trip to France in 1853–54, and *The Lackawanna Valley* is one of the earliest and clearest examples of Barbizon influence on his art. In the 1850s Barbizon art was not compatible with American taste, as evidenced by the critic, evidently accustomed to the careful, precise style of most American landscape paintings, who found a painting by Inness in the broad and allusive Barbizon mode so illegible that to him it resembled green cheese and soft tallow.[11] Among the many things we do not know about *The Lackawanna Valley* is why the railroad commissioned it of an artist who was not only young (Inness was in his early thirties) and without reputation, but who had also recently returned from France under the influence of a style that had in

America, and to some extent even in France, the disagreeable flavor of modernity. The railroad's directors probably selected Inness because, being young and relatively unknown, he would work cheaply. And they chose him, perhaps, not on the basis of his most recent art, but with knowledge only of earlier preBarbizon works markedly different and distinctly more conventional in style (figure 64).

According to Inness's son, the railroad was not pleased with *The Lackawanna Valley*. It omitted the firm's initials at first and did not show enough tracks. He does not report that the railroad was also dissatisfied with the painting's style, but it is possible. It has been suggested that the painting was rejected outright by the railroad.[12] That seems unlikely: Inness surely would have said so, and he was, after all, paid for it. Even so, the railroad may not have liked the painting, and if it was the first part of a larger set, the railroad may have insisted that the remaining paintings be executed in a more conventional style. That would explain why the precision and polished smoothness of the two Delaware Water Gap Paintings are found in no other paintings that Inness made at the same time.

The company's preference for the style of the Water Gap paintings may have been determined in part by its commercial utility. Both Daingerfield and

Inness's son reported that *The Lackawanna Valley* was to be used for advertising. So far as we know it was not. If that was the railroad's plan, it may have been thwarted by a style that was, in its painterly breadth, unsuitable for reproduction. But in 1859 the Montclair *Delaware Water Gap* was reproduced faithfully in a lithograph by Currier & Ives (figure 65). This is not advertisement in the strictest sense, but it is close; Currier & Ives lithographs were often converted into advertisements.[13] This print could have been the advertisement that Daingerfield and George, Jr. mentioned, displaced to another painting of the set.

The railroad company may have found Inness's interpretation of the subject of *The Lackawanna Valley* as unpalatable as its style. It commemorates the railroad's founding by an image of unusual frankness, a blunt depiction of what railroad builders did to nature that might almost take as its text the cutting and slashing, leveling and defacing that Daniel Webster, with similarly unembarrassed frankness, described about ten years earlier.[14] Railroad companies were clearly sensitive to this issue. They were anxious to have artists sanction railroad-making and tried to show that rather than desecrating nature, the railroads actually brought more people, more easily, into its undisturbed presence. That, of course, was the purpose of the famous artists' excursion organized by

64
George Inness, *The Old Mill,* 1849. Oil on
canvas, 30 × 42 in. The Art Institute of
Chicago. William Owen and Erna Sawyer
Goodman Collection.

65
Currier & Ives, *View on the Delaware:*
"Water Gap" in the Distance, 1860. Litho-
graph. Library of Congress.

the Baltimore & Ohio Railroad in 1858.[15] It is possible, therefore, that in the difference between *The Lackawanna Valley* and the two Water Gap paintings, the editorial hand of the railroad company is visible; for in the Water Gap paintings the offensive candor of *The Lackawanna Valley* has been censored and sanitized, its roughness of meaning polished away just as thoroughly as its roughness of style. All traces of the railroad's destructiveness have been replaced, or subsumed, by images of conventional pastoral serenity. Nature's beauty and man's works are linked in perfect harmony, and each instance of that untroubling relationship is given with almost encyclopedic thoroughness.

If *The Lackawanna Valley* belonged to a set, it took that form, of course, primarily because of the commercial and documentary needs of the company that commissioned it. But artistic precedent for working in sets and series was a strong one in the 1850s. It was established by Thomas Cole, whose five-part *Course of Empire* (1836, New-York Historical Society), four-part *Voyage of Life* (1840 and 1842, Munson-Williams-Proctor Institute and National Gallery of Art), and narrative pairs like *Departure* and *Return* (figures 66, 67) and *Past* and *Present* (1838, Amherst College) were chief parts of his artistic legacy. Artists who followed Cole tried their

hand at similar narrative configurations, such as Jasper Cropsey's *Spirit of War* (National Gallery of Art) and *Spirit of Peace* (Woodmere Art Gallery) in 1851.[16] Inness never accepted Cole's influence as openly or as readily as Cropsey, Church, or Gifford did, but there can be no question that he felt it. If he did not actually paint Colesian series in the early 1850s, the character of a number of his paintings points unmistakably to his knowledge of them. *Peace and War* of 1848 (Private Collection) and *March of the Crusaders* of 1850 (figure 68) are thoroughly redolent of Cole's *Departure* and *Return*, for example, and other paintings of that period show Cole's influence as well. That influence abated in the later 1850s, particularly after Inness's trip to France and his conversion to the Barbizon landscape style. It did not disappear, however, for only a resurfacing of Cole's influence can explain Inness's three-part series *The Triumph of the Cross* of 1867.[17]

Through Cole's use of the pictorial device of series or pendant sets, it became identified with historical narration. And it may have been precisely for this sense of history that the D.L.& W. wanted a set of paintings, not just a single one. A set could express historical process, not just commemorate a single

event, and that process could convey an argument. For instance, presenting the railroad as the catalyst for the serene interaction and bountiful collaboration of nature and machinery, in a state of almost inevitable ethical and aesthetic rightness, would identify technological enterprise with the inexorable and disinterested operations of history. From this point of view, it is possible to think of the D.L.& W. set as a two-stage Course of Empire, with *The Lackawanna Valley* as the Savage State and the Water Gap paintings the Consummation. But here the pessimism of Cole's cyclical view of history has been modernized, recast in the terms of technological progress and an optimistic future.[18]

Despite considerable recent discussion of the meaning and intention of *The Lackawanna Valley*, "the picture's interpretation remains open, and it is impossible to read it 'correctly.' " In short, according to Barbara Novak, "It is a singular and somewhat mysterious picture."[19] There is no "correct" reading of *The Lackawanna Valley*, of course, but the painting's meaning is not quite as elusive, as mysterious, as Novak says, nor as relative to changing tastes and times. To be sure, neither Inness himself nor his contemporaries explained *The Lackawanna Valley*. It was not publicly exhibited during the artist's lifetime

66
Thomas Cole, *The Departure*, 1837. Oil on
canvas, 39½ × 63 in. The Corcoran Gallery
of Art. Gift of William Wilson Corcoran,
1869.

67
Thomas Cole, *The Return*, 1837. Oil on canvas, 39¾ × 63 in. The Corcoran Gallery of Art. Gift of William Wilson Corcoran, 1869.

68
George Inness, *March of the Crusaders,*
1850. Oil on canvas, 36¼ × 48⅜ in. Fruit-
lands Museums, Harvard, Massachusetts.

and therefore generated no interpretive commentary. However, there is a body of evidence that, if it does not yield a detailed reading of the painting's content and Inness's purposes in painting it, testifies to the frame of mind and framework of meaning in which it was made. That evidence is the subject matter and style of *The Lackawanna Valley* itself and of other Inness paintings that precede or are contemporary with it.

About twenty years after painting *The Lacka-wanna Valley*, Inness praised the type of "civilized landscape" it represented: "I love it more and think it more worthy of reproduction than that which is savage and untamed. It is more significant. Every act of man . . . marks itself wherever it has been."[20] Inness declared that preference just as boldly in his earliest paintings. In them, he never painted "savage and untamed" nature; his scenes were almost always populated and depicted acts and emblems of civilization that exemplified the human domination of nature. In *Sunshower* (1847, Santa Barbara Museum of Art), for example, the foreground contains a reaper and a shepherdess, who symbolize a nature tamed and shaped to human purposes by cultivation and husbandry. *The Woodchopper* (1849, Cleveland Museum of Art) presents an explicit symbol of the human subjugation of nature, and the woodchopper's by-product, the tree stump, figures in *The Lament*

(1846, Mrs. Anton Hulman) as the cause of the Indian's distress and the symbol of his doom. In *Midsummer Greens* (1856, Private Collection) the stump is also a symbol of civilization, and the picnic party in the distance represents nature tamed for human use and pleasure. Finally, in *Surveying* (1846, Location unknown), nature is plotted and organized by human reason for human designs.

The Lackawanna Valley, therefore, is only a more explicit and forceful rendering of the kind of civilized subject Inness depicted in a succession of paintings. It is clear that Inness knew what the subject meant and that his feelings about its meaning were not neutral. Some of Inness's contemporaries had misgivings about civilization and progress; he did not. Civilization's transactions with nature were never so openly and insistently presented in the work of any of his contemporaries, and Inness repeatedly affirmed the "marks" left by "every act of man" on the landscape. What is more, the unequivocal frankness with which he depicted the railroad's encounter with nature in *The Lackawanna Valley*, the warmth and brightness of the painting's light and the clarity of its atmosphere, forbid insinuations of doubt or irony or criticism.

But why did Inness care? Why did that subject attract him so? Perhaps because civilized landscape

was *modern* landscape, different on one hand from the wilderness which, although for many of his American contemporaries the highest form of landscape subject matter, was by the 1850s part of America's mythological past, not its visible present; and different, on the other, from the mere civility of pastoral landscape in the Claudian tradition. Civilized landscape—particularly a landscape like *The Lackawanna Valley*, in which the instrument of civilization was the railroad, "type of the modern" as Walt Whitman said in the 1850s, the "merciless embodiment of the Present and the Practical" as Bayard Taylor described it in 1852[21]—was a legible sign, almost an emblematic proclamation, of an affiliation with the modern present and a rejection of the mythologized past.

All the evidence of Inness's artistic behavior suggests that he understood very early that art was essentially artificial; that art and nature were different things and that paintings were not necessarily pictures; that it was the function, perhaps even the obligation, of the artist, through the formal reorganization of its materials, to interpret nature aesthetically and expressively and not merely depict it. Civilized landscape, nature shaped by creative intelligence, was thus the counterpart of Inness's modern—indeed, modernist—determination to transform nature into art, to impress his artistic will on nature and use its materials for his own artistic purposes, just as reapers and shepherdesses, woodcutters and surveyors, and of course, railroad builders, used and remade nature according to human design. The subject matter of Inness's pre-Barbizon art instinctively reflected that understanding. But in the suggestive breadth and energetic handling of Barbizon style, as displayed in *The Lackawanna Valley*, Inness discovered artistic means by which nature could be even more freely and directly reorganized into art.

When Inness first encountered Barbizon art in the early 1850s, it was, he surely knew, the most modern form of landscape painting. Inness's art had from the first been modern in instinct and intention; adopting the Barbizon style made it modern in appearance as well. Shortly before he painted his most explicitly modern subjects in *The Lackawanna Valley* and the Water Gap paintings, therefore, his art assumed its most explicitly modern form. That those two occurrences were not unrelated, that in *The Lackawanna Valley*, particularly, modernity of subject and modernity of style were issues of correlative meaning and comparable pertinence, is suggested by the unprecedented pictorial quality of the painting. It is the clearest sign that something about its subject touched Inness in a direct and special way, as though

its stylistic conviction is the direct outgrowth and visible manifestation of Inness's belief in what he depicted, and in what that stood for.

Another painting virtually begs to be considered in relationship to *The Lackawanna Valley—St. Peter's, Rome* (figure 69). *The Lackawanna Valley* depicts the characteristically mid-nineteenth-century contest between nature and the machine in peculiarly American terms—with an American spaciousness, an American forthrightness, and in a clean, clear, hopeful American light. After a relatively recent trip to Europe, the subject might have seemed to Inness quintessentially American. And it might have occurred to him to reinforce its Americanness by painting a pendant of its equally quintessential European counterpart. The paintings are composed and constructed in similar ways, and each has as its most prominent feature a large domed building. In one case the building was the most famous piece of religious architecture in the West, St. Peter's basilica, whose monumentality is the symbol of European fixity and, seen as if through the mists of time, of the Old World past. The roundhouse in *The Lackawanna Valley* is its New World counterpart, secular and utilitarian, a shrine of the greatest implement of American progress and enterprise, the railroad, and, seen in the clear morning light, the symbol of futurity.

69
George Inness, *St. Peter's Rome,* 1857. Oil
on canvas, 30 × 40 in. The New Britain
Museum of American Art. Charles F. Smith
Fund.

Notes

1

"His Art His Religion," *New York Herald*, August 12, 1894. An altered version of this text was published in the sale catalogue *Oil Paintings & Water-Colors by George Inness. Collection of the Artist's Daughter, Mrs. Jonathan Scott Hartley* (New York: American Art Association, Inc., 1927), 66, lot 76; it was the source of LeRoy Ireland's citation in his catalogue raisonné *The Works of George Inness* (Austin, Texas, 1965), 28, no. 110.

2

George Inness, Jr., *Life, Art, and Letters of George Inness* (New York, 1917), 108, 111.

3

Elliott Daingerfield, *George Inness: The Man and His Art* (New York, 1911), 16–17.

4

The early years of the 1850s were stringent ones, so much so that in 1852 Inness wrote to a potential donor, "three shillings is all I possess in the world and I know not where to get more" (Letter to Samuel Gray Ward, New York, November 21, 1852. Samuel Gray Ward Papers, Houghton Library, Harvard University). His situation was not unremittingly dire in the 1850s, but a seventy-five dollar commission would have been welcome, particularly in the "hard times" for artists that a writer in *The Crayon* commented on in 1857 (IV, December, p. 378).

5

See Marjorie Dakin Arkelian, "George Inness: His Life, Signature Years, and the California Highlights," *George Inness Landscapes: His Signature Years 1884–1894* (Oakland, CA: The Oakland Museum, 1978), 21–22.

6

There are, of course, a number of places named Mexico in the United States. Mexico, Pennsylvania, a town on the Juniata River near Harrisburg, is the closest to the offices and works of the D.L.& W. at Scranton. Inness painted on the Juniata River in 1856, at the same time—perhaps on the same campaign—that he painted *The Lackawanna Valley*.

7

History of the City of Scranton (Scranton, 1867), 50. The D.L. & W.'s second annual report, issued in 1855, looked forward to the completion of the roundhouse the following year by predicting, "It will be a noble structure."

8

In an earlier discussion of the painting ("George Inness and the Hudson River School: *The Lackawanna Valley*," *The American Art Journal* II [Fall 1970]: 51), I was unnecessarily ingenious in explaining the discrepancy between its supposed date of 1855 and the roundhouse's completion in 1856, suggesting that Inness might have known the building from descriptions or architect's renderings. Avoiding the discrepancy by questioning the painting's date did not occur to me.

9

Infrared reflectography shows precisely the same squaring in the painting.

10

Stephen R. Edidin, Curator of the Montclair Art Museum, was kind enough to examine the date of the Montclair *Delaware Water Gap*. That date has always been given as 1859 (as in Ireland, *Works*, 41, no. 168, and *The American Painting Collection of the Montclair Art Museum* [Montclair, 1977], no. 171). Close scrutiny, however, shows it clearly reads 1857. Two things seemed to support an 1859 date. One was the unnecessary assumption that the Montclair painting and the Currier & Ives lithograph after it, published in 1860, were closely related in date. Another was Ireland's feeling that the Montclair *Delaware Water Gap* was the painting of that title in the 1859 exhibition of the National Academy of Design. But the NAD painting might have been the one exhibited also in 1859 at the Royal Academy in London (Ireland, *Works*, 37, no. 145).

11

The Knickerbocker XLV (May 1855): 533.

12

Susan Danly Walther (ed.), *The Railroad in the American Landscape: 1850–1950* (Wellesley, MA: The Wellesley College Museum, 1981), 79, no. 8.

13

For example, the *American "Express" Train* (1855) was made into an advertisement for the Adams Express Co. See *Currier & Ives: A Catalogue Raisonné* (Detroit, 1984), I, nos. 0142, 0046.

14

Speech at the Opening of the Northern Railroad to Grafton, New Hampshire, August 28, 1847, in *The Works of Daniel Webster* (Boston, 1851), II, 412. Barbara Novak finds *The Lackawanna Valley* "a shocking picture" (*Nature and Culture: American Landscape and Painting 1825–1875* [New York, 1980], p. 172).

15

See Kenneth W. Maddox, "The Railroad in the Eastern Landscape: 1850–1900," in *The Railroad in the American Landscape: 1850–1950*, 28–33.

16

William Sonntag painted a four-part *Progress of Civilization* in 1847 (unlocated). In 1848, Gifford exhibited paintings entitled *The Past* and *The Present*.

17

Of its three parts, only one, *The Valley of the Shadow of Death* (Vassar College Art Gallery), survives.

18

A particularly stubborn objection to the proposition that the three paintings were a set is their own history. If the paintings were at one time a group, they surely did not descend as one. *The Lackawanna Valley* may have been owned by the railroad until it was sold with a lot of office furniture, but the other paintings were both privately owned through most of the nineteenth century. For that there is no easy or entirely satisfactory explanation.

19

Novak, *Nature and Culture*, 174.

20

"A Painter on Painting," *Harper's New Monthly Magazine* LVI (February 1878): 461.

21

Walt Whitman, "To a Locomotive in Winter," in *Leaves of Grass*; Bayard Taylor, "The Erie Railroad," in *The Home Book of the Picturesque* (New York, 1852), 143.

3 Andrew Joseph Russell's *The Great West Illustrated*

Susan Danly

The importance of content is demonstrated by the fact that photographs which have survived from the past and which ever increase in value and prestige are those endowed with content and documentary interest, as well as beauty. The primitive trestle bridge of Lincoln's time is not a beautiful object, but it is certainly a beautiful photograph, because it tells us so poignantly about our country's technological birthpains: this is our past as Americans, organized in a most lucid manner.[1]

In the post–Civil War decade, the event that most captured the imagination of Americans was the construction of the transcontinental railroad. Like many, the photographer Andrew Joseph Russell saw the railroad as a practical means both to reunify the country and generate economic growth:

The great Rail Road problem of the age is now solved. The Continental Iron Band now permanently unites distant portions of the Republic, and opens up to Commerce, Navigation and Enterprise the vast unpeopled plains and lofty mountain ranges that now divide East from West.[2]

From the beginning of railroad construction in 1865, photography played an important role in documenting and publicizing its progress, educating the public in the geography and geology of the West, advertising the scenic attractions along its route, and providing aesthetic images of the western landscape. One of several important photographers[3] to work for the western railroads, Russell produced small stereographic views and large albumen prints, glass lantern slides and photographically illustrated books—the largest body of work to record the building of the Union Pacific Railroad. His album *The Great West Illustrated*, published in 1869, the year the transcontinental railroad was completed, is an outstanding example of the advances, both technical and aesthetic, made in landscape photography dedicated to the program of promoting rail travel.

This essay analyzes Russell's photographs and their multiple functions as expressions of the nineteenth-century ideology of progress. By examining Russell's choice of people and places to photograph and by placing his work within the context of other forms of visual art, we can more fully recognize the extent of his contribution to the history of photography. The often self-contradictory elements of his imagery imbue these photographs with a historical and aesthetic tension that reaches beyond the circumstances of their origin and gives the work an added importance for the modern viewer.

Raised in Nunda, New York, in the picturesque Genessee Valley, Russell initially established himself as a landscape and portrait painter in the early 1850s.[4] But with the outbreak of the Civil War, he began to experiment with new forms of picture making. Russell started work on a huge diorama of war scenes, based on engravings after Mathew Brady's photographs, and by the winter of 1862 was exhibiting his *Panorama of the War for the Union* in various towns in upstate New York.[5] Russell's choice of subject and presentation was significant, for they later became two of his primary concerns as a photographer—the documentary and panoramic landscape.[6]

In the fall of 1862, Russell joined the Union Army and was dispatched as a government artist to the U. S. Military Railroad.[7] Under Egbert Guy Faux, a photographer trained in Brady's studio, he learned the techniques of the collodion wet-plate process. Although the physical conditions were harsh, the army provided Russell with the resources for experimenting with a wide range of photographic negatives. Close study of Russell's images from his Civil War album[8] reveals that he developed a sense for the aesthetic as well as the documentary aspects of the photographic medium. He used bridge structures to organize panoramic landscapes and natural elements such as trees and riverbanks to establish a strong vertical and horizontal framework in his compositions. In his feeling for contrasts of light and dark

and the selective view of the camera lens, Russell displayed his power as a photographer (figure 70). But these photographs primarily served a documentary function, as they were used to illustrate General Herman Haupt's reports on the U. S. Military Railroad Construction Corps. They include a variety of scenes of bridge construction, track repairs, demolition, and railroad equipment, as well as portraits of officers and landscapes.

From his Civil War experience, Russell gained an appreciation not only for railroad engineering, but also for the important role of the camera in documenting history. Recalling his years as a military photographer, Russell later emphasized his sense of historical mission:

The memories of our great war come down to us and will pass on to future generations with more accuracy and truth-telling illustration than that of any other previous struggle of ancient or modern times: and the world is indebted to the photographic art and a few enterprising and earnest men, who are not afraid of exposure and who could laugh at fatigue and starvation, could face danger in all shapes, and, were at all times ready to march, often between two armies, in the trenches, on the ramparts, through the swamps and forests, with the advance guard, and back again at headquarters—not a flank movement, but the willing and indefatigable artist at his post of danger and adventure.[9]

It must have been a similar sense of "danger and adventure" that lured Russell from New York to the plains of the American West in 1868 to photograph the construction of the Union Pacific Railroad. While there is no documentary evidence that Russell was hired directly by the Union Pacific, the railroad was ultimately responsible for publishing Russell's most important work, *The Great West Illustrated*. The leather-bound album (figure 71) consists of fifty carefully selected and elaborately mounted photographs, each accompanied by a short descriptive text. While some albums were presented as gifts to railroad investors and management, others were sold for fifty dollars each to the public.[10] To the investor and general public alike, the album was the visual expression of the nineteenth-century belief in the providential progress of industrial technology and man's ability to overcome the obstacles of nature by dramatic feats of engineering. As the preface to the Russell album acknowledges, the West was not to remain an untamed wilderness, but was a geographic region ripe for economic exploitation:

It is therefore believed that the information contained in this Volume . . . is calculated to interest all classes of people, and to excite the admiration of all reflecting minds as to the colossal grandeur of the Agricultural, Mineral and Commercial resources of the West.[11]

The sites included in the album by no means represent a complete journey on the route of the Union Pacific.[12] The album is limited to the last third of the route, to a stretch of country between Laramie, Wyoming, and Salt Lake City, Utah. Of the fifty views, only seventeen are scenes of actual railroad construction. The remaining thirty-one include townscapes, panoramic landscapes, geological studies of unusual rock formations, and two outdoor group portraits. Accompanying each photograph is a brief description of the particulars of the landscape, such as the height, color, and geological properties of the terrain. In scenes of railroad building, the captions stress man's engineering accomplishments, while in the landscapes the "architecture of nature" is emphasized.

The photographs themselves also represent contrasting impressions of western landscape: on one hand we see a natural terrain formed by powerful geological forces and on the other a man-altered landscape, carved up by railroad cuts and bridged by tremendous spans of wooden trestle work. Russell conveys these contrasting views in individual images, such as those of *Skull Rock* (figure 72) and the *Dale Creek Bridge* (figure 73), which are next to each other in the album, and within single images, such as the *East End of Tunnel No. 3, Weber Valley* (figure 74). In these photographs the human figures are

70
Andrew Joseph Russell, *Aqueduct Bridge Looking Toward D.C.*, c. 1863. Albumen print. Library of Congress.

THE GREAT WEST ILLUSTRATED

IN A SERIES OF

PHOTOGRAPHIC VIEWS ACROSS THE CONTINENT;

TAKEN ALONG THE LINE OF THE

UNION PACIFIC RAILROAD,

WEST FROM OMAHA, NEBRASKA.

WITH AN ANNOTATED TABLE OF CONTENTS, GIVING A BRIEF DESCRIPTION OF EACH VIEW; ITS PECULIARITIES, CHARACTERISTICS, AND CONNECTION WITH THE DIFFERENT POINTS ON THE ROAD.

BY A. J. RUSSELL.

RHODE ISLAND HISTORICAL SOCIETY

VOL. I.

PUBLISHED BY AUTHORITY OF THE UNION PACIFIC RAILROAD COMPANY.
NEW YORK: OFFICE, 29 NASSAU STREET.
1869.

71
Frontispiece to *The Great West Illustrated*, 1869.

72
Andrew Joseph Russell, *Skull Rock*. From *The Great West Illustrated*.

73
Andrew Joseph Russell, *Dale Creek Bridge.*
From *The Great West Illustrated.*

74
Andrew Joseph Russell, *East End of Tunnel No. 3, Weber Valley.* From *The Great West Illustrated.*

either dwarfed by the scale of nature or, paradoxically, they swarm over mountains, industriously building tunnels and bridges.

Russell began work on the project in the summer of 1868. He and Samuel Bowles, a well-known journalist, had been traveling together on an excursion sponsored by the Union Pacific. In his book *Our New West*, Bowles explained the railroad's importance:

There will speedily be other railroads across our Continent. The rivalries of sections, the temptations of commerce, the necessities of our political system, will add at least two more lines within a generation's time. But this, the first, will forever remain the one of history; the one of romance. Its construction in so short a time was the greatest triumph of modern civilization, of all civilization indeed. [13]

The "temptations of commerce" were also evident in the construction of the Union Pacific itself, and Russell's photograph of railroad and government officials at Fort Sanders in July 1868 documents one of the most important conflicts that arose during the railroad's construction. Generals Ulysses S. Grant, Philip Sheridan, and William Harney met with Union Pacific officers to settle a dispute that had halted construction. Grenville Dodge, the railroad's chief engineer, and Thomas Durant, a vice president in charge of financial matters, had disagreed over the choice of routes. While Dodge argued for the most

direct route across the high plains of Wyoming, Durant favored a circuitous route that would add more track mileage and thus increase the profits of the Credit Mobilier, the financial group that had received government subsidies for construction costs. Grant, then campaigning for the presidency of the United States, had traveled west in order to get the project back on schedule. [14] Russell's photograph of the confrontation between representives of the railroad and the government is a document that transcends conventional portrait photography (figure 75). Flanked by the ethereal halation of the American flags, [15] the figures are stretched along a picket fence in a frieze-like composition. Russell managed to capture the tensions between the adversaries by isolating their poses and expressions. Characteristically, he used the architectural framework of the background building to frame the individual heads and give a strong underlying structure to the composition.

With agreement on the route settled, Russell went on to photograph construction in western Wyoming and Utah, and in February 1869 he returned to New York to print his negatives. The *Philadelphia Photographer* reported that he "presented twelve very fine 10 × 13 prints of views on the Union Pacific

Railroad, principally in Utah" to an audience of New York's leading photographers, including Charles Bierstadt and Abraham Bogardus. [16] Meanwhile, during the winter of 1868–69, construction on the railroad had been halted at the mouth of Echo Canyon in eastern Utah because of bad weather and a dispute with the Central Pacific Railroad over competing claims for construction subsidies from the government. The disproportionate number of photographs of eastern Utah included in the Russell album would seem to support a claim to this region by the Union Pacific.

When Grant assumed the presidency in March 1869, he quickly moved to settle the dispute and set a date for the completion of the transcontinental route. Russell returned to the West for this historic occasion, and he was present on May 10, 1869, for the ceremony of the joining of the two railroads at Promontory Point, Utah. Three of Russell's photographs of the festivities were reproduced as wood engravings in the June 5 edition of *Frank Leslie's Illustrated Newspaper* to accompany the lead article on the event. [17] For many nineteenth-century Americans, it was Russell's image of the two engines (figure 76) face to face on the single track that epitomized the century's greatest triumph of technology over nature.

75
Andrew Joseph Russell, *Fort Sanders*. From *The Great West Illustrated*.

76
Andrew Joseph Russell, *East and West Shaking Hands at the Laying of the Last Rail*, 1869. Albumen print. Yale University, Beinecke Rare Book and Manuscript Library.

While in the West, Russell also contributed an article to *Anthony's Photographic Bulletin*. In "On the Mountains with Tripod and Camera," he describes his campsite in the Uintah Mountains (figure 77) with an explorer's appreciation of the western wilderness:

Eleven thousand feet above the level of the sea, in the very heart of the Rocky Mountains, is a great amphitheatre. In this distant and unknown locality, it was my fortune to be found the 15th day of August, 1869. At my feet lay Spectre Lake, surrounded by a great variety of evergreens, while behind rose lofty and perpendicular bluffs, some of them three thousand feet in height. I arrived here the evening of the 14th of August, with my camera, selected a good cover under a huge overhanging rock, made a good mattress, spread down my blankets, threw a few armfuls of wood on the fire, and turned in (as the saying goes) for the night. [18]

Russell was accompanied by a guide and two assistants whom he dubbed Tripod Tom and Jim Focus. One of these assistants probably was Stephen J. Sedgwick, a New York teacher and public lecturer. [19] Sedgwick had contacted Thomas Durant in March 1869 "to make arrangements with the Union Pacific Railroad Company to deliver illustrated lectures on the line of the road," [20] and by the spring of 1870 he was lecturing on the New York lyceum circuit, using Russell's stereographs, projected as lantern slides,

for illustrations. Throughout the next decade, Sedgwick published and distributed Russell's photographs in his *Catalogue of Stereoscopic Views of Scenery in all Parts of the Rocky Mountains between Omaha and Sacramento*. [21]

Russell apparently made little distinction between his work as a painter and as a photographer. In the preface to *The Great West Illustrated*, he is referred to as "the artist who photographed the views contained in his work," and, indeed, his wife listed Russell's occupation at the time of his death in 1902 as "artist." [22] The nineteenth-century American photographer had less difficulty assuming a position in the art world, for distinctions between fine and popular art had yet to be codified. This fact was readily observed by Dr. Hermann Vogel, the eminent German photographer, on a visit to America in 1870:

In Germany, where prejudice so often hinders free development, the photographer is generally but little esteemed, and rarely considered an artist. Here in America where such difference in rank is unknown, he enjoys a much higher position if he is able to fill it. Here the photographer is the chief representative of creative art, and is not forced to submit to the arrogance of artists. [23]

That Russell saw an alliance between painting and photography is evident in his use of the picturesque mode to reconcile the contradictions raised by

77
Andrew Joseph Russell, *Major Russell's Bedroom, Uintahs*, 1869. Stereographic view. Union Pacific Historical Museum, Omaha.

the intrusion of technology into the wilderness.[24] In the picturesque, the human element is usually subordinated to the features of the landscape; buildings and figures enliven or reinforce the elements of nature, but they are never the principal subjects. That landscape photography could be adapted to this traditional mode of pictorial representation was recognized as early as 1854 in an article significantly entitled "Photography as a Fine Art":

Here we have collected into a focus the choicest productions of this wonderful art, contributed by practitioners of various countries and fully representing the great state of perfection at which photography has arrived. Every department of art and nature is laid under contribution, and each adequately represented. Nature, animate and inanimate; leafless tree with its perplexing anatomy of branches and twigs, or crowned with its luxuriant foliage; the corn-field, the rural lane, the copse and dell, the lofty battlemented castle or lowly cottage, the bridge, the stream, are mirrored before us with picturesque effect, and microscopic fidelity.[25]

In *Castle Rock* (figure 78) Russell featured a similar variety of picturesque forms: leafy vegetation, castellated peaks mirrored in the placid waters of a gracefully curving river, and the lone fisherman—forms that can be found again and again in paintings and prints from this period. This site on the Green River was considered one of the most picturesque spots on the route of the Union Pacific and was often used to

78
Andrew Joseph Russell, *Castle Rock, Green River Valley.* From *The Great West Illustrated.*

101

draw analogies between man-made and natural structures that coexisted in the western landscape:

And all throughout this region fantastic forms abound everywhere, the architect of nature exhibited in sport. An eastern journalist—a traveler here in the first days of the Pacific Railway—has best enumerated the varied shapes. All about one, he says, "lie 'long, wide troughs, as of departed rivers; long level embankments, as of railroad-tracks or endless fortifications."[26]

Following the advice of contemporary photography critics, Russell frequently used a curving roadway or riverbed to organize his picturesque compositions. In *Source of the Laramie River* (figure 79) and *Echo Canyon,* he placed tree and rock formations to one side of the composition to create a diagonal division of the photograph into dark and light triangular sections. Edward L. Wilson, the editor of the most widely read photography journal of the period, *The Philadelphia Photographer,* particularly recommended such picturesque formulas in a series of articles entitled "Art Principles Applicable to Photography."[27] Based on the theoretical writings of Reynolds, Ruskin, and Burnet, these articles discussed principles of mathematical and aerial perspective, composition, and lighting. They were also illustrated with engravings after paintings by seventeenth-century Dutch landscape painters, which fit

79
Andrew Joseph Russell, *Source of the Laramie River.* From *The Great West Illustrated.*

Wilson's recommendation to photographers "to study the works of others, and to imitate it when it is good." He continued:

Do not be confined to works of photography, however, there is much, very much, outside of it, worthy of study, in the multitude of engravings and drawings to be seen or had almost anywhere. Some of the grandest studies of light and shade are to be found in the engravings in old books to be had at the book stands.[28]

While Russell organized his picturesque views around natural elements, his panoramic views focus attention on landscapes ordered by human structures. His views of Coalville and Salt Lake City (figure 80) convey a strong sense of abstract order, particularly when he sets the expansiveness of the landscape against the structure of civilization. The gridwork of streets and the simple geometry of buildings featured in these townscapes emphasize man's ability to create an environment that established civilized order in the American wilderness.

The natural world is perhaps most enigmatic in Russell's photographs of rock formations. In these views, the more traditional pictorial formulas of the

80
Andrew Joseph Russell, *Salt Lake City.* From
The Great West Illustrated.

picturesque and the panorama are of less importance. Russell relied instead on the more specifically photographic character of his medium. The ability of the camera to capture the texture of the rock surfaces, the silhouetting of dark forms against the blank sky, and the odd juxtaposition of human and natural forms are aspects of the photographic image that Russell exploited to great effect. In *Hanging Rock* (figure 81) Russell went to great lengths to arrange the camera angle, secure an extreme depth of field, and heighten the contrasts of light and dark. Comparison with another view taken at this site (figure 82) shows the degree to which Russell selected, rather than merely recorded, his images of the western landscape.[29]

In contemporary travel guides, the unusual rock formations of the West were often identified by names that elicited associations with monumental architecture of the past. Through photography the architectural feats of ancient Egypt and medieval France became familiar to many Americans during the 1860s. With the invention of the paper and glass-plate negative processes, techniques more suited to landscape photography and mass reproduction, photographers began to explore the outlying reaches of European colonial empires in Africa, the Middle East, and Asia in search of new and more

81
Andrew Joseph Russell, *Hanging Rock*. From *The Great West Illustrated*.

exotic subjects.[30] These photographs replaced lithography as a source of illustrations for travel literature.

Russell's work demonstrates a consciousness of the achievements of European photography in the 1850s and 1860s. His *Sphinx of the Valley* (figure 83), for example, clearly reflects the impact of popular travel photographs of the Middle East (figure 84), which were widely distributed in the United States as stereographic views, lantern slides, and book illustrations.[31] The contrast in scale between the figures and the rock formations, the isolation of these monumental forms within the picture frame, and the historical associations of their names place Russell's work within the context of European precedents. As Americans became better acquainted with the deserts in the West, they soon discovered natural monuments they believed rivaled those of Egypt:

What a wild land we live in! A few puffs of a locomotive had transformed us from civilization to solitude itself. This was the "great American desert." . . . A mysterious land with its wonderful record of savages and scouts, battles and hunts. We had a vague idea then that a sphynx and a score of pyramids were located somewhere on it.[32]

Often the chauvinist ideology of America's superiority over Europe was expressed by references to both her landscape and technological achievements.

82
Andrew Joseph Russell, *Hanging Rock, Mouth of Echo Canyon,* 1869. Stereographic view. Union Pacific Historical Museum, Omaha.

83
Andrew Joseph Russell, *Sphinx of the Valley.*
From *The Great West Illustrated.*

84
Francis Frith, *The Sphinx and the Great
Pyramid.* From *Lower Egypt, Thebes and the
Pyramids,* 1857. The J. Paul Getty Museum.

After his 1868 excursion on the Union Pacific, Schuyler Colfax wrote of the transcontinental railroad:

If our people, who now go to Europe for pleasure, travel and observation, knew a tithe of the enjoyment we experienced in our travels under our own flag, far more of them would turn their faces toward the setting sun; after exploring the Switzerland of America, the Rocky Mountains, with their remarkable Parks and Passes, go onward to that realm which fronts the Pacific, whose history is so romantic, and whose destiny is so sure; and which that great Highway of Nations, the Pacific Railroad, will this spring bring so near to all of us on the Atlantic slope.[33]

In his photograph of tunneling in Weber Canyon (figure 74), Russell seems to call attention to parallels between America's mountains and the Alps. As in A.-R. Bisson's view of Mt. Blanc (figure 85), Russell used the backdrop of the mountain face to frame the climbing figures, and he further emphasized their importance by placing the hole of the tunnel in the center of the composition.

The most direct European precedent for Russell's work was the railroad photography of Edouard-Denis Baldus, who produced several albums for the French railroads in the mid-1850s.[34] While there is no explicit evidence that Russell knew of Baldus's railroad albums, the work of the two photographers is related in both subject matter and photographic approach.

85
Auguste-Rosalie Bisson, *Ascension au Mont-Blanc*. From *Le Mont-Blanc et Ses Glaciers. Souvenir du Voyage de LL. l'Empereur et l'Imperatrice,* Paris, 1862.

They share a reliance on the graphic delineation of forms, a love of strong contrasts of light and shade, and a sense of abstract, geometric order. However, Baldus's railroad scenes could never be mistaken for Russell's precisely because of the subtle differences in their subject matter, for unlike any other visual medium, photography remains grounded to its subject. Baldus's imagery bespeaks a civilized European landscape, while Russell's celebrates the raw, primitive character of the American wilderness. One has only to compare the refined classical formality of Baldus's photograph of a viaduct (figure 86) with the rough-hewed improvisation emphasized in Russell's view of the Dale Creek Trestle (figure 73) to realize the cultural differences between European and American railroads as represented by these two photographers.

Early American landscape photography may be indebted to European precedents for the typology of travel photography and even for specific formal schema, such as the picturesque or panoramic mode, but the dictates of the American landscape itself, the frequent use of photography for more expressly commercial purposes, and the particular associations of wilderness and industrial progress in

86
Edouard-Denis Baldus, *Landscape with Viaduct at Chantilly.* From *Chemin de Fer du Nord; Ligne de Paris à Boulogne; Album de vues photographiques,* 1855. International Museum of Photography at George Eastman House.

108

nineteenth-century American art set Russell's photographs apart from those of his European counterparts. Moreover, the richness of Russell's images derives from this interweaving of the several functions of a photograph. Russell's photographs were explicitly documentary: they recorded the construction techniques, engineering, and rolling stock used to build the Union Pacific Railroad and provided scientific records through their close observation of the geological structures of the West.[35] In addition they served as advertisements and educational tools designed to promote travel on the transcontinental railroad by appealing to members of the upper middle class, who could afford to travel in the luxury of the Pullman car; to the lower middle class, who traveled vicariously through stereoscopic viewers and lantern slide lectures; and even to members of the working class, who packed into the immigrant trains, seeking employment promised in the developing towns and agricultural areas of the West. Finally, these photographs functioned as an important source for illustrations in newspapers and travel literature, giving visual expression to the popular belief in Manifest Destiny and the ideology of capitalist expansionism.

The visual force of Russell's compositions makes these photographs compelling works of art as well. In some landscapes Russell draws on the older European tradition of the picturesque (figure 79), while in others, images of the strange rock forms in the West (figure 81) and of railroad engines and tracks, Russell displays an aesthetic that is more camera-conscious. Again and again he makes known the presence of his camera; shadows cast by the tripod, the darkroom tent, and the cumbersome box itself, intrude into the view of his lens (figure 78). Russell's use of strong shadows, his silhouetting of dark forms against empty skies, and his reliance on a geometric underpinning in his compositions were elements of a photographic aesthetic much discussed in the journals of his day. The graphic sharpness of his photographic vision combined with the starkness of the landscape itself to produce imagery that is characterized by strength and austerity.

The subtle complexities of Russell's photographs derive not only from the rigorous formalism of his style, but also from the interaction between that style and the tensions within the imagery itself: the vastness of the American West literally put into perspective by the railroad track; the geometry of new cities juxtaposed with the panoramic vista of mountains; man dwarfed by the monuments of nature, while technology stands triumphant in the wilderness. These contradictions add another layer of meaning to Russell's work and point to Russell's valuable contribution to the development of landscape photography as a means of visual communication. While the nineteenth-century viewer favored his choice of picturesque valleys and marvelous rock formations that rivaled European scenery, the modern viewer admires the abstraction and ironies of his compositions.[36] This historical reinterpretation not only reveals a wealth of information about the production and meaning of art in the age of aesthetics and enterprise, but also helps account for today's postmodernist interest in early photography.

Notes

1

Berenice Abbott, *A Guide to Better Photography* (New York: Crown Publishers, 1941), 166–167.

2

A. J. Russell, "Correspondence from Russell to E. W. Packard, May 13, 1869, Echo City," Nunda *News* 10, no. 22 (May 29, 1869), n.p.

3

Other photographers who sold views of the Union Pacific Railroad during the 1860s and 1870s included John Carbutt, W. H. Jackson, and T. C. Roche. Alexander Gardner photographed on the route of the Kansas Pacific Railroad; and C. R. Savage, A. A. Hart, and Carlton Watkins were the principal photographers on the Central Pacific Railroad. See Weston Naef and James Wood, *Era of Exploration, The Rise of Landscape Photography in the American West, 1860–1885* (New York: The Metropolitan Museum of Art, 1975), 43–49.

4

The Nunda *News* listed him as one of the town's three local artists in 1851, and by 1855 he held a position as Professor of Chirography (penmanship) at the Nunda Literary Institute. Russell's extant paintings are family portraits (now in the Oakland Museum), but he also painted landscapes. See the Nunda *News*, December 13, 1851, and December 15, 1860; the latter article mentions a series of landscapes Russell painted for a prominent New York lawyer, Robert Bruce VanValkenberg.

5

Nunda *News*, December 14, 1862.

6

For a discussion of the relationship of panoramas and dioramas to the origins of photography, see Helmut and Alison Gernsheim, *L. J. M. Daguerre, The History of the Diorama and the Daguerreotype*, 2nd ed. (New York: Dover Publications, 1968) and Peter Galassi, *Before Photography* (New York: The Museum of Modern Art, 1981).

7

The most comprehensive history of Russell's Civil War photographs is an unpublished paper by Susan Williams, "Andrew J. Russell, United States Military Railroad Photographer, 1863," in the Union Pacific Railroad Archives, Omaha, Nebraska. A brief discussion of this subject is also found in William Gladstone, "Captain Andrew J. Russell: First Army Photographer," *Photographica* 10 (1978): 7–9; and in A. J. Russell, *Russell's Civil War Photographs* (New York: Dover, 1982).

8

Prints from the Civil War album are located in the National Archives and Library of Congress in Washington, D.C.; in the Virginia Historical Society; and on loan to the San Francisco Museum of Modern Art.

9

A. J. Russell, "Photographic Reminiscences of the War," *Anthony's Photographic Bulletin* 13 (1882): 212–213.

10

The exact number published is not known, but there are at least eleven extant albums and three incomplete sets in both public and private collections. See Susan Danly

Walther, "The Landscape Photographs of Alexander Gardner and Andrew Joseph Russell" (Ph.D. dissertation, Department of Art History, Brown University, 1983).

11

A. J. Russell, *The Great West Illustrated* (New York: The Union Pacific Railroad, 1869).

12

The fifty plates in the album were carefully selected from over two hundred glass-plate negatives, now in the collection of the History Department of the Oakland Museum. Vintage prints from those negatives are in the collection of the Beinecke Library at Yale University.

13

Samuel Bowles, *Our New West* (Hartford: Hartford Publishing Company, 1869), 68.

14

J. R. Perkins, *Trails, Rails and War: The Life of General G. M. Dodge* (Indianapolis: Bobbs-Merrill Company, 1929), 196–222. This biography of Dodge is illustrated with Russell photographs from the collection of the Union Pacific Railroad. A more scholarly history of Dodge and the Union Pacific Railroad is Stanley P. Hirschson, *Grenville M. Dodge* (Bloomington: Indiana University Press, 1967).

15

There are slight variations in this print from album to album. In some, only the central group of figures is included and the flags are not visible.

16

"New York Correspondence," *Philadelphia Photographer* 6 (1869): 88–89.

17

"Completion of the Union Pacific Railroad," *Frank Leslie's Illustrated Newspaper* 28 (June 5, 1869): 1, 183–185. Russell is credited in the photograph captions, and the article states: "The engravings we give are the faithful reproduction of the scenes prominently associated with the completion of the road. They are strict copies of the photographs taken expressly for *Frank Leslie's Illustrated News* at Promontory Point on that eventful 10th of May, and we can imagine no pictures more interesting to the civilized world."

18

A. J. Russell, "On the Mountains with Tripod and Camera," *Anthony's Photographic Bulletin* 1 (1870): 33–34. A continuation of this article appeared in the August 1870 issue, 128–130, and a description of Russell's camera in July 1870, 117–118.

19

For a discussion of Sedgwick and Russell, see William D. Pattison, "Westward by Rail with Professor Sedgwick: A Lantern Journey of 1873," *The Historical Society of California Quarterly* 42 (1960): 335–349, and "The Pacific Railroad Rediscovered," *Geographical Review* 52 (1962): 25–36.

20

Letter dated March 24, 1869, from George Opdyke, banker to Thomas Durant, in Sedgwick papers, collection of A. C. Combes, Pittsfield, Massachusetts.

21

There were at least four editions of this catalogue published between 1873 and 1879. Copies are in the collection of the Oakland Museum and the Beinecke Library at Yale University.

22

National Archives, Pension Records filed October 9, 1902.

23

"Photography in America," *The Photographic News* 14 (1870): 534.

24

For further discussion of this problem as it pertains to both painters and photographers, see Barbara Novak, *Nature and Culture* (New York: Oxford University Press, 1980), 157–200; and Leo Marx's essay in this volume.

25

"Photography as a Fine Art," *Illustrated Magazine of Art* 3 (1854): 1.

26

E. L. Burlingame, "The Plains and the Sierras," in *Picturesque America* 2, ed. William Cullen Bryant (New York: 1874), 174. The "eastern journalist" quoted here is Samuel Bowles.

27

Edward Wilson, "Art Principles Applicable to Photography," *The Philadelphia Photographer* 4 (1867): 337–338, 371–374; 5 (1868): 49–52, 71–73, 117–118, 265–267, 331–332, 367–369, 438–439.

28

Philadelphia Photographer 5 (1868): 438.

29

Recent attempts to recreate this image have underscored Russell's selectivity in composing this photograph. See Mark Klett, "Rephotographing Nineteenth Century Landscapes," in *That Awesome Space: Human Interaction in the Intermountain Landscape*, ed. E. Richard Hart (Salt Lake City: Sun Valley Center for the Arts and Humanities, 1981), 63.

30

Naef and Woods, 22–27; Robert Hershkowitz, *The British Photographer Abroad: The First Thirty Years* (London: Robert Hershkowitz, Ltd., 1980); Clark Worswick and Ainslee Embree, *The Last Empire: Photography in British India, 1855–1911* (Millerton, NY: Aperture, Inc.); and Nigel Cameron, *The Face of China: As Seen by Photographers and Travelers, 1860–1912* (Millerton, NY: Aperture, Inc.).

31

Frith's work in particular was well received, for reviews see "Egypt and Palestine," *The Art-Journal*, n.s. 4 (1858): 229–230; "Frith's Swiss and English Views," *The Philadelphia Photographer* 4 (1867): 193.

32

W. E. Webb, *Buffalo Land* (Philadelphia: Hubbard Bros., 1872), 118.

33

Bowles, ix–xi.

34

Weston Naef, *After Daguerre: Masterworks of French Photography, 1848–1900 from the Bibliothèque Nationale* (New York: The Metropolitan Museum of Art, 1980), nos. 13, 14; and Andre Jammes and Eugenia Parry Janis, *The Art of French Calotypes* (Princeton: Princeton University Press, 1983), 139–142. Baldus's railroad albums are also found in the collections of The International Museum of Photography at George Eastman House and The J. Paul Getty Museum.

35

Russell's photographs were used as illustrations in F. V. Hayden, *Sun Pictures of Rocky Mountain Scenery* (New York: J. Bien, 1870).

36

See for example Max Kozloff's discussion of Russell's work in "The Box in the Wilderness," in *Photography and Fascination* (Danbury, NH: Addison House, 1979), 60–75.

4

Man-Made Mountain: "Gathering and Governing" in H. H. Richardson's Design for the Ames Monument In Wyoming

James F. O'Gorman

On February 27, 1873, Oakes Ames, member from Massachusetts, sat in the seat in the House of Representatives he had occupied for a decade and listened while his colleagues condemned him for allegedly attempting improperly to influence other members by offering them stock in the Credit Mobilier of America at a price below par. After the vote, it is said, many of them crowded around to explain their ballots as acts of political expediency. Just over two months later Ames died in disgrace, surrounded by his family and friends at North Easton, Massachusetts.[1]

So ended the career and life of a remarkable and still controversial nineteenth-century manufacturer, politician, and capitalist, who had a major role in the creation of the transcontinental railroad, that thin belt of wood and iron that bound East and West into a unit upon its completion in 1869 just as the outcome of the Civil War had rebound North and South just four years earlier. As the partner of his brother Oliver (1807–77) in the operation of the highly successful Ames Shovel Company of North Easton, Oakes (1804–73) had entered Congress in 1862, the year in which it granted the Union Pacific Railroad its first charter (figure 87).[2] By the end of the Civil War no track had been laid, although a limited liability construction company, the Credit Mobilier, had been established in 1864. During the next

five years, until the driving of the Golden Spike at Promontory Point, Utah, where the Union Pacific locomotive bumped "buffalo-catchers" with that of the Central Pacific, the Ames brothers and their New England colleagues gradually gained control of both the railroad and the construction company. Oliver served as acting president of the line from 1866 and as president from 1868 to 1871, after which he continued to sit as a director until his death. Oakes assumed personal responsibility for constructing the road in 1867 and continued to direct the flow of capital into the process. Some of that capital came from his congressional peers, and that eventually led to his censure early in 1873.

History sees that censure as a politically useful act growing out of the election campaign of 1872 rather than a just reaction to illegal moves on the part of Oakes. In this, history merely echoes Oakes's friends and family, who at the earliest possible moment sought to counteract the effects of censure by memoralizing the man. At North Easton in 1879 his children began construction from the design of H. H. Richardson of the Oakes Ames Memorial Hall, and on the occasion of its dedication in 1881, they published a long refutation of the charges brought against him years earlier.[3]

87
Railroad Kings, Wood engraving. From William M. Thayer, *Marvels of the New West* (Norwich, CT: The Henry Bill Publishing Company, 1888).

Memorial Hall celebrates Oakes as a leading citizen of North Easton; his career as a railroad builder was memorialized in a more fitting spot. Meeting in Boston on March 10, 1875, the Union Pacific stockholders requested the directors of the line, who included Oakes's brother and his son, "to take measures . . . for the erection, at some point on the line of the road, of a suitable and permanent monument" to Oakes Ames, "in recognition of his services in the construction of the Union Pacific Railroad, to which he devoted his means and his best energies."[4] The intent was clearly to reaffirm the corporation's belief in Oakes's innocence, and it was probably for that reason that the project languished while a suit against the Credit Mobilier to recover "illegal" profits supposedly resulting from the scandal wound its way up to the Supreme Court.[5] On January 9, 1879, that body handed down an opinion which in effect vindicated Oakes, and at the end of the year the commission to design the railroad monument entered the Brookline, Massachusetts, office of H. H. Richardson.[6] Construction began in September 1880, and the memorial, now commemorating the deceased Oliver as well as Oakes, was dedicated in October 1882.

Although paid for by the railroad, the Ames Monument was clearly a commission from the Ames family, for whom Richardson had begun to work as early as 1877. (In that year he designed the Oliver Ames Free Library at North Easton for Oliver's descendants, including Frederick L. Ames, who had replaced his father on the board of the Union Pacific.) Surviving correspondence regarding the monument, which is mainly concerned with the portraits of the brothers by Augustus Saint-Gaudens applied to the east and west faces, was directed by Richardson's office to Oakes's son, Oliver III.[7] For both F. L. and Oliver III, Richardson also provided other designs, including the famed Gate House at North Easton for F. L. and an unbuilt town house for the Back Bay in Boston for Oliver III, both from 1880.[8]

Although Richardson might have chosen to memorialize Oakes Ames's reputation as a railroad financier with a monument incorporating realistic depictions of him, his brother, engines, and tracks he opted instead for a generalized form which, in Emerson's phrase, "nestles in nature." The site selected for the Ames Monument was at the summit of the Union Pacific line, a spot near Sherman Station in the Wyoming Territory between Cheyenne and Laramie (figure 88).[9] With both line and station now removed, the location is a high, lonely, wind-swept,

88
Andrew Joseph Russell, *Sherman, Front Street*, c. 1868–69. Union Pacific Historical Museum, Omaha.

James F. O'Gorman

89
Jean Baer O'Gorman, *Oakes and Oliver Ames Monument, Albany County, WY, from the South,* 1983. Courtesy of the photographer. The monument was designed in 1879–80 and erected in 1880–82.

vast, and barren meadow dotted in summer with colorful wildflowers (figures 89, 90). The site is animated by the shifting lights and shadows of scudding clouds and framed by spectacular geological images. Visible to the distant south and west are the Rocky Mountains, dominated by Long's Peak, and to the north, the Black Hills. And "in the intermediate space are groups of lower peaks, or cones rising like steps to the higher ranges," to quote F. V. Hayden's 1870 description of the view.[10] The pyramidal stone monument was clearly designed and erected to echo at scale the rich formations of the divine architect or his scientific handmaiden, geology. But, serene and silent amidst this continental landscape, it is at once appropriate for its site and clearly a work of artifice; it is based upon both geometry and geology; it is both man-made and mountain.

Almost certainly Richardson never saw the site, never in fact traveled west of St. Louis or Chicago. His frequent collaborator, the landscape architect Frederick Law Olmsted, who had crossed the West, might have relayed its natural wonders, and his frequent builder, O. W. Norcross, who took a crew of skilled workmen from Massachusetts to Sherman to erect the monument, might have described the location; but the one would have been too general and the other, presumably, too late. When in 1880 he designed the monument, Richardson needed a concrete

90
Jean Baer O'Gorman, *Ames Monument from the Northeast,* 1983. Courtesy of the photographer.

conception of the place. He needed visual images from which to work in order to create the shape he did.

The exploration of the "New West," as it was called in the years after the Civil War—exploration intended to disclose appropriate paths for the railroad, unveil the mineral resources of the region, and provide military information for use against the Indian—revealed in words and pictures a vast new visual realm as well. The awe-inspiring Yosemite and Yellowstone replaced the East's Niagara and Natural Bridge as sources of wonder at the majesty of genesis or geology, depending upon one's religious or scientific inclination. The words of a Samuel Bowles or F. V. Hayden, the paintings of a Bierstadt or Moran, the photographs of a Watkins, Jackson, or Russell revealed a world of natural forms that far outshone—in American eyes—the man-made wonders of the Old World.[11] "Nature's architecture" was not an invention of these writers, of course, since it occurs in Europe at least as early as the seventeenth century and recurs, for example, in John Ruskin's *Seven Lamps of Architecture*,[12] but it provided Americans with native images to rival the cathedrals of Cologne and Milan. Here certainly was inspiration for forms of building that, although they could scarcely escape the history of architecture, might be freshened and naturalized by American nature. Emerson, who as

early as "The American Scholar" of 1837 had bid his compatriots to free themselves of the "long apprenticeship to the learning of other lands," had in "The Young American" of 1844 predicted that the inspiration of the new West would have this effect:

Lucky for us, now that steam has narrowed the Atlantic to a strait, the nervous, rocky West is intruding a new and continental element into the national mind. . . . I think we must regard the *land* [his emphasis] as a commanding and increasing power on the citizen, the sanative and Americanizing influence, which promises to disclose new virtues for ages to come.[13]

Richardson wrote few words of theory, so we must speculate about his intentions. We can guess that Emerson meant something to him, or that his closest associates saw him in relation to Emersonian thought, because of the epigraph from the essay "Art" placed on the title page of M. G. Van Rensselaer's memorial volume on the architect.[14] From a host of verbal hints and from many of his buildings, we can assume that Richardson sought to adapt traditional architectures to North American themes.[15] For rural work, and first of all for the Ames Monument, that meant an inversion of "nature's architecture" to an architecture crystalized from nature, an architecture based upon geological forms revealed by

the era of exploration. The Ames Monument has Egyptian ancestors, but I want to suggest here that it derives its primary impact from the regeneration of that inherited form through the geometrical reinterpretation of its natural neighbors.

Any number of Richardson's associates might have induced him to study the images created by the exploration of the West. F. L. Olmsted, who seems to have been Richardson's environmental mentor, had worked in the shadow of Yosemite and helped establish the National Park at Yellowstone in 1872.[16] Henry Adams, Richardson's friend and future client, included geology among his intellectual interests.[17] The geologist Clarence King was among Adams's closest friends and might have met the architect through the historian. King, a follower of Ruskin, leader of the government's Fortieth Parallel Survey (1867–77), and first director of the U.S. Geological Survey (1879–81), combined art and science in his thinking; and in his *Mountaineering in the Sierra Nevada* (1871, 1872, 1874), he drew parallels between American mountain scenery and European architecture.[18] But New West imagery was ubiquitous in the 1870s. It was to be found everywhere from government scientific reports to expensive, limited-edition photographic portfolios, to the illustrated popular press, to "coffee-table" publications, to stereographic cards. It was certainly no more possible then to be ignorant of the marvels of the New West, to appropriate the title of William Thayer's book of 1888,[19] than it is now to be innocent of the face of the moon or the color of Mars.

One need not have read government survey reports or visited the National Academy of Design exhibitions to learn about western physical forms. A "coffee-table" production such as the two-volume *Picturesque America*, edited by William Cullen Bryant and issued in 1872–74, contains hundreds of views of "nature's architecture" spread from the coast of Maine to the coast of California. Richardson or an associate might have found inspiration in the wood engraving of Pilot Knob in northern California (figure 91).[20] Although the site is far more dramatic than the high meadow at Sherman summit, and the magnitude of the Knob larger than the monument, the correlation in profiles between the two forms seems too close to be mere coincidence.

Yet the characteristics of the high meadow itself seem to have inspired the shape of the monument, so it is doubtful that the architect would have relied specifically upon the image of the California Knob. He could have learned about the area around Sherman summit by turning to other pictorial sources, especially ones generated by the construction of the

91
Wood engraving after R. Swain Gifford, *Pilot Knob, California*. From William Cullen Bryant, editor, *Picturesque America* (New York: D. Appleton and Company, 1872–74).

Union Pacific itself. The photographer A. J. Russell documented its westward march and issued, in 1869, *The Great West Illustrated,* an album of fifty views taken in the vicinity of the line as it snaked its way across southern Wyoming and on to Promontory Point.[21] These photographs record both the works of man as he bridged canyons and leveled hills, and the works of nature to be found along the route. In these contrasting views the works of man seem frail and transitory;[22] perhaps in reaction Richardson sought to create a man-made form seemingly as permanent as the natural forms it conventionalized. *Skull Rock* (figure 72) is especially attractive in this regard, not only because it is a startling pyramidal formation of weathered granite, but also because, according to F. V. Hayden's *Sun Pictures,* illustrated with Russell's *Great West* photographs, it was one of the "granitic ruin-like piles that give the peculiar distinction to the plateau surface of the Laramie Mountains,"[23] that is, to the area around Sherman.

The photographs in Russell's album were but a small selection of those he took of the Union Pacific between 1867 and 1869.[24] The remainder were, however, known, at least in the Northeast, from the "Illustrated Course of Lectures . . .[on the] Scenery Between Omaha and San Francisco taken . . . for [the] Union Pacific Railroad" given during the 1870s

by S. J. Sedgwick, who seems to have gained control of Russell's negatives.[25] *Skull Rock* does not appear by name in the catalogue of Sedgwick's stereographic cards, although *High Rocks, near Sherman Station* does, but there were in his list at least three views of another outcropping, Reed's Rock, which he describes as "a pile of granite about a quarter of a mile west of the station [at Sherman] and within a stone's throw of the tracks, rising from the ground as clean and regular as though built by man" (figure 92).[26] Surely, here was inspiration for monumental design!

The specific sources of Richardson's ideas may never be known, but his intention to use geological references at Sherman summit cannot seriously be doubted. This is affirmed by F. L. Olmsted, who in a letter to Van Rensselaer after the architect's death wrote that he "never saw a monument so well befitting its situation, or, a situation so well befitting the special characteristics of a particular monument." He explained:

[It is] on the peak of a great hill among the great hills. . . . A fellow passenger [on the Union Pacific] told me that . . . it had caught his eye . . .[but] he had supposed it to be a natural object. Within a few miles there are several conical horns of the same granite projecting above the smooth surface of the hills. . . . At times the monument is under a hot fire of little missiles driven by the wind. But I think they will only improve it.[27]

That ornamental forms in architecture ought to derive from nature was a commonplace of nineteenth-century aesthetic thought. But even John Ruskin, the writer most closely associated with the tenet, did not propound the idea in isolation. He is at pains, in fact, in *The Seven Lamps,* to recognize a duality in the creative act. At the beginning of the "Lamp of Power" he asserts that "what ever is in architecture fair or beautiful, is imitated from natural forms; and what is not so derived . . . depends for its dignity upon arrangement and government received from human mind."[28] This duality of geology and geometry, or what Ruskin labels "gathering and governing," recognizes art—and architecture—as not merely real but ideal, as not merely the product of imitation but of cultivation as well. Other nineteenth-century writers on ornamental art provide us with processes for idealizing nature. In *The Grammar of Ornament,* for example, Owen Jones proceeds from the principle that "true art consists in idealizing, and not copying, the forms of nature."[29] He includes among his many propositions two of special interest here: "all ornament should be based upon a geometrical construction," and "natural objects should not be used as ornaments, but conventionalized representations founded upon them sufficiently suggestive to

120

convey the intended image." That Jones writes of floral ornament need not detain us, for his principles could be adapted to larger forms as well.[30]

If Richardson did indeed "gather" in the photographs of A. J. Russell and others information about the geological imagery at the site of his monument, he modified these images by "governing" them, by imposing a geometrical order on revealed natural form. He may even have taken a cue from a passage in Hayden's *Sun Pictures*, in which these "massive piles, like the ruins of old castles . . . scattered all over the summit" are described as "once angular masses, probably nearly cubical blocks, and they have been rounded to their present form . . . by exfoliation. Nature," Hayden concludes, "seems to abhor all sharp corners or angles."[31] Richardson, I suggest, reversed the process of nature by creating his monument as an angular reshaping of the granite piles he found in A. J. Russell's photographs.

There is every reason to suppose that Richardson agreed with Owen Jones's principle of conventionalized nature.[32] He had been educated in rational planning at the Ecole des Beaux-Arts in Paris, and often during the 1870s, as in Trinity Church in Boston (1872–77) whose plan is based upon a series of

92
Andrew Joseph Russell, *Reed's Rock*, c. 1869. Albumen print. Yale University, Beinecke Rare Book and Manuscript Library.

squares, organized architectural forms according to regular geometries.[33] Ruskin had already recognized the power of such simple forms when he recommended a "choice of form approaching to the square for the main outline" of a building.[34] The Ames Monument is said to measure sixty feet square in plan and rise sixty feet into the air.[35] It is, then, contained within a cube, one of the perfect solids.

Not only the salient dimensions herald the monument as artifice. Richardson and his builder Norcross took great pains to construct it from local granite, but they cut that granite into dressed shapes and laid them in regular patterns (figure 93). There is a base course of massive blocks from which the pyramid rises, and its battered walls are offset midway to the truncated apex. Below the offset the stone is rock-faced random ashlar; above, rock-faced horizontal ashlar. The offset itself is marked by four smooth-faced "shoulders" at the four corners resting upon two, thin, continuous layers of stone. The monument, then, was constructed with the same exquisite sense of scale and attention to detail that marks Norcross's other work for the architect.[36]

Whether or not some such process of "gathering and governing" occurred on the drawing board in Richardson's Brookline office, that is exactly what happened at the site near Sherman summit. The Ames Monument was actually erected from stones cut from Reed's Rock (figure 94).[37] The natural formation some seventy feet high was removed and reshaped by Norcross's workmen to create the conventionalized granitic outcropping dedicated to the memories of Oakes and Oliver Ames.[38] It is no wonder, then, that this man-made mountain appears among the marvels of William Thayer's New West (figure 95).[39]

93
Jean Baer O'Gorman, *Ames Monument, Detail*, 1983. Courtesy of the photographer.

94
Anonymous, *Reed's Rock*, c. 1881. Wyoming State Archives, Museums and Historical Department. "Quarrying" is about to commence.

95
Wood engraving after a photograph of Ames monument from the northwest, c. 1882. From Thayer, *Marvels of the New West*.

Notes

1

See Jay B. Crawford, *The Credit Mobilier of America* (Boston: C. W. Calkins and Co., 1880), 214 ff.; Hubert Howe Bancroft, *Chronicle of the Builders of the Commonwealth*, 6 vols. (San Francisco: History Co., 1891–92), V, 633–634; Charles Edgar Ames, *Pioneering the Union Pacific* (New York: Appleton-Century-Crofts, 1969), 488 ff.

2

There is no modern biography of either Oakes or Oliver. For the Union Pacific, see, in addition to works cited in note 1, John P. Davis, *The Union Pacific Railway* (Chicago: S. C. Griggs and Co., 1894); Edwin L. Sabin, *Building the Pacific Railway* (Philadelphia and London: J. B. Lippincott and Co., 1919); Nelson Trottman, *History of the Union Pacific* (New York: The Ronald Press Co., 1923); Robert William Fogel, *The Union Pacific Railroad* (Baltimore: Johns Hopkins Press, 1960); and Wesley S. Griswold, *A Work of Giants* (New York: McGraw-Hill, 1962).

3

Oakes Ames. A Memoir with an Account of the Dedication of the Oakes Ames Memorial Hall at North Easton (Cambridge, MA, 1883). This contains a "Forbes Albertype" of the Wyoming monument seen from the northeast (the depot at Sherman Station) that was certainly the source of the wood engraving published by Thayer (see note 19 and figure 95). The photographer is not named (see note 39). See also Jeffrey Karl Ochsner, *H. H. Richardson. Complete Architectural Works* (Cambridge, MA: The MIT Press, 1982), 204–207.

4

Oakes Ames, 50–51. Recent attempts to locate original drawings and documents concerning the commissioning, design, and construction of the monument have proven futile.

5

Ames, *Pioneering*, 531 ff.

6

Mariana Griswold Van Rensselaer, *Henry Hobson Richardson and His Works* (Boston: Houghton, Mifflin and Co., 1888), 140; Ochsner, 212–213.

7

Ochsner, 183–187. The letters are at the Easton Historical Society (copies in the files of the author). The square portrait plaques are not very well integrated with Richardson's design; these letters record Oliver's dissatisfaction with them. See also John H. Dryfhout, *The Work of Augustus Saint-Gaudens* (Hanover, NH: University Press of New England, 1982), 122–123 (where the orientation of the monument is given incorrectly).

8

Ochsner, 217–219, and 216. Ochsner catalogues a host of other works by Richardson for the family.

9

See H. R. Dietrich, Jr., "The Architecture of H. H. Richardson in Wyoming," *Annals of Wyoming* 38 (April 1966): 49–53.

10

F. V. Hayden, *Sun Pictures of Rocky Mountain Scenery* (New York: J. Bien, 1870), 60. The photographs by Jean Baer O'Gorman (figures 89, 90, 93) were taken in July 1983 on a trip to the site made possible by a grant from Wellesley College.

11

See Samuel Bowles, *Across the Continent* (Springfield, MA: S. Bowles and Co., 1865), 75 ff. Bowles, who produced other similar works, such as *Our New West* (Hartford, 1869) and *The Switzerland of America* (Springfield, 1869), was the brother of Benjamin F. Bowles, for whom Richardson designed a Springfield house in 1873 (Ochsner, 129). See also Weston J. Naef and James N. Wood, *Era of Exploration* (Boston: New York Graphic Society, 1975).

12

John Ruskin, *The Seven Lamps of Architecture*, 2d ed. (London: Smith, Elder, and Co., 1855), 65.

13

R. W. Emerson, *Nature, Addresses and Lectures* (Boston: Houghton, Mifflin and Co., 1904), 83, 369–370.

14

See note 6. Van Rensselaer's study was sponsored by F. L. Olmsted and Charles Sprague Sargent, the dendrologist (see Cynthia D. Kinnard, "The Life and Works of Mariana Griswold Van Rensselaer" [Ph.D. dissertation, Johns Hopkins, 1977], 135 ff.).

15

Van Rensselaer (57), for example, tells us that Richardson often remarked that "it would not cost me a bit of trouble to build French buildings . . . but that is not what I want to do."

16

See Laura Roper, *FLO: A Biography of Frederick Law Olmsted* (Baltimore: Johns Hopkins University Press, 1973); J. F. O'Gorman, *H. H. Richardson and his Office: Selected Drawings* (Cambridge, MA: Harvard University Library, 1974), 29–30.

17

See David H. Dickason, "Henry Adams and Clarence King," *The New England Quarterly* XVII (June 1944): 229–254.

18

See Thurman Wilkins, *Clarence King, a Biography* (New York: Macmillan and Co., 1958).

19

William M. Thayer, *Marvels of the New West* (Norwich, CT: The Henry Bill Publishing Co., 1888).

20

W. C. Bryant, ed., *Picturesque America: or, the Land We Live in*, 2 vols. (New York: D. Appleton and Co., 1872–74), II, 421.

21

A. J. Russell, *The Great West Illustrated in a Series of Photographic Views Across the Continent* (New York: Union Pacific Railroad Co., 1869). It seems reasonable to assume that the Ames family owned one or more copies of this work and could have made it available to Richardson.

The copy in the Boston Public Library once belonged to Charles Francis Adams, Henry's brother, president of the Union Pacific in the mid-1880s, and chairman of the building committee of Richardson's Crane Memorial Library at Quincy, Massachusetts, a work coeval with the Ames Monument (Ochsner, 226–231).

Russell's photographs were also published in a smaller version by Alfred Mudge and Son of Boston (Beinecke Library, Yale University). See Susan Danly Walther, "The Landscape Photographs of Alexander Gardner and Andrew Joseph Russell" (Ph.D. dissertation, Department of Art, Brown University, 1983), 58 ff.. I am greatly indebted to Ms. Danly for guidance through the bibliography of western photography.

22

Naef and Woods, 45.

23

Hayden, 60.

24

There are additional views at the Beinecke Library, the Oakland (California) Museum, and the Union Pacific Railroad Museum in Omaha.

25

S. J. Sedgwick, *Announcement of . . . Illustrated Course of Lectures and Catalogue of Stereoscopic Views of Scenery . . . between Omaha and San Francisco taken . . . for [the] Union Pacific Railroad*, 4th ed. (Newton, NY: S. J. Sedgwick, 1879). For Sedgwick, see Walther, 76–78.

26

Images of Reed's Rock appear as numbers 83, 84, and 86 in Sedgwick's Series No. 3 (his catalogue is not paginated). Reed's was named for Samuel B. Reed (1818–91), construction engineer with the Union Pacific (Ames, *Pioneering*, 146–147 and *passim*).

27

Library of Congress, Olmsted Papers, General Correspondence, Box 18, 6 February 1887. A slightly inaccurate version is given by Van Rensselaer, 72. For a recent, dramatic characterization of the impact of wind in the area, see John McPhee, "Annals of the Former World," *The New Yorker*, 24 February 1986, 38–71.

28

Ruskin, 64.

29

O. Jones, *The Grammar of Ornament* (London: B. Quaritch, 1868), 154, 5–6.

30

See J. F. O'Gorman, *The Architecture of Frank Furness* (Philadelphia: Philadelphia Museum of Art, 1973), 36–37.

31

Hayden, 59.

32

The books of both Jones and Ruskin were included in Richardson's working library; see J. F. O'Gorman, "An 1886 Inventory of H. H. Richardson's Library," *Journal of the Society of Architectural Historians* XLI (May 1982): 150–155.

33

See H. H. Richardson, *A Description of Trinity Church* (Boston: Trinity Church, 1877), 11–12.

34

Ruskin, 71.

35

Alternative dimensions given by newspaper accounts and railroad museum releases are 65 by 65 feet and 60 by 65 feet. Neither much alters my point.

36

See J. F. O'Gorman, "O. W. Norcross, Richardson's 'Master Builder,' " *Journal of the Society of Architectural Historians* XXXII (May 1973): 104–113.

37

Ochsner, 212–213.

38

The height of Reed's is estimated from the figures in Russell's photograph. W. H. Jackson also photographed Reed's; see Naef and Woods, 49, fig. 64. (This cannot be Skull Rock, as labeled, as can be seen by comparing this photograph with Russell's *Skull Rock*, figure 72. The latter was some 300 feet high.) Others who photographed the Union Pacific route and whose work appears in stereographic views include C. R. Savage and Eadweard Muybridge.

39

Thayer, 416; the illustration is a wood engraving by Kilburn & Cross after the albertype published in *Oakes Ames* (see note 3). Susan Danly suggests W. H. Jackson and Carlton Watkins as the photographers whose work appears engraved in this volume.

5 City Railways/ Modernist Visions

Dominic Ricciotti

Like their predecessors, twentieth-century artists in America found inspiration in the railroad. But instead of the older theme of the railroad-in-the-landscape, they frequently turned to the changing technological circumstances presented by the emerging American city. Their paintings of subways, elevated trains, and trolleys remind us how thoroughly the city was replacing the wilderness in the imagination of American artists, modernists and others alike. At issue in works of the modernists Max Weber and Joseph Stella, however, is a consciousness of the new urban landscape as a complete "technological system." This is the phrase Leo Marx employs in his comprehensive essay in this volume to consider the prototypical significance of the motif of the railroad in George Inness's prophetic painting *The Lackawanna Valley* (figure 58). But if this picture, in Marx's words, "is the first to convey a sense of the new machine technology as a determinant and a visible emblem of a new kind of large-scale, expansionary, corporate enterprise," then the paintings of Weber and Stella embody a more advanced stage of the same process. In their canvases, the city railroads are but one feature of the larger technological whole they endeavor to treat comprehensively. Beginning somewhat tentatively with Weber's *New York* (figure 98) and culminating brilliantly with Stella's series *New York Interpreted* (figures 101–105), the abstract complexities of modern technological civilization find their analogy in modernist pictorial form.

Charles Sheeler, though not as radical a modernist as Weber or Stella, nevertheless shares with them certain formal values and technological concerns. Having undergone a modernist apprenticeship around the time of the 1913 Armory Show, when experimentation with advanced European art accelerated in this country, Sheeler gradually moved toward his characteristic Precisionist manner. Although Precisionism was by modernist standards a conservative style, Sheeler's paintings in that mode do have a place here; they illustrate his alternative to a thoroughgoing European modernism that conflicted with his profound commitment to American experience.

Not surprisingly, the increase in images of the city railways, in a variety of styles, toward 1920 accorded with the population shift toward the city at the same time. The transcontinental railroads were of course a major factor in the urbanization process; they not only stimulated the growth of cities across the nation, but were being adapted to use within cities as well.[1]

The Machine Abstracted

In *The American Scene* (1907), Henry James likened New York City to

some colossal set of clockworks, some steel-souled machine-room of brandished arms and hammering fists and opening and closing jaws. The immeasurable bridges are but as the horizontal sheaths of pistons working at high pressure, day and night, and subject, one apprehends with perhaps inconsistent gloom, to certain, to fantastic, to merciless multiplication.[2]

The passage reveals James's less than enthusiastic attitude toward the American city, one not necessarily shared by all American artists. Still, James's metaphor illuminates the conceptions of modernists in rendering the city in mechanical terms. Subways and trains exemplified the dynamism of the modern city, and modernist pictorial strategies for representing this dynamism disclosed the character of the urban machine. Significantly, Weber and Stella eschewed direct representation of the city trains. What interested them was less the objective presence of the trains than their power, their terrific speeds, and the sensations they aroused—realities that seemed to demand expression in the new idioms of advanced art.

Rejecting the notion of literal description in his watercolors of the city, John Marin might have been speaking for others, too, when he justified using a modernist style to describe "the great forces at work" in the city.[3] He wrote that his watercolors were "made in an effort to put down the different Street & City movements as I feel them in such a way that what appears on the paper shall have a life of its own akin to the movement felt."[4] Like Weber, Stella, and others of the modernist generation, Marin strove to correlate the sensory stimuli of the modern city with affective aesthetic form.

In view of Marin's desire to portray "city movements," it is surprising that he was not more interested in the urban railways. *Lower Manhattan* of 1920 (figure 96) appears to be his only major foray into the subject.[5] For Marin, the technological aspirations of the age were more apparent in the great skyscrapers than in the new forms of transportation. Since he had worked in an architectural office before turning to painting, his interest in buildings is understandable. In *Lower Manhattan*, however, the skyscrapers are somewhat less emphatic than in most of his city pictures. In fact, the surging diagonal of the el tracks establishes the dominant note of the composition.[6]

With the exception of Sheeler's *American Landscape*, the railway images under discussion here demonstrate in some fashion the stated aims of Marin. Although individual stylistic solutions vary, the works nonetheless share a dynamic vocabulary involving diagonals, curves, repetitions, or other devices designed to impart a sense of the motions or powerful energies of the machine. Yet only Sheeler's works actually depict trains. Marin's summary style may well be meant to suggest an actual train speeding along his thrusting tracks in *Lower Manhattan;* aside from this, the viewer is confronted in other paintings by highly abstracted motifs or by subway tunnels and platforms. The experience of the railways is as much felt, or implied, as seen.

As the first modernist movement to embrace machine aesthetics, Italian Futurism played a major role in providing Americans with models for pictorializing the new modes of mechanized travel in the modern city.[7] The Futurists produced a singular body of well-articulated theories; their first manifesto (1909) stated:

We declare that the world's splendour has been enriched by a new beauty; the beauty of speed. . . . We shall sing . . . of factories suspended from the clouds by their strings of smoke; of bridges leaping like gymnasts over the diabolical cutlery of sunbathed rivers; . . . of broad chested locomotives prancing on the rails, like huge steel horses bridled with long tubes; of the gliding flight of aeroplanes.[8]

Not until a few years later, however, did the Futurists realize their aim of creating a "style of motion." Umberto Boccioni, Giacomo Balla, Carlo Carrà, and Gino Severini, to name the major figures of the

96
John Marin, *Lower Manhattan,* 1920. Water-
color, 21⅞ × 26¾ in. Collection,
The Museum of Modern Art, New York.
The Phillip L. Goodwin Collection.

group, insisted on rendering "the *dynamic sensation,*
that is to say, the particular rhythm of each object,
its inclination, its movement, or to put it more exactly, its interior force."[9]

Celebrating the technological eruptions of the age,
the Futurists tested their theories in numerous paintings of speeding automobiles and trains (figure 97),
bouncing omnibuses, clanging trams, and busy ter-
minals, among other nontechnological subjects. The
Futurists had an international following, and it is not
surprising that American modernists responded to
their style and to their ideas. In Marin's case it was
more the latter.[10] Stella and Weber, on the other
hand, took up the stylistic vocabulary of the Futurists more directly and on occasion produced works
close to Futurist models. For example, Weber's *Rush
Hour, New York* (figure 99) is formally quite similar
to Boccioni's *Forces of a Street* (1911, Private Collection, on loan to the Kunstmuseum, Basel).[11] But
while Stella and Weber were the most ardent American proponents of Futurism at this time, neither artist practiced the style exclusively.[12]

Only Stella, among the American modernists, was
directly acquainted with Futurist painting. On a visit
to Paris in 1912 he saw the famous Futurist exhibition at the Bernheim-Jeune galleries. It was this exhibition, particularly when it was shown in London
in March of that year, that generated much interest

97
Gino Severini, *Red Cross Train Passing a Village,* 1915. Oil on canvas, 35 × 45¾ in. Solomon R. Guggenheim Museum, New York. Photo: Myles Aronowitz.

in Futurism in the United States. Popular journalistic accounts were soon followed by serious critical appraisals, and illustrations of key Futurist paintings frequently accompanied both types of writings.[13] Photographs were in fact Weber's and Marin's only means of visual access to the style, for no Futurist paintings were then being exhibited in New York. Though initially invited to participate, the Futurists were not represented in the Armory Show.[14]

Weber, meanwhile, had been experimenting with a Futurist vocabulary for several years when in 1913 he undertook the first clearly modernist interpretation of the American intra-urban rails: *New York* (figure 98). The composition stems from an earlier, more realistic series of cityscapes, viewed from the upper reaches of a skyscraper. To designate the trains, Weber uses a serpentine form (the snake image was a popular one for the els).[15] The form passes through the impacted space of lower Manhattan, where the largest concentration of tall buildings and rail lines were then located. Weber also includes the graceful arcs of Brooklyn Bridge, which, aside from its import as an urban symbol, was a vital link in the city's transportation network.

Exploiting the Futurist technique of interfusing simultaneous perspectives, Weber lays out some of the buildings of *New York* flatly while he depicts others obliquely. The "endless electric coil," to use Henry

98
Max Weber, *New York*, 1913. Oil on canvas, 40 × 32 in. Thyssen-Bornemisza Collection, Lugano, Switzerland.

James's phrase, at once surrounds and penetrates the buildings. The seemingly instantaneous speeds with which the traveler could make his way through the city were new experiences to which Weber tries to give symbolic expression. As the Futurists wrote: "Time and space died yesterday. Already we live in the absolute, since we have already created speed, eternal and ever present." [16] Appropriating the dizzying kinetics of the Futurist idiom in *New York*, Weber found metaphors for the capacity of the trains to "annihilate space and time."

Both the *idea* and the experience of rapid movement were key to the near-abstract conception of *New York*. [17] The painting could not contrast more with the nineteenth-century image of the railroad-in-the-landscape seen from on high in an open space. The arrested and the literal have given way to the dynamic and the abstract, though by continuing the high vantage point, Weber preserves an incidental continuity with the older tradition. Once an alien intrusion into a pre-industrial landscape, the train in *New York* is assimilated by the technological environment spawned in part by the railroad. [18] Weber's depiction of the city as a technological maze effectively transmits the complexity of the new environment, which was no doubt bewildering to the throngs of newcomers to the city, most of whom were coming from rural areas.

Weber painted *Rush Hour, New York* (figure 99) two years later. During the interval his understanding of Futurist form and of the potential of abstraction had matured. The functional geometries in the picture suggest something of the "colossal set of clockworks" invoked by Henry James. The work is a paradigm of locomotion; in choosing the twice-daily rush through the city, the artist dramatized those peak periods when the urban machine churned most forcefully. *Rush Hour* embodied the Futurist principle of "universal dynamism"—that the world is continually in a state of flux. [19] Yet Weber also intended his language to convey the psychic experiences of modern life. "Dynamic force or power involved in art expression becomes," as he wrote, "a psychic force." Accordingly, such force had to be embodied in form. "The electric engine is powerful," added Weber, "but it is also, in its power . . . a plastic truth." [20]

Abandoning the high, landscape point of view of *New York*, Weber descends from the skyscraper perch of the earlier work to encounter the trains more directly: in a subway tunnel. The net gain is a tumultuous immediacy. While no trains are actually represented, Weber's Futurist vocabulary is *of* the machine. To articulate the energies of the powerful trains simultaneously roaring in and out of a station, Weber recreates through a pattern of sharp angles

and zigzags the sequential motions of braking, acceleration, and velocity. A series of flickering arches fuse with the pattern to enact the swift passage through the tunnel. At the same time, highly kinetic spatial fields result from Weber's deft use of what the Futurists called "*force-lines* . . . the prolongations of the rhythms impressed upon our sensibility by . . . objects." [21] In *Rush Hour*, such lines take the form of the perspective orthogonals of platforms and other architectural features of the station, experienced not from a fixed point in time or place, but as if from the moving cars. The station explodes with the thunder of the passing machine.

Rite of Passage

Weber and Stella were European immigrants, like countless others at this moment in American history. As newcomers living in New York City, they were especially sensitive to America's new urban-industrial civilization; but Stella's interest in the machine was more consuming. In 1913 he undertook his notable series of paintings inspired by the mechanized amusements of Coney Island; shortly thereafter he turned to the Brooklyn Bridge, *the* monument to urban technology, and was soon portraying the industrial scene as well. But the series *New York*

99
Max Weber, *Rush Hour, New York*, 1915. Oil
on canvas, 36¼ × 30¼ in. National Gallery
of Art, Washington. Gift of the Avalon
Foundation, 1970.

Interpreted (figures 101–105), which he painted between 1920 and 1922, is his artistic testament to modern urban technology.

For our purposes, it is significant that Stella chose to include subway imagery in both *New York Interpreted* and the earlier *Brooklyn Bridge* (figure 100), the celebrated painting in the collection of Yale University Art Gallery. Central to both are the motions generated within the colossal city and the idea of movement toward it. The symbols of subway tunnels hence become crucial. In the Yale picture, whose thematic conceptions Stella will develop further in *New York Interpreted*, highly prominent tunnels occupy the composition's lower half; placed logically beneath the span, they suggest the network of subways linked to it. The tunnels substitute for the trains themselves, and their orthogonals graphically embody the motions generated by the speeding machines. They intersect with beaming arc lights and with intimations of the bridge's cables—forms creating a Futurist version of "the interplay of forces represented by an abstraction of lines," as Montgomery Schuyler once described the bridge.[22] By virtue of Futurist simultaneity, the spectator oscillates between a distant perspective of the bridge and a sensation of being thrust through it to the city of skyscrapers and smokestacks beyond the span. Aureoles of red and green at the tunnels add a coloristic

133

100
Joseph Stella, *Brooklyn Bridge,* 1917–18. Oil
on canvas, 84 × 76 in. Yale University Art
Gallery. Gift of Collection Société Anonyme.

symbolism to this movement, representing, as Stella himself suggested, the traffic lights measuring the passage through time as well as space.[23]

In the Yale painting, Stella expresses the clearly religious connotations that Brooklyn Bridge had for him. Long fascinated by John Roebling's engineering masterpiece, in the early twenties he called the bridge a "shrine containing all the efforts of the new civilization of AMERICA." Standing on the span at night, he "felt deeply moved, as if on the threshold of a new religion or in the presence of a new DIVINITY."[24] The bridge as shrine was obviously suggested by Roebling's Gothic towers, and in his picture Stella makes the symbolism explicit. Not only did he place the towers in the center of the composition to underscore their iconic significance, but he also added a third tower to suggest a single tripartite tower of a Gothic cathedral. If perceived separately, the three towers, containing three pairs of arches set one above the other in diminishing scale, also appear to recede in space, which enhances the sensation of movement through the span. The apparent dichotomy between the static image of the pseudocathedral tower and the Futurist kinetics surrounding it thus takes on plausible meaning: to move across the "threshold of a new religion" through the "shrine" of the towers is to participate in a ritual of

passage to the city beyond, and hence to the "new civilization of AMERICA—the eloquent meeting point of all forces arising in a superb assertion of their powers, in APOTHEOSIS."[25]

Stella also clarified the role of the tunnels in the painting. From the span he noted

here and there lights resembling suspended falls of astral bodies or fantastic splendors of remote rites—shaken by the underground tumult of the trains in perpetual motion, like the blood in the arteries—at times, ringing as alarm in a tempest, the shrill sulphurous voice of the trolley wires—now and then strange moanings of appeal from tug boats, guessed more than seen, through the infernal recesses below.[26]

Stella saw the city railways as protagonists in a *ritual* "Drama" enacted on the bridge in the "mysterious depth of night."[27] The subways, the vital "arteries" of the city, serve to rationalize the mystic motions of the span itself—to facilitate its metaphor of bridging to a new culture. For Stella, an immigrant from a rural region in southern Italy, American urban civilization was new in both an historical and a personal sense.

New York Interpreted literally gave Stella a larger canvas on which to elaborate the iconographic program of the Yale picture. Consisting of five muralsized paintings, the series is an epic summation of Stella's interest in the city. He described how while

"at the Battery, all of a sudden [there] flashed in front of me the skyscrapers, the port, the bridge, with the tubes and the subways." In response, "I got hold of five big canvases to be clasped in a long rectangular one. I selected this most elementary geometrical form as the most appropriate frame for the simultaneous action of these mechanical essentials chosen."[28]

Stella begins his New York sequence with *The Port* (figure 101), dense with its docks, electrical wires, and industrial installations. *The White Way I* (figure 102), which follows, is an abstract maze that represents the brilliant illuminations of Times Square. *The Skyscrapers* (figure 103) is directly in the center, next to *The White Way II* (figure 104). *The Bridge* (figure 105), a variation on the Yale painting, closes the series. As Irma Jaffe has shown, Stella composed the New York series in the form of a twentieth-century "altarpiece," after the manner of Italian late-Medieval and Renaissance polyptychs.[29] He also raised the height of the center panel (by almost a foot) to make the conception clear.[30] He thus transfers some of the religious meaning of the *Brooklyn Bridge* to his chosen format.

Stella also transfers several motifs from the Yale painting, adapting them accordingly. He uses the cathedral-like spires of the skyscraper architecture

101

Joseph Stella, *New York Interpreted: The Port,* 1922. Oil on canvas, 88½ × 54 in. The Newark Museum.

102

Joseph Stella, *New York Interpreted: The White Way I,* 1922. Oil on canvas, 88½ × 54 in. The Newark Museum.

103

Joseph Stella, *New York Interpreted: The Skyscrapers,* 1922. Oil on canvas, 99¾ × 54 in. The Newark Museum.

104

Joseph Stella, *New York Interpreted: The White Way II,* 1922. Oil on canvas, 88½ × 54 in. The Newark Museum.

105

Joseph Stella, *New York Interpreted: The Bridge,* 1922. Oil on canvas, 88½ × 54 in. The Newark Museum.

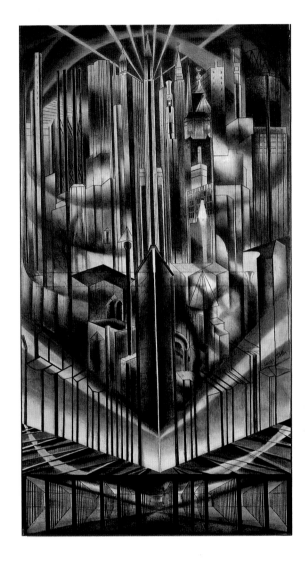

of the period much as he used the bridge's towers. The frontality and height of the skyscrapers along the series' vertical axis, for instance, lend the proper hieratic tone, similar to the metaphorical shrine of the bridge's towers in the Yale painting. By contrast, in *The Bridge* Stella puts greater emphasis on the forms of the arches within the towers, particularly by bringing one of the towers up to the pictorial surface. Framing a tracery of steel cables, the arches allude to the lancets of Gothic stained glass windows; "from arcs and ovals darts the stained glass fulgency of a cathedral," Stella exclaimed.[31] But the configuration of Gothic arches within the pictorial frame also seems to offer an analogy with a cathedral portal, alluding once again to the idea of passage. Seen through this symbolic portal, the perspective of the gridiron of the span propels the spectator toward the city, much as the subway tunnels had in the Yale picture.

Though seemingly a secondary element in his composition, the imagery of subway tunnels is vital to Stella's overall theme. He declared: "The flux of metropolitan life continually flows, as the blood in the arteries, through the subways and tubes used for the predella of my composition."[32] In positioning tunnels at the base of *The Skyscrapers* and of the

White Way paintings beside it, within the "predella" of his technological altarpiece, Stella creates a metaphor for the topographical relationship between the subterranean city of tunnels and the metropolis of streets and towers above. It seems as if the artist, taking his cue from the way earlier Italian predellae iconographically support the images above them, has constructed a pictorial analogy for the economic support the subways gave to the activities of the modern city. The altarpiece/predella device thus carries a meaning apart from its religious implications.[33]

The varying forms and subject matter of the three centermost panels, moreover, are visually united by the band of subway tunnels extending across their bases. Adjoining *The Port* and *The Bridge*, the two outermost paintings, the predella tunnels also help link these panels conceptually: the subways share with the New York port and Brooklyn Bridge a primary means of passage to, or travel and communication within, the great metropolis. While *The Bridge* continues the theme of the Yale picture, Stella no longer limits the meaning of the subways to the significance of Brooklyn Bridge alone; removed from the precise context of the bridge, the subways are now part of the larger urban whole.

The Port, meanwhile, calls attention to those historic circumstances that made New York, to quote

Stella, "what she now is, the center of the world."[34] The city's natural harbor had facilitated much of the trade, commerce, and industry that led to its economic leadership; and a multitude of immigrants from Europe, including Stella himself, entered through the port of New York. Moreover, because the Battery (the original title of *The Port*) and Brooklyn Bridge are at the opposite sides of Manhattan, west and east, they are positioned at the extreme left and right in the series, denoting a geographical relationship consistent with the topographical relationship between the subways and the city.[35] Stella has thus organized his series according to a spatial experience of Manhattan; the overall idea of transportation/communication becomes more lucid within this spatial context and results in a highly coherent composition. Most importantly, the subway imagery of *New York Interpreted* contributes to Stella's comprehensive view of the city.

In "interpreting" New York City according to its technological artifacts, Stella again reveals his sympathies with Italian Futurism. But in contrast to his earlier works, including *Brooklyn Bridge*, he modifies his Futurist approach; he employs a much harder linearity to portray the "steely" effects of New York. "Mathematically precise," as he claimed his style to be, "the abstract [is] opportunely inserted [in] to realism."[36] Such adjustments between abstraction and representation would soon come to characterize the new Precisionist style.[37] Not coincidentally, Sheeler painted *Church Street El*, one of his first mature Precisionist works, at the time Stella began *New York Interpreted*.

Dynamism versus Classicism

In *Church Street El* (figure 106), Sheeler also portrayed the city trains in the context of Manhattan's towering peaks.[38] Originating in several photographic projects on which he was working around 1920, the painting makes use of a sharp downward perspective to view a train tracing a path through one of the city's canyons.[39] The work is unusual in Sheeler's oeuvre because it carries a dynamic organization (along with a dramatic light) that he will quickly give up for the more classical compositions that characterize his work of the next several decades.[40] Here, a speeding train lends the painting a rationale entirely suited to Sheeler's design: the directional thrust of the train and tracks contributes to a series of movements fanning outward from New York's cavernous depths. With its bird's-eye viewpoint and conceptual similarities to a natural landscape of gorges and peaks, Sheeler's painting is comparable to Weber's *New York* (figure 98), but whereas Weber

106
Charles Sheeler, *Church Street El,* 1920. Oil on canvas, 16⅛ × 19⅛ in. The Cleveland Museum of Art. Purchase, Mr. and Mrs. William H. Marlatt Fund.

telescopes the time and space of all of lower Manhattan, Sheeler presents a single location in stilled time, in keeping with the camera vision he was evolving at this point in his career.

That photographer's sensibility was a principal component of his maturing Precisionist style, but modernist aesthetics played another major role. Sheeler, like other Precisionists such as Charles Demuth and Louis Lozowick, was attracted to the urban-industrial scene in a formal sense because technological artifacts lent themselves to quasi-Cubist interpretation. The vernacular forms of the machine, to whose inherent geometry Cubist aesthetics drew attention, could be portrayed more or less straightforwardly (as Sheeler's camera might have recorded them) while retaining their "Cubist" integrity. Cubism tempered Sheeler's camera vision by encouraging a process of abstract simplification;[41] by this means he synthesized a distinctly personal version of Precisionism. In *Church Street El*, the semi-abstract design harmonizes the steel-edged linearity of tracks and train with the hard geometrical shapes of the urban environment. At the same time, the clearly representational forms suggest the degree to which the first period of American modernism was drawing to a close, not merely for Sheeler, but for an entire generation of artists.

By the time Sheeler painted *American Landscape* (figure 107), the balance between abstraction and representation became weighted toward the latter. Yet in moving toward a greater realism, Sheeler also began to evolve an ideal vision of the technological landscape. Comparing the factory to a Gothic cathedral in 1922, he posited one way to create an "authentic expression" for America: "since industry concerns the greatest numbers, finding an expression for it concerns the artist."[42] This concern became a moral imperative for Sheeler; his view of an egalitarian America embraced technology as something of a spiritual force. Coming to recognize the potentially idealizing character of Cubist-derived form, which he seamlessly embedded in his realism, Sheeler presented the industrialized "American landscape" as a "modern Arcadia."[43] He offers stillness, a clear, rarefied light, crisp shapes defined by subtle contour lines, and above all a highly rational composition. There is neither grime nor confusion in Sheeler's technological utopia.

American Landscape is in fact a cityscape. The painting describes the industrial suburb of River Rouge, the site outside Detroit of a newly opened plant of the Ford Motor Company. Henry Ford chose this location, as he did all his factory sites, for its rural setting; he wanted his employees and their families to have "a chance to breathe God's fresh air."

Moreover, he claimed he built his cars so that everyone could enjoy "hours of pleasure in God's great open spaces."[44] Paradoxically, the one man who was radically changing urban-industrial America with the private automobile turned his back on the cities to embrace the virtues of the land.

Sheeler was not insensitive to the ironies of the Ford undertaking. He chose not to portray River Rouge in urbanistic terms, as he did, for example, in *City Interior* (1936, Worcester Art Museum), and his title makes clear that he opted instead to conceive of the American landscape as a "natural" vista. He does so by referring to the landscape conventions of the past. As with its companion piece, *Classic Landscape* of 1931, which was purchased by the Ford family, Sheeler invokes the classical tradition while simultaneously emphasizing its transformation by a contemporary machine aesthetic. *American Landscape* exhibits all the hallmarks of classical design, transposed to the industrial city.

The river and railroad occupy the characteristic foreground plane of classical landscape painting, while the apparatus at the right serves as the requisite *coulisse* or "wing." Factory structures and coal heaps, in place of the usual classical architecture or groups of trees, occupy the rising middle ground;

107
Charles Sheeler, *American Landscape,* 1930.
Oil on canvas, 24 × 31 in. Collection,
The Museum of Modern Art, New York.
Gift of Abby Aldrich Rockefeller.

and the smokestack approximates the distant focal point normally created by a mountain peak.[45] Comparing *American Landscape* to a 1927 photograph and to a watercolor of 1928 (figure 108), both of which apparently served as models for the painting, makes clear Sheeler's intention of defining the industrial scene according to classical conventions.[46] The earlier efforts offer much closer views than the painting, which, in keeping with a classical spatial system, adds more breadth and depth. The result is that in the painting, Sheeler drops the newer convention of landscape intimacy, generally followed since the advent of Impressionism.

For all its deliberate classicism, Sheeler's image of the landscape is nonetheless "American" because it acknowledges the economic transformation of the land while recalling through its design a vision of a once natural landscape. But this association also carries with it a recollection of earlier landscape art in America. Indeed, the American tradition in landscape painting had accommodated various classical conventions, albeit in forms suited to a naturalistic depiction of the nation's wilderness. Some of these classical survivals are evident in those earlier paintings employing the railroad-in-the-landscape motif: Thomas Doughty's *A View of Swampscott, Massachusetts* and George Inness's *The Lackawanna Valley,*

108
Charles Sheeler, *River Rouge Industrial Plant,* 1928. Watercolor, 8 × 11¼ in. Museum of Art, Carnegie Institute. Gift of G. David Thompson.

while more panoramic than Sheeler's work, are just two examples inviting formal comparison with *American Landscape*.

Exchanging the purities of nature for the man-made world of technology, *American Landscape* "is the industrial landscape pastoralized."[47] The intrusion of the machine into the "garden," however, has apparently been reversed.[48] Now it is the river, the one vestige of a natural perspective, that seems the alien element. The river, paralleled by the railroad, passes through the mechanical "scenery," nourishing the factories with the materials it brings and disposing of their wastes.

American Landscape denies the railroad the dynamism and force of the modernists' interpretation (and even of Sheeler's own in *Church Street El*). Aside from his representational style, Sheeler's classical vision—his Arcadianism—set him apart from artists like Weber and Stella, who seized upon the railways as symptomatic of the changing tenor of cultural experience wrought by the emergent city. As newcomers to the United States, they largely ignored American nature, the *American* past. Unlike Sheeler, they found little relevance, perhaps, in forging an aesthetic or historical connection with native traditions. Stella's admiration for Poe and Whitman not-

withstanding, his interest in the past centered on the Italian tradition, which he wished to reconcile with the American technological present. What occupied both him and Weber were the new pictorial and expressive problems that modern technology posed. They therefore looked to contemporary Europe, to advanced art, particularly Futurism. Cubist geometrical conventions and the trend toward abstraction were also decisive in the search for a machine aesthetic. Though Precisionism may have been a compromise with the more radical elements of modernism, it too was central to this endeavor. Like many of his generation, Sheeler attempted to "make a genuine culture out of industrialism,"[49] looking at the same time for a "usable past."[50]

In *American Landscape*, Sheeler succeeded in harmonizing the man-made world of technology with nature, by recourse to those artifices imposed on nature in a more humanistic age. In the end, Sheeler may have contributed a more lasting legacy to American art than Weber or Stella because of his success in assimilating European modernism to a more traditional, native realism. Sheeler proved the durability in modern American art of the traditions of landscape painting and dramatized the potency of a revived—though clearly transformed—realism.

Notes

1

Sam Bass Warner, Jr., *The Urban Wilderness: A History of the American City* (New York: Harper and Row, 1972), 88–98. For information on intra-city transport, see George Rogers Taylor, "The Beginnings of Mass Transportation in Urban America, Parts I, II," *Smithsonian Journal of History* 1 (Summer–Autumn 1966): 35–90, 31–54.

2

Henry James, *The American Scene*, ed. Leon Edel (Bloomington: Indiana University Press, 1968), 75.

3

From a statement in *Camera Work* (April–July 1913); reprint, Dorothy Norman, ed., *The Selected Writings of John Marin* (New York: Pellegrini and Cudahy, 1949), 4.

4

Quoted in *John Marin*, essays and contributions by Frederick S. Wight, et al. (Berkeley: University of California Press, 1956), n. (from the section by Wight).

5

Larry Curry lists an etching, *St. Paul's against the El* (1930) in *John Marin, 1870–1953* (Los Angeles: Los Angeles County Museum of Art, 1970), 55.

6

The horse in the lower right corner of figure 96 is a wry commentary on the revolution in modern transportation technology.

7

I have written elsewhere on the relationship of Futurism to the city railway theme in American art at this time; see Dominic Ricciotti, "The Revolution in Urban Transport: Max Weber and Italian Futurism," *American Art Journal* 16 (Winter 1984): 48, 50–51, 56–60.

8

"The Initial Manifesto of Futurism," *Le Figaro*, Paris, February 20, 1909; reprint, Joshua C. Taylor, *Futurism* (New York: Museum of Modern Art, 1961), 124.

9

"The Exhibitors to the Public," prefatory essay to the *Exhibition of the Italian Futurist Painters* (London: Sackville Gallery, 1912), 128.

10

Marin's links to Futurism are discussed in Sheldon Reich, *John Marin: A Stylistic Analysis and Catalogue Raisonné* (Tucson: University of Arizona Press, 1970), I:56–58. Emphasizing that Marin's forms do not closely resemble those of the Futurists, Reich makes a strong case for the influence of their theories on Marin and cites the possible circulation of the various Futurist texts among the New York vanguard at the time the Armory Show was being organized.

11

The Boccioni work is reproduced in Ricciotti, 46; see also the discussion of the relationship of *Rush Hour* to it, ibid., 56–59; for Weber's previous Futurist involvement, ibid., 48–50. One of Stella's best-known paintings, *Battle of Lights, Coney Island* (1913–14; Yale University Art Gallery) is apparently based on Severini's *Dynamic Hieroglyph of the Bal Tabarin* (1912; Museum of Modern Art). On the influence of Futurism in Stella's work, see John I. H. Baur, *Joseph Stella* (New York: Praeger, 1971), 29–37.

12

Like most American modernists of this period, Weber and Stella experimented with a variety of styles. Aside from their more or less Futurist works, notable are Weber's Cubist-related efforts and Stella's pictures anticipating the Precisionist aesthetic.

13

For the more popular Futurist criticism, see John Oliver Hand, "Futurism in America, 1901–1914," *Art Journal* 41 (Winter 1981): 337–342; for some of the serious criticism, Ricciotti, 56–57.

14

Several possible reasons for the Futurists' absence are given in Hand, 342, n. 23.

15

Ricciotti, 53; see also the accompanying photograph of the "snake-curve" at Coenties Slip in lower Manhattan.

16

"Initial Manifesto," 124.

17

Ricciotti, 53.

18

The locomotive as an intrusion into the landscape is an image defined by Leo Marx, *The Machine in the Garden: Technology and the Pastoral Idea in America* (New York: Oxford University Press, 1964), 29 and passim.

19

The quoted phrase appears in "Futurist Painting: Technical Manifesto," leaflet, Milan, April 11, 1910; reprint, Taylor, 125.

20

From Weber's unpublished essay, "Plastic Expression," c. 1912, The Max Weber Papers (Washington, D.C. [and regional centers]: Archives of American Art, Smithsonian Institution), microfilm NY59–6, frame 132. For further discussion of this essay, see Ricciotti, 59, 62.

21

The force-lines concept is explained in "Exhibitors to the Public," 128. For its application to *Rush Hour*, see Ricciotti, 56.

22

Quoted in Alan Trachtenberg, *Brooklyn Bridge: Fact and Symbol*, 2nd ed. (Chicago: University of Chicago Press, 1979), 88. I am enormously indebted to the work of Trachtenberg on Brooklyn Bridge and on the city in general; see also, Trachtenberg et al., eds., *The City: American Experience* (New York: Oxford University Press, 1971), vii–xi. I am grateful, too, to have been a participant in an NEH Summer Seminar for College Teachers on the American City which Trachtenberg conducted at Yale in 1978.

23

Joseph Stella, "Discovery of America: Autobiographical Notes," *Art News* 59 (November 1960): 65.

24

Joseph Stella, "The Brooklyn Bridge (A Page of My Life)," *transition* 16–17 (June 1929): 87–88. This essay was privately printed by Stella earlier in the decade and was illustrated with the five paintings of *New York Interpreted* plus *Brooklyn Bridge*. Hart Crane, who admired Stella's Brooklyn Bridge paintings and whose own verses ("To Brooklyn Bridge," from *The Bridge*, 1930) were somewhat inspired by Stella's essay, was instrumental in getting the latter published.

25

Ibid.

26

Ibid., 88.

27

Ibid.

28

Stella, "Autobiographical Notes," 65.

29

Irma Jaffe, *Joseph Stella* (Cambridge, MA: Harvard University Press, 1970), 69–70. Jaffe devotes her entire chapter 7 to *New York Interpreted*; my analysis gratefully builds on hers. She outlines the formal evolution of the series's composition from the Yale picture on pages 71–72.

30

For a composite photograph of all five paintings (reproduced to the same scale), which reveals more fully their altarpiece character, see "The Voice of the City," *The Survey* 51 (October 15, 1923): 141. The title of this article was the original title of the series; see pages, 142–46 for the original titles of the individual panels.

31

Stella, "Autobiographical Notes," 66.

32

Ibid.

33

When *New York Interpreted* was first exhibited in the early twenties, the title of what is now *White Way I* was *The Great White Way, Leaving the Subway*, which directly acknowledged the subway context of the series. "We turn to either side [of the skyscrapers]. We feel the subway, the sensation as we leave it to enter the blaze of Broadway," read a contemporary description in a Société Anonyme brochure (*Stella*, 1923; reprint, *Selected Publications. Société Anonyme* [New York: Arno Press, 1972], 2:4).

34

Stella, "Autobiographical Notes," 65.

35

The cartographic analogy is both completed and seemingly thwarted by Stella's reference in *The Skyscrapers* to the Flatiron Building (ibid., 66). Located at the intersection of Broadway and Fifth Avenue, the street which divides Manhattan in half along its north-south axis, the Flatiron is properly situated at the precise center of the series.

That Stella views the Flatiron from the north in *The Skyscrapers*, showing its distinctive triangular form, however, requires that *The Bridge* be placed at the left instead of the right of the series. In opting for the most characteristic view of the Flatiron, Stella violates the geographical consistency that he seems to aim for. I believe that whatever geographical ambiguities exist in the series are justified by Futurist simultaneity; in fact, Stella wrote of the "simultaneous action" of the series, implying multiple or shifting perspectives on the great city (ibid., 65). See also the unsigned article, "Painting the 'Simultaneousness of the Ambient'," *Literary Digest* 44 (March 23, 1912): 590–591.

36

Stella, "Autobiographical Notes," 65–66.

37

In the preface to the catalog of his pioneering exhibition, Martin Friedman writes that Stella's style is among the "important related directions and influences on the Precisionist idea." See *The Precisionist View in American Art* (Minneapolis: Walker Art Center, 1960), 9.

38

At this time John Sloan also combined the two themes in *The City from Greenwich Village* (1922;). Similarly, one of the major literary works of the decade, John Dos Passos's *Manhattan Transfer* (1925), an epic novel that features the mechanized movements of the city as an organizing metaphor, takes full advantage of skyscraper imagery. Like Stella in *New York Interpreted*, Dos Passos aims at a total view of the city.

39

One of Sheeler's projects was the short film *Manahatta*, on which he collaborated with Paul Strand. The relationship of one of the final frames in the film to *Church Street El* is described in Dickran Tashjian, *Skyscraper Primitives: Dada and the American Avant-Garde, 1910–1925* (Middletown, CN: Wesleyan University Press, 1975), 221–223. The frame in question is reproduced in Susan Fillin-Yeh, "Charles Sheeler: Industry, Fashion, and the Vanguard," *Arts* 54 (February 1980): 157, figure 14.

40

See Robert Allerton Parker, "The Classical Vision of Charles Sheeler," *International Studio* 84 (May 1926): 68–72.

41

Van Deren Coke, *The Painter and the Photograph* (Albuquerque: University of New Mexico Press, 1964), 33.

42

Quoted in Tashjian, 221.

43

Friedman, 36, referring to Sheeler's *Classic Landscape* (1931). Also apt here is the assertion: "The fact that the River Rouge paintings . . . look like photographs almost leads one to forget the complex role played by the artist's hand" (Fillin-Yeh, 158).

44

Quoted in Roderick Nash, *The Nervous Generation: American Thought, 1917–1930* (Chicago: Rand McNally, 1970), 158. See Nash's entire discussion of Ford, whom he characterizes as a "Symbol of an Age," on pages 153–163.

45

This summary of classical landscape design is based largely on the discussion of Claude in Kenneth Clark, *Landscape into Art* (London: John Murray, Ltd., 1949; reprint, Boston: Beacon Press, 1961), 64. Clark's assessment of Poussin's "ideal landscape" (65–69) is also useful in considering figure 10.

46

The photograph is reproduced in Fillin-Yeh, 156, figure 10. It was one of the well-known group Sheeler took of the River Rouge plant, on which he based his industrial landscapes of the 1930s.

47

Marx, 356. Interpreting *American Landscape* from a literary perspective, Marx's view is consistent with the art-historical perspective of Friedman with regard to his statement about Sheeler's vision of a "modern Arcadia."

48

See note 18.

49

Lewis Mumford, "The City," *Civilization in the United States: An Inquiry by Thirty Americans*, ed. Harold D. Stearns (New York: Harcourt Brace, 1922), 12.

50

In literary circles during the 1920s, a revisionist attitude toward America's past influenced such works as William Carlos Williams's *In the American Grain* (1925) and Hart Crane's epic poem *The Bridge* (1930), as well as the writings of Van Wyck Brooks. See Frederick J. Hoffman, *The Twenties: American Writing in the Postwar Decade* (New York: Viking Press, 1955), 120–62. Because Sheeler had associations with literary figures, including Williams, he may well have come under the revisionist thinking of the decade. In formulating my concluding remarks on Sheeler, I have benefited from Alan Trachtenberg, "Cultural Revisions in the Twenties: Brooklyn Bridge as 'Usable Past'," *The American Self*, ed. Sam B. Girgus (Albuquerque: University of New Mexico Press, 1981), 58–75.

6 Charles Sheeler's *Rolling Power*

Susan Fillin-Yeh

To bring things closer is . . .[a] passionate 20th century trend.
Walter Benjamin, *A Brief History of Photography*

I've been working on the railroad all the live-long day.
American Folk Song

Charles Sheeler's *Rolling Power* has both an art history and a commercial one. As an oil painting (figure 109), the work is embedded in a dense network of associations with art produced by other Americans and Europeans of Sheeler's generation. As one of his realist depictions of machine subjects, *Rolling Power* also reflects ideas Sheeler developed in drawings, paintings, and photographs over the thirty years since his first depiction of an industrial subject in 1909. But the painting has another special life in the world of journalism. It was commissioned by *Fortune* Magazine in 1938 and was simultaneously presented to the public as a reproduction in the December 1940 issue of *Fortune* (figure 110) and as an art object at Edith Halpert's Downtown Gallery.[1] For *Fortune's* readers, few of whom would ever see the actual painting, *Rolling Power* derived its meaning from its *context*—from the other images Sheeler presented in his "Portfolio"[2] entitled "Power" and from its presentation within the pages of *Fortune* itself. As it appears in the magazine, *Rolling Power*

looks like a photograph, is labeled as a painting, and is presented as a reproduction. The image possesses the complexity and ambiguity of "the work of art in the age of mechanical reproduction."[3]

Fortune's editorial purpose, as stated in the inaugural issue in 1930, was "to reflect industrial life in ink and paper and word and picture as the finest skyscraper reflects it in stone and steel structure."[4] From the beginning, the magazine was intended as a luxury product, not a throwaway. Its heavy paper, fine type, and color illustrations were, like the goods it advertised, aimed at the business world. *Fortune's* editors fabricated a toned-up version of the business world's image of itself: a world of power, where the twin gods of science and industry had replaced traditional religion, where, as Henry Adams had noted, the Virgin had been replaced by the dynamo.[5] And it was the dynamo that Sheeler presented in his "Portfolio": a train, a plane, hydroelectric and steam turbines, an electrical transmission tower, and a water wheel—mechanisms that could have appeared on any schoolchild's list of modern machinery.[6] *Fortune's* editors wished to show that engineering's marvels need not be exotic. These "instruments of power," they wrote, "are not strange, inhuman . . . material [but] forms that are more deeply human than the muscles of the human torso because they trace the firm pattern of the human mind."[7]

Here is an anatomical study revealing the driving mechanism of a Hudson-type locomotive, designed to haul heavy New York Central passenger trains up to possible speeds beyond 100 miles per hour. In this canvas the sometimes subtle difference between painting and photographs may best be examined. Sheeler, himself a photographer of high distinction and perhaps the first to exhibit both his paintings and his photographs on an equal artistic footing, puts the difference in these words: "Photography is nature seen from the eyes outward, painting from the eyes inward." And a critic of his work has written, "We know, upon consideration that nature was never quite like that, so luxuriant, so bountiful, so rich in design, yet nothing seems to have been altered . . ." "The over-illumination of this painting ('Eagle . . . as Sheeler, "is the great designer."), the pristine shade . . ., the clearly ruffled, the clear outlines of the machinery, so as no photograph could the physical sensation of tractive effort, the pull at the drawbars of 45,000 locomotive . . . they provide a contrast with an exchange of goods, seen possible only to those who lived on the margins of the . . .

109
Charles Sheeler, *Rolling Power,* 1939. Oil on canvas, 15 × 30 in. Smith College Museum of Art, Northhampton, Massachusetts.

110
Rolling Power as illustrated in *Fortune,* December 1940.

If, as Walter Benjamin asserted, mechanical reproduction stripped an object—specifically a work of art—of its "aura," its "unique physical presence," *Fortune*'s editors were going to invest it with a metaphysical one. Though it is doubtful the editors ever read Benjamin, their approach to persuasion embodies some of his ideas, preserving them in the language of American business culture while documenting the economic upturn of the late 1930s. For example, Benjamin spoke about "aura" withering in picture magazines because of the existence of a "plurality of copies." But "plurality" was valued by *Fortune*'s readership of businessmen and would-be industrialists, for whom features like the "Portfolio" were exemplars of the benefits of mass circulation. And so, *Rolling Power* and the other images of the "Portfolio" had a special impact, retaining their "aura" in ways Benjamin perhaps could not have predicted. *Fortune*'s packaging gave the "Portfolio" privileged-object status: it was printed on shiny paper stock to distinguish it from sections immediately preceding and following it, the same paper used elsewhere in the magazine for expensive multicolor advertisements, images which made commercial goods look like works of art. A self-contained unit in the magazine, the "Portfolio" was intended to evoke portfolios of painting reproductions published by the *Dial* and other art and literary magazines in the 1920s, as well as the luxury portfolios photographers (including Sheeler) made up to market their work in the teens.

The text that accompanies Sheeler's "Portfolio" promotes Benjamin's original definition of "aura," because not only the images but also the artistic intentions are described in religious terms. "The artist put a devout intensity into painting," the editors assert, and they proclaim that Sheeler's painting of a Boulder Dam transmission tower "is as truly a religious work as any altarpiece, stained glass window or vaulted choir."[8] Furthermore, "The heavenly serenity of Sheeler's style brings out the significance of the instruments of power he here portrays. . . . They are exquisite manifestations of human reason."[9] The statement reveals more about editorial complacency than about the similarities between altars and turbines. But if culling the past for religious metaphors suggests something of *Fortune*'s essential conservatism, *Fortune*'s editors were also tapping sentiments rooted deep in American popular culture—a reservoir of responses to machinery and industrialization, phenomena which Sheeler's imagery also considers.

Comparing the "Portfolio" paintings with any number of commercial advertisements in *Fortune* gives other information about influences on religiosity. Couched in the psychological language of persuasion first developed in the 1920s, the advertisements testify to a belief in the powers of science and engineering. Even so, captions and images in *Fortune* advertisements deal in miracles and mysteries. They are themselves a secularized, even trivialized variety of religious experience. This, at any rate, is the message of advertisements such as one for a new high-vacuum pump in the same issue of *Fortune* as the Sheeler "Portfolio" (figure 111). "We work in 'interlunar' space," runs the caption, a banner of text superimposed on the image of a factory bathed in moonlight and under a starry sky."[10] Floating like the diagram of a constellation in the sky is a cross-shaped, semi-abstract rendering of a pumping apparatus. The constellation theme appears in other advertisements in the same issue. An advertisement that has as its title "Brave New World" is a description of the potential good to be derived from an alliance between business and scientific exploration, an alliance that will enable "humanity [to] evolve into a free society."[11]

Such advertisements are germane to a discussion of *Rolling Power* because they illustrate the extraordinary similarity between the way *Fortune* handled its advertisements and the Sheeler paintings. With the exception of the one nineteenth-century subject,

Sheeler's painting of a waterwheel, all the "Portfolio" subjects are duplicated in the advertisements.[12] Furthermore, the "Portfolio" exhibits the same relationship between image and text as the advertisements. It is not only that Sheeler's paintings, reproduced as pages juxtaposing images and text, look a great deal like the *Fortune* advertisements; but in adding captions to the paintings, which usually hang without text, the layout of the "Portfolio" also emphasizes the paintings' similarities to photographs.

The interface between paintings and photographs, a relationship of a quarter century's duration by the time of the *Fortune* "Portfolio," is a central concern of Sheeler's art. His fascination with photographic vision goes back to the earliest stages of his career, and he defined his involvement as modern. Because he came to feel that a sharply focused vision could—unlike the Cubist-derived language of geometric displacement favored by many contemporaries—be avant garde, Sheeler evolved a cool and impersonal painting style, a technique and attitude responsive to mechanically defined standards: his paintings are characterized by structured images and polished surfaces. Paintings and photographs alike have machine-related subjects, beginning in the 1920s and

111
"We work in 'interlunar' space," *Fortune*, December 1940, p. 17.

150

especially after 1929, when they testify to Sheeler's belief that realism could provide a viable, up-to-date alternative to abstraction.[13] *Rolling Power* and the whole *Fortune* "Portfolio," among the last of Sheeler's realist paintings concerned with mechanically derived standards for realism,[14] close a chapter of dialogue with twentieth-century modernism because of the way in which those images are influenced by photographic processes and by values Sheeler defined as belonging to photography.

Sheeler's earliest decisions about what photographs should look like are confirmed in *Rolling Power*. First, there is the matter of distance. *Rolling Power* stems from early photographs in which Sheeler began to treat subjects in close-up. Sheeler was encouraged in his decision to shrink the space between himself and his subjects by Alfred Stieglitz. Indefatigable promoter of photography as an art, Stieglitz was an influential member of the Wanamaker jury, which, in 1918, awarded Sheeler his first important recognition for photography—a prize for the photograph *Bucks County Barn* (figure 112). A stark photograph that documents the variations on white and weathered clapboard barn siding, *Bucks County Barn* may have been particularly appealing to Stieglitz. Stieglitz's own Lake George photographs of the 1920s and 1930s (figure 113) examine the textures and structuring of white clapboard siding,

Charles Sheeler

112
Charles Sheeler, *Buck's County Barn,* 1916. Photograph. International Museum of Photography at George Eastman House.

113
Alfred Stieglitz, *Grape Leaves and House, Lake George,* 1934. Photograph. International Museum of Photography at George Eastman House.

which is often photographed in close-up. Stieglitz, like Sheeler, placed his camera close—just far enough away from his subject to inform the viewer about the expanse, ordering, and variations in the white painted surfaces and the architectural organization of walls and windows. In such photographs, the whole is suggested but not revealed. The photographs also decline to concentrate on elements of architectural closure. This approach reappears in *Rolling Power*'s exaggerated close-up horizontality.

Paul Strand's photographs are also part of *Rolling Power*'s artistic heritage. Strand's close-up views of camera apparatus, lathes, and other machine shop equipment, subjects which anticipate *Rolling Power*'s drive wheels and connective shafts, reveal the aesthetic integrity of machinery. The sensibility which led Strand to buy an Akeley movie camera in 1920 and then to photograph his purchase is Sheeler's as well. Strand photographs of the camera, especially photographs of its cranking mechanism (figure 114), are monumentalized images that predict *Rolling Power.* For both Strand and Sheeler, photographs of machinery were the means for gaining aesthetic control over unaesthetic material, for redefining beauty in the images of functional objects.[15] Such photographs bypass standard definitions of the utilitarian, but the result is not art for art's sake. As with Stieglitz photographs, which give

114
Paul Strand, *Double Akeley, New York, 1922.* Photograph. Copyright 1976 The Paul Strand Foundation, as published in Paul Strand, *Sixty Years of Photographs* (Aperture, 1976).

twentieth-century versions of symbolist ideas of essential and spiritual form, the images of Strand and Sheeler are faithful to the world in which detailed visual facts predominate. But the photographs are also autonomous: because the camera does not record the object's surroundings, the photograph compels the viewer to contemplate the object.

Sheeler photographs like *Bucks County Barn* are not the only early works which, despite a delicately calibrated inner coherence, do not seem to stop at their own boundaries. The sensibility is derived from film vision—specifically from the movie *Manahatta*, which Sheeler filmed with Strand in 1920. A tribute to New York City inspired by Walt Whitman's poem (lines from the poem appear as subtitles for images of the harbor, crowds, and skyscrapers), *Manahatta* shows the city in episodes that are studies in visual extremes. A still image at the skyline repeats as a chorus.

Sheeler ultimately took from *Manahatta* a new sense of imagery, the panned or panning image produced by a movie camera moving across the urban terrain. Such images differ morphologically from images composed within the ground glass lens of a still camera. The images in *Manahatta* are not framed; or, to put it differently, they are images that are framed continuously, sequentially, as the camera moves. Shifting constantly, the boundaries tend to

disappear. This is the vision in Sheeler photographs of the 1920s, which show buildings as portions, as vertical or horizontal swathes (figure 115) even when the artist could as easily have chosen to center the subject, to fix the instant when the given subject was contained within his view. It is also the sensibility behind *Rolling Power*, where Sheeler gives us the side view of a railroad car. The image lacks an internal frame, is determinedly on the horizontal and on the verge of stretching. Conceptually as well as compositionally, the implication is of a whole line of railroad cars extending into the distance.

Rolling Power is more than just like a photograph. It embodies a dialogue between painting and photography at least in part because it was taken from a photograph—one of Sheeler's own. Its source is probably *Drive Wheels* (figure 116) which is a nearly identical though cropped version of *Rolling Power*.[16] *Rolling Power* fits with a group of paintings based on photographs in which the artist almost certainly used a photographic device—the *camera obscura*—to translate from one medium to the other.[17] The paintings, which appear sporadically in the 1920s and consistently after 1929 (beginning with the painting *Upper Deck*), result from Sheeler's conviction that camera vision was preferable to vision as recorded

115
Charles Sheeler, *New York,* 1920. Gelatin silver print, 9¹¹⁄₁₆ × 7¾ in. The Museum of Fine Arts, Houston.

116
Charles Sheeler, *Drive Wheels,* 1939. Photograph, 6¹¹⁄₁₆ × 9¹¹⁄₁₆ in. Smith College Museum of Art. Gift of Mrs. Holger Cahill (Dorothy C. Miller '25), 1978.

by the human eye. "No drawing can give you the actuality," he wrote in 1937.[18] Paintings of the 1930s enact concerns that were first worked out in the artist's *Self-Portrait* of 1923 (figure 117). In that work, the artist gave himself the image of a telephone, a piece of machinery that set contemporary standards for ease and speed of communication. The *Self-Portrait* was Sheeler's statement of artistic stance, his first formulation of an aesthetic idealizing machinery. Within this context, the *Self-Portrait* invokes photography at several levels. With its dramatic contrasts of light and dark, Sheeler's rendition looks like a black-and-white photographic print. At the same time, the portrait suggests a photographic negative. Sheeler shows parts of his torso reflected on a window pane, and the image—pale, ghostly, and floating—is that of glass negative plates still in use in the 1920s.[19] The *Self-Portrait* is also photographic in its crisp and non-painterly surfaces and in its veristic approach to detail.

The *Self-Portrait* thus introduced an aesthetic of camera vision that was rendered literal in *Rolling Power.* But *Rolling Power* differs from past work in the extent to which Sheeler was willing to go public about his painterly use of photographs. Although he had exhibited paintings with photographs in the teens, the most he would say about their relationship

Susan Fillin-Yeh

117
Charles Sheeler, *Self-Portrait*, 1923. Conté
crayon, gouache, and pencil on paper,
19¾ × 25¾ in. Collection, The Museum of Modern Art, New York.
Gift of Abby Aldrich Rockefeller.

was that "photography is nature seen from the eyes outward, painting from the eyes inward."[20] That comment was included in the *Fortune* magazine text accompanying the reproduction of *Rolling Power*, for *Fortune*'s editors apparently felt the need to explain the look of Sheeler's paintings. Though poetic, Sheeler's explanation is also somewhat ambiguous, especially given some ten years of paintings and photographs in which the images are identical. Even in 1939, on the occasion of his Museum of Modern Art retrospective exhibition, when Sheeler gave an official statement about connections between his paintings and his photographs, he hedged: although paintings and photographs could look alike, he said that the paintings were composites. Much later, Sheeler made explicit the relationship between the two forms in *Rolling Power:* "Since I could not camp beside the locomotive for the three months required to paint it, I made a photo."[21]

Sheeler's description offers a glimpse, as it were, into his studio. The comment seems at first to be a variant on nineteenth-century definitions of photography's functions. It gives an optimistic inflection to, for instance, Baudelaire's definition of photography as a tool for scientists, which removed it from the world of artistic expression.[22] But Sheeler's sensibility was different; his admiration for and utilization of applied technology, his involvement with industrial subjects, were part and parcel of his art-making. As he wrote in his *Autobiography,* "The language of the Arts should be in keeping with the Spirit of the Age, if statements are to be authentic."[23] Yet Sheeler's specialized expectations for photography are more than merely twentieth-century updates of nineteenth-century theories. To begin with, Sheeler photographs consistently decline the camera's potential to represent motion. They project, instead, an impassioned immobility, surprising for an artist of his generation, steeped in Cubism and Futurism.

Even photographs of industrial subjects that draw considerably on what is ultimately a Cubist-derived interest in geometric form have nothing to do with Cubistic spatial disjunctions. The important series of photographs taken at the Ford automobile plant at River Rouge in 1927 are representations of a stable universe in which everything has its place. In photographs and paintings alike, Sheeler's vision of industry is startling. It is almost antithetical to twentieth-century images of the subject, which characteristically comment on the tensions between workers and machines or give a kinetic image of machinery. Instead, Sheeler gives us machines without their operators, machines at rest. They tend to be embedded in architecture, locked into the factory-scape with its railway tracks, walkways, and blast furnaces. They seem, in fact, like still-lifes. If the puff of steam in the photograph *Drive Wheels*, for instance, fails to convince us that the locomotive engine Sheeler photographed can attain speeds of up to 100 m.p.h., it is probably because Sheeler has presented his subjects in relationships of extraordinary stability. The machinery of *Drive Wheels* recalls the immobilized subjects of daguerreotypes, subjects Walter Benjamin once described by saying, "They grew . . . into the image."[24]

Rolling Power is thus informed by the artist's unwillingness to tamper with the visual presence of the industrial world, by an aesthetic reluctance given literal expression because the painting is a photographic quotation, an imprint from the world as seen in a camera lens. The painting is also evidence for Sheeler's positivist philosophical stance—the belief that faithfulness to appearances expresses something important about reality. Sheeler's aesthetic also has to do with repetition and mass production. *Rolling Power* and paintings of its type are the doubles of photographs, and Sheeler's vision of his art was also doubled: "We get," he wrote, "the vision of the facts as well as the facts."[25] The image thus occupies an ambiguous position with reference to the viewer, and its meanings are rendered even more equivocal vis-à-vis the other images in *Fortune* which it resembles. In those images—paintings and photographs alike—

verisimilitude was valued because of direct and indirect relationships to news about production and consumption.

Disjunction and ambiguity also characterize the response to *Rolling Power* as a painting. *Rolling Power* is small (15 by 30 inches). The image is a dense little assemblage of wheels and shafts. The painting is nearly monochromatic, a study in the various colors of metal, and its tonality is heavy and leaden. The imagery of *Rolling Power* encourages the fantasy that the painting is as heavy, as concrete, and as compact an object as the railroad cars it represents. All of this is of interest because of the peculiar relationship between the painting and the eye of the viewer. *Rolling Power* is oddly inaccessible, for the image that Sheeler presents is one whose breadth exceeds the capacities of the human eye. The effect is marked because of the painting's myriad details, which encourage the viewer to peer at it closely. The viewer who stands close enough, though, to actual train wheels and gears to take in the visual information *Rolling Power* contains could see only an area approximated by the painting's center and not its sides. The image is also one which, although it is presented frontally as if at eye level, is actually low to the ground. Such displacements are those of camera vision. (Sheeler's comment about camping out beside the locomotive to photograph the subject of *Rolling Power* may have real physical significance, for it implies a position close to the ground.) Yet Sheeler's painting at first glance suggests that the viewer unequipped with a camera could see this scene unaided. These factors make experience of the painting a built-in exercise in the distinctions between what the eye can see and photovision. The painting's details, which interest the viewer in close examination, undermine confidence in the naked eye.

Other meanings of *Rolling Power* are less paradoxical because they connect with Sheeler's other railroad images. Perhaps the earliest appearance of the railroad motif in Sheeler's work is *Church Street El* (1920), a painting that gives an aerial view of subway trains, tracks, and ties (figure 106). Based on a still photograph of the subject that Sheeler made when he and Paul Strand were filming *Manahatta*, *Church Street El* also recalls an earlier photograph by his friend Morton Schamberg of a railroad station tracks and roofs. *Rolling Power* is also related to some seventeen photographs, drawings, and paintings derived from his trip to River Rouge in 1927: railroad tracks and cars figure in *American Landscape* (1930; figure 107), *Classic Landscape* (1931; figure 118), *City Interior* (1936), *Ballet Méchanique* (1931), and in the photographs *Storage Bins at the Boat Slip* (1927) and *Salvage Ship* (1927).

In all of these images, though, railroad imagery is part of the urban or industrial landscape. *Rolling Power* differs from them all in its absence of setting. Sheeler pares the image of a locomotive to its wheels and drive shafts; only the crop line that cuts the image at top and sides suggests the locomotive's total expanse, and Sheeler permitted only the cut ends of the railroad ties which appear below the wheels to hint at the landscape the train could move through. But the image represents more than a transformation of Sheeler's past work. The painting is also a radical departure from representations of trains in nineteenth- and twentieth-century American paintings and photographs, not only as a close-up, but also because the image is presented as a side view. Sheeler gives the image of a train as a wall of machinery exactly parallel to the viewer's plane of vision, while other images of locomotives are almost invariably set in the picture space on the diagonal. It differs, for example, from almost archetypal photographs like Alfred Stieglitz's *The Hand of Man*, (figure 30) in which the railroad tracks recede along the orthogonals of conventional perspective systems. Nor can

118
Charles Sheeler, *Classic Landscape*, 1931.
Oil on canvas, 27⅞ × 36 in. Private
collection.

Rolling Power be related to Ashcan school or American Scene railroad paintings, which invoke travel or the sensation of speed. *Rolling Power* also differs from other representations of railroads in the advertisements of the 1920s and 1930s, in which they are glamorized and streamlined icons of dynamism.[26]

Not that Sheeler's image is devoid of streamlining. In choosing this subject, Sheeler could hardly have avoided the image of streamlining, for the image he chose was the New York Central Line's famous train, the Twentieth Century Limited. The creation of industrial designer Henry Dreyfuss in 1938, this special "Hudson-type" locomotive was a powerful exercise in psychology.[27] The project was undertaken to revive and popularize train travel. The Twentieth Century Limited's exterior (figure 119) and interior were streamlined in elegantly simple curved and rounded forms that represented the most advanced thinking about the effects of design on not only the function of objects, but also their sales appeal. Given Dreyfuss's input, the machinery in *Rolling Power*, with its curves and smooth surfaces, its grays and silver matte and shiny contrasts, looks suitably up-to-date. It is not surprising that the image even suggests the streamlined, redesigned office furniture of the period, a reference that must have been satisfying to *Fortune*'s subscribers.

119

Henry Dreyfuss, *New York Central Railroad. Twentieth Century Limited.* The Henry E. Huntington Library and Art Gallery.

Rolling Power is not the first streamlined image in Sheeler's oeuvre. Eight years earlier, the painting *Home Sweet Home* had been a sly reference to the streamlining aesthetic of contemporary industrial designers. In *Home Sweet Home*, the streamlined volumes of a recent-model furnace replace the open hearth as the traditional center of domesticity (figure 120). The painting answers furnace advertisements of the 1930s, which attempted to demonstrate that grimy and coal-filled basement spaces could be remodeled into hygienic Formica-covered "recreation" rooms.[28]

Such concerns, though, are latent in *Rolling Power*. In fact, the drive wheels Sheeler took for his subjects are the only parts of the Twentieth Century Limited locomotive that lack a streamlined casing. Sheeler's ideological interest in machinery, as well as his artistic admiration for machines, for their logic and organization, predicted his choice of the image of machinery undisguised. But it is the way in which the image first notes and then departs from contemporary conventions for photographs, for paintings, and for the paraphernalia of modern life that gives it its particular importance and its special place among Sheeler's railroad images.

120
Charles Sheeler, *Home Sweet Home*, 1931.
Oil on canvas, 36 × 29 in. © 1987 The
Detroit Institute of Arts. Gift of Robert H.
Tannahill.

Notes

1

Halpert timed the exhibition to capitalize on *Fortune*'s publicity.

2

"Portfolio," an "essay" of paintings or photographs, was a regular feature of the magazine. Among the artists whose work was featured were Walker Evans, Margaret Bourke White, Reginald Marsh, and Charles Burchfield.

3

See Walter Benjamin, "The Work of Art in the Age of Mechanical Reproduction," in *Illuminations* (New York: Schocken, 1976), 217–251, first published in *Zeitschrift für Sozialforschung*, V, I, 1936.

4

Fortune 1:1 (February 1930): 38.

5

Henry Adams, *The Education of Henry Adams* (New York: Modern Library, 1931), 379–390.

6

Constellations of similar images appear in Thomas Hart Benton's murals (for example, the New School murals of 1931), where the motif suggests the murals' educational imperatives.

7

"Power: A Portfolio by Charles Sheeler," *Fortune* 22:6 (December 1940), following p. 72, unpaginated.

8

Ibid.

9

Ibid.

10

Fortune 22:6 (December 1940): 17.

11

Ibid., 10.

12

See ibid., 2, 6, 36, 38, 119, 156, 159, 163.

13

See S. Fillin-Yeh, "Charles Sheeler: Industry, Fashion and the Vanguard," *Arts Magazine* 54:6 (February 1980): 154–158, for a discussion of realism and Sheeler's commercial photography. See also Charles Sheeler, "A Brief Note on the Exhibition," in *Charles Sheeler: Paintings, Drawings Photographs* (New York: Museum of Modern Art, 1939), 10.

14

Sheeler's paintings after the transitional years 1943–45 played with photographic effects to achieve semi-abstractions (he structured works with doubled, superimposed, and off-register images which look like double exposures of stacked negatives). See, for examples, Martin Friedman, Bartlett Hayes, and Charles Millard, *Charles Sheeler* (Washington, D.C.: Smithsonian Institution Press, 1968), 133, 135–146.

15

For a statement of Strand's aesthetic position, see "Photography and the New God," *Broom* III (1922): 252–258.

16

Rolling Power and *Drive Wheels* are invariably linked in Sheeler literature; see, for example, Charles W. Millard, "Charles Sheeler: American Photographer," *Contemporary Photographer* VI: 1 (1968). However, the fact that most Sheeler paintings based on photographs are near duplicates of their sources suggests that a photograph closer to *Rolling Power* than *Drive Wheels* may also exist.

17

Sheeler's use of the *camera obscura* is documented by his contemporaries Matthew Josephson and William Carlos Williams. See S. Fillin-Yeh, "Charles Sheeler and the Machine Age" (Ph.D. dissertation, The Graduate Center, City University of New York, 1981), 105–155. Throughout his career, Sheeler based paintings on photographs. *Still Life: Zinnia and Nasturtium Leaves* (1918; photograph 1915) is one of the earliest. During the 1920s, paintings such as *Church Street El* (1920) represented simplified versions of forms derived from photographs. *Church Street El* comes from the movie *Manahatta*. It has been suggested by Dr. Naomi Rosenblum (*Conversation*, November 1980, discussing her Ph.D. dissertation "Paul Strand," The Graduate Center, City University of New York, 1979) that the painting was based on a photograph taken with a still camera during the filming of *Manahatta*. Sheeler probably discovered subjects for photographs as a result of his involvement in capturing images with a movie camera (only a still camera, Dr. Rosenblum feels, would capture a scene with sufficient sharpness to make it useful as a painting study). Another work based on photographs is *Offices* (1920); the photograph (c. 1920) was published in *Vanity Fair* (January 1921): 72. The lithograph *Delmonico Building* (1926–27) has a photograph source published in

Vanity Fair (November 1926): 72. *Delmonico Building* sets a pattern for 1930s paintings in which image and polished style alike come from photographs, and the correspondence is exact. Paintings like *Upper Deck* (photograph c. 1927) are exactly like their photograph sources. *Classic Landscape* (1931), *American Landscape* (1930), and *City Interior* (1936) take sections from photographs. (It is the opinion of Mary Jane Jacob, *The Rouge* (Detroit: Detroit Institute of the Arts, 1978), 33–43, that at least in 1927 there were photographs, now lost or inaccessible, which were the exact images of each of these paintings. One might also posit photograph sources for *Americana* (1931), in which the sharp angle of vision suggests photographic vision, and in *Home Sweet Home* (1931) because they are interior views of Sheeler's home, which he often photographed (see *Charles Sheeler, Paintings Drawings, Photographs* [New York: Museum of Modern Art, 1939], 12). *Cactus* (1931) and the entire *Power* series are based on photographs. Black-and-white conte crayon drawings including *Chartres, Industrial Architecture, Ballet Méchanique, Interior Buck County Barn, Interior with Stove*, and *Katherine* are nearly *trompe l'oeil* evocations of black-and-white photographs.

18

See Sheeler, manuscript *Autobiography*, 1937, New York, Archives of American Art, Nsh 1, frame 113.

19

Glass imagery also recalls the headless torsos of Marcel Duchamp's *Large Glass* (1911–21), an influential work. See S. Fillin-Yeh, "Charles Sheeler's 1923 Self-Portrait," *Arts Magazine* 52:5 (January 1978): 106–09.

20

The comment appeared first in Sheeler's manuscript *Autobiography*, frames 94–98, and was incorporated in Constance Rourke's *Charles Sheeler: An Artist in the American Tradition* (New York: Harcourt Brace and Company, 1938), 119–121.

21

Sheeler, as quoted from a typewritten note (February 11, 1963) in the files of the Museum of Modern Art, New York. See Millard, footnote 61.

22

See Charles Baudelaire, "The Modern Public and Photography," (1859) in Alan Trachtenberg, ed., *Classic Essays on Photography* (New Haven: Leete's Island Books, 1980), 83–89.

23

Sheeler, manuscript *Autobiography*, frame 101.

24

Walter Benjamin, "A Short History of Photography," (1931), in Trachtenberg, 204.

25

Sheeler, as quoted in Katherine Kuh, *American Artists Paint the City* (U.S. Pavilion, Venice Biennale, 1956), 35.

26

See Jeffrey L. Meikle, *Twentieth Century Limited: Industrial Design in America 1925–1939* (Philadelphia Temple University Press, 1979), and Susan Danly Walther, *The Railroad in the American Landscape* (Wellesley College Art Museum, 1981), 127. A particularly conflated image

of streamlining and fashionable glamor appears in a photograph by Toni Frissell for the *Vogue* cover for November 15, 1939. Examples in painting include Edward Hopper's *Compartment Car C* (1938; IBM Corporation, Armonk, New York). An Albert Renger-Patzsch photograph from *Das Deutsche Lichtbild*, Berlin, reproduced in *Creative Art* II: 1 (April 1928): 301, is an excellent example of the dynamic image of drive wheels that Sheeler eschewed.

27

For a discussion of the Twentieth Century Limited's ambience, see Meikle, 177.

28

For a contemporary discussion, see Sheldon and Martha Cheney, *Art and the Machine* (New York: McGraw Hill, 1936), 225, 233.

7 Edward Hopper's Railroad Imagery

Gail Levin

When asked why he selected certain subjects over others, Edward Hopper replied, "I do not exactly know, unless it is that I believe them to be the best mediums for a synthesis of my inner experience."[1] His continuing interest in railroad imagery, a repeated motif in Hopper's art from his childhood sketches to *Chair Car* of 1965, his penultimate painting, suggests very personal associations. He depicted trains still and moving, interior and exterior views, stations, platforms, ticket windows, conductors, tracks, tunnels, bridges, viaducts, signal towers, urban and rural views, American and European trains, commuter and long-distance trains, freight and passenger cars, railroad crossings, views from trains, and views of trains and trucks passing through the landscape. The many railroad images reveal a variety of meanings, some of them related to events in Hopper's life, others referring to sources of inspiration he found in earlier art or literature.

Any investigation of recurring themes in Hopper's art must begin with his childhood.[2] Hopper himself recognized the consistency within his work when in 1935 he wrote:

In every artist's development the germ of the later work is always found in the earlier. The nucleus around which the artist's intellect builds his work is himself; the central ego, personality or whatever it may be called, and this changes little from birth to death. What he was once, he always is, with slight modification. Changing fashion in methods or subject matter alter him little or not at all.[3]

Hopper grew up in Nyack, New York, where in 1882 he was born into a solidly middle-class family. Nyack was then a prosperous port town on the Hudson River with train connections to New York via the Hoboken, New Jersey, ferryboat. New York City, less than forty miles away, represented civilization, America's culture capital, while Nyack meant provincialism, a cultural wilderness.

Hopper's mother encouraged both Eddie, as he was called, and his sister Marion to develop an interest in art and the theater. When Hopper graduated from Nyack High School in 1899, he had already been actively sketching for years and had been signing and dating work since the age of ten. He intended to become an artist, but his parents prevailed upon him to study commercial illustration, which they felt would offer a more secure income. He began to commute daily to New York City to attend the Correspondence School of Illustration. A year later he entered the New York School of Art, where he eventually studied painting with William Merritt Chase, Kenneth Hayes Miller, and Robert Henri.

In 1900 Hopper sketched the *Culvert at Orangeberg*, depicting a site in Rockland County near

Nyack. In this charcoal sketch, he employed railroad tracks on a diagonal axis from the lower left corner into the distance, much as he would later align the highway in *Route 6 Eastham* (1941). In both compositions, the route is flanked by grassy banks with trees and has one or more utility poles on the left side. These scenes, devoid of human presence, are animated only by the play of light and shadow. The deserted tracks and the empty road, recurrent motifs in Hopper's work, convey a desire for escape—a longing to be some other place. Hopper once admitted, "To me the most important thing is the sense of going on. You know how beautiful things are when you're traveling."[4]

After art school, Hopper wanted to travel to Europe to see the works of the great masters firsthand. He left for Paris in October 1906 and remained in Europe until the following August. He was immediately fascinated by the infinite charms of Paris and the *joie de vivre* of the French. He depicted them in the streets, in cafés, and even in train stations. Men, women, and children fill his sketch *The Railroad* (1906), which also includes soldiers, whose costume fascinated him. The train coaches in this sketch are typical European ones of the period, with outside running boards and a door for each compartment.

Hopper may well have sketched this at the Gare d'Orsay, a short walking distance from his home on rue de Lille.

Hopper did not easily forget his European experience. Years later he recalled that America "seemed awfully crude and raw when I got back," and he admitted, "It took me ten years to get over Europe."[5] Hopper painted *Valley of the Seine* in 1908 after returning from his first trip abroad and his longest stay in France (figure 121). Although a recollection of the French countryside, this canvas calls to mind works by nineteenth-century painters of the Hudson River school such as Thomas Cole or Jasper Cropsey. Hopper's vast panoramic view, with the river winding through a valley flanked by mountains, suggests antecedents like Cole's *The Oxbow*, acquired by the Metropolitan Museum in 1908, the year of Hopper's painting.[6] In both, the viewer has a bird's eye perspective and the winding river leads the viewer to the horizon and the impressive expanse of sky. Yet while Cole celebrated the American wilderness, placing himself in the sublime uncultivated forest, Hopper saw man's encroachments on nature—the train crossing a viaduct and the village of orange-roofed white houses—as positive and picturesque. Hopper's *Valley of the Seine* also recalls Cropsey's *Starrucca Viaduct* of 1865, where man and nature, the

train and the landscape, are harmoniously accommodated, in part through the graceful, dramatic arches of a viaduct.

Before he left for Europe, Hopper had already begun his career as an illustrator, which lasted nearly two decades. By working in an advertising agency three days a week, he paid for his two additional trips abroad, in 1909 and 1910. Hopper dismissed this aspect of his career. He claimed to have been a poor illustrator because he was not interested in the right subjects: "I was interested in architecture, but the editors wanted people waving their arms." He was also fascinated by trains, and they occur in his illustrations for *System* magazine, *Associated Sunday Magazine*, *Wells Fargo Messenger*, *The Express Messenger*, and *Farmer's Wife*. He probably found the trade magazines requiring factual representations more appealing than some of the more exotic fiction or the movie posters he was called upon to illustrate.

Among the early unpublished illustrations Hopper produced are two of trains. *The Port* probably documents Hopper's own shipboard passage to France and the connecting train to Paris. In his grisaille illustration of a man *Jumping on a Train*, Hopper depicted what was for him an unusual scene of dramatic action. The image strongly suggests a story at

121
Edward Hopper, *Valley of the Seine,* 1908.
Oil on canvas, 26 × 38 in. Whitney
Museum of American Art. Josephine N.
Hopper. Bequest. Acq. 70.1183.

a pivotal moment, and this may have been intended for a film poster. Hopper's recording of the scene is convincing: this is the back of a caboose around 1890; even the utility pole necessary to send the train's signals is visible.

As Hopper distanced himself from the influence of the French Impressionists, his palette darkened once again to resemble more closely that of his contemporaries from the New York School of Art, their teacher Robert Henri, and other members of "The Eight" like John Sloan and George Luks. For his subjects, Hopper also turned to what he observed around him. His *Railroad Train* of 1908 was perhaps inspired by his own daily trip from Nyack to New York City, where he worked in his studio before returning each evening to his family home (figure 122). His representation of a moving train recalls his pen and ink sketch of about 1900, which also depicts a caboose pulled by a train. In the painting, however, Hopper has cropped the train at the picture's edge, a lesson he might have learned from the work of Edgar Degas, instead of relying on the awkward perspective of his sketch. The painterly surface and broken brushstrokes in *Railroad Train* demonstrate the lingering effect of his encounter with French Impressionism. With few exceptions (an illustration for *Associated Sunday Magazine* of April 19, 1914, and a sketch

122
Edward Hopper, *Railroad Train*, 1908. Oil on canvas, 24 × 29 in. Addison Gallery of American Art, Phillips Academy, Andover, Massachusetts. Gift of Dr. Fred T. Murphy. Photo: John C. Lutsch.

168

for an oil painting, *East River*, of about 1930, for instance), the trains that Hopper portrayed, like most of his images, are notably still.

That stillness often derives from a simplified composition. *The El Station* (1908) and *Dawn in Pennsylvania* (1942) both have tracks stretching across the foreground at an angle into the middle distance and both use contrasting vertical accents—chimneys in the former and smokestacks in the latter (figure 123). Although critics have often mentioned affinities between Giorgio de Chirico's metaphysical paintings and Hopper's cityscapes,[7] such similarities are most likely coincidental, for as *The El Station* indicates, Hopper had formulated the essentials of *Dawn in Pennsylvania* in his 1908 composition. Furthermore, the urge to reduce details in a work such as *Dawn in Pennsylvania* stems from Hopper's disdain for illustration, which he was able to give up completely in 1925, rather than from any important debt to De Chirico. A comparison of one of Hopper's working drawings for *Dawn in Pennsylvania* reveals changes he made to simplify his composition, such as the elimination of the luggage cart from the left wall, as well as changes in architectural design and scale (figure 124).

Hopper's *The El Station* expresses his interest in the sense of imminent change that characterizes train stations. In contrast to Claude Monet, whose *Gare St. Lazare* of 1877 depicts a station full of life and activity, emphasized by the steam engine's puff of smoke, Hopper favored the quiet moment of anticipation, when the station is deserted or nearly empty. He charged such scenes with drama, conveyed through light and through the shadows cast by ordinary structures, but the result is an aura of eerie expectation.

Hopper's railroad stations also express the air of waiting and longing that so often accompanies the immobilized figures in his works. Whether waiting for a train, a play to begin, or for someone to return or something to happen, Hopper's characters nearly always seem to be frozen in place before the action begins. Several etchings depict passengers waiting in train stations, including a posthumously printed plate from about 1915–18 and *The El Station* of about 1919–23. In *The Conductor*, another etching of about the same date, the figure leans against the car rail, waiting.

The figures in Hopper's train interiors, however, all seem to have found some way to escape the tedium of waiting. They have begun their journey to somewhere else, which, perhaps, releases them. They read, look at one another or out the window, and even talk. Hopper's first train interior appeared as an illustration for *System* magazine on September 22, 1912. There, a man stands in a commuter train reading the advertisements near the ceiling, while seated passengers read their newspapers. His next two train interiors also depict commuter-train passengers. In *Associated Sunday Magazine* for November 16, 1913, a standing man and seated woman communicate while the man behind her reads his newspaper. In the December 1917 *Farmer's Wife*, a conductor interrupts a woman's gaze out the window. The vaulted train interiors in both illustrations are similarly furnished. In *Night on the El Train*, an etching of 1920, a couple engrossed in a serious discussion confront one another. Their twisted postures add to the tenseness of the drama.

Hopper's first painting of a train interior was *Compartment C, Car 293* of 1938 (figure 125). The work is important for understanding another category of Hopper's railroad imagery—the views seen while traveling in trains. A solitary woman is engrossed in her reading, while the landscape passing outside the window goes unobserved except by the viewer of the painting itself. One of Hopper's working drawings for this painting shows that he initially considered having the woman turn and look out the window rather than read. In the 1921 etching *House Tops*, a woman is absorbed in the constantly changing views of urban roof tops (figure 126). Her view is framed by the

123
Edward Hopper, *Dawn in Pennsylvania*,
1942. Oil on canvas, 24¼ × 44 in. Daniel J.
Terra Collection, Terra Museum of American
Art, Chicago.

124
Edward Hopper, Drawing for the painting
Dawn in Pennsylvania, 1942. Conté crayon
on paper, 11⅟₁₆ × 15 in. Whitney Museum
of American Art. Josephine N. Hopper Bequest. Acq. 70.852.

125
Edward Hopper, *Compartment C, Car 293,*
1938. Oil on canvas, 20 × 18 in. IBM
Corporation, Armonk, New York.

126
Edward Hopper, *House Tops,* 1921. Etching,
6 × 8 in. Philadelphia Museum of Art. The
Harrison Fund.

train's window, and what she sees is thus filtered by the moving train.[8] It reflects the actual experience of train travel, where the train's velocity dissolves the foreground, so that the traveler's perception of the world outside the window becomes panoramic, even cinematic.[9]

The scenery also becomes merely backdrop after a while. Ralph Waldo Emerson, whose writing Hopper read and admired, recorded just such a sensation in his journal in 1843: "Dreamlike traveling on the railroad. The towns which I pass between Philadelphia and New York make no distinct impression. They are like pictures on a wall. The more that you can read all the way in a car a French novel."[10] Hopper presented the landscape, such as that in *Compartment C, Car 293* or *Railroad Sunset* of 1929 (figure 127), as seen through a machine ensemble—either from a train's window frame or from behind the telegraph pole and signal tower essential to the railroad's operation. This, as Wolfgang Schivelbusch has so incisively noted in his study of trains in the nineteenth century, results in the traveler's alienation from the landscape.[11] The poles and wires "interpose themselves, both physically and metaphorically, between the traveler and the landscape.[12] Thus, Hopper shows a woman, who, like Emerson, is bored by the view of the landscape from the train, ignores it, and loses herself in reading. He is also emphasizing the boredom of those more affluent individuals who isolate themselves in first-class compartments. Passengers in crowded cars, as in Daumier's *Third Class Carriage* of 1856, could enjoy the company and conversation of others.[13]

In a collection of poems Hopper treasured, Paul Verlaine described a view from a train much like the one represented in *Railroad Sunset* or even *Railroad Crossing* (1922–23)—the landscape punctuated by the railroad and telegraph poles:

The scene behind the carriage window-panes goes flitting past in furious flight; whole plains with streams and harvest fields and trees and blue are swallowed by the whirlpool, whereinto the telegraph's slim pillars topple o'er, whose wires look strangely like a musical score.[14]

Hopper's watercolor *Toward Boston* (1936) presents a similar view of nature dominated by the train, the tracks, the utility poles, and wires. Furthermore, in his etching *The Railroad* (1922), man's presence is seemingly diminished by the great unseen rumbling locomotive.

Many of Hopper's paintings present a specific time of day.[15] That the times he chose carried definite associations for him is suggested by his stated fondness for certain poems by Verlaine, Goethe, and Robert Frost. Hopper repeatedly quoted in French from Verlaine's "La Lune Blanche," which praises

173

127
Edward Hopper, *Railroad Sunset*, 1929. Oil
on canvas, 28¼ × 47¾ in. Whitney Mu-
seum of American Art. Josephine N. Hopper
Bequest. Acq. 70.1170. Photo: Bill
Jacobson.

128
Edward Hopper, *Hotel by a Railroad*, 1952.
Oil on canvas, 31¾ × 40⅛ in. Hirshhorn
Museum and Sculpture Garden, Smith-
sonian Institution. Gift of Joseph H. Hirsh-
horn Foundation, 1966. Photo: John
Tennant.

evening as "C'est l'heure exquise" or that "exquisite hour."[16] Hopper evidently saw evening as essentially melancholy, suggesting lost opportunity or the death of a dream. This can be seen in paintings like *Summer Evening* (1947), which depicts the end of a summer romance, or *Cape Cod Evening* (1939), which reveals the twilight of a relationship where communication no longer exists. Thus, his decision to make both the view from *Compartment C, Car 293* and that in *Railroad Sunset* an evening sky is symbolically significant. We are reminded once again of Verlaine's image of the traveler in poems from his *Romances sans paroles*, which describe views like those in Hopper's painting:

How much this pale landscape, O traveler,
mirrors your pale self there,
and how mournfully in the lofty leaves
your drowned hope grieves![17]

Train travel for Hopper is also a metaphor for the passage of time and the inevitable lost opportunity that results. The most overt reference to the longing and the melancholy Hopper associated with railroad imagery is in the painting *Hotel by a Railroad* of 1952 (figure 128). Years of dissatisfaction and an inability to communicate are poignantly expressed within the most intimate setting of this aging couple's hotel room. The proximity of this cheap hotel to the train tracks implies a depressing ambiance filled with noise and smoke. The woman is reading, apparently ignoring her husband's wanderlust. Bleak and wistful, impatiently waiting to depart, he gazes longingly out the window at the railroad tracks. In the record books Hopper's wife Jo kept, she noted: "Wife better watch husband & tracks below window."[18] This comment and the somber mood of the painting suggest the husband's flirtation with either escape or suicide. When, late in life, Hopper was asked if he was a pessimist, he responded, "A pessimist? I guess so. I'm not proud of it. At my age don't you get to be?"[19]

Hopper was continually intrigued by the vistas one caught while riding in trains, and he expressed his interest in such works as *House by the Railroad* (1925) and *New York, New Haven and Hartford* (1931). The railroad tracks, which set off the architecture in both of these paintings, lead the viewer's eye beyond the confines of the picture, but they also seem to suggest the continuity, mobility, and rootlessness of modern life, as the trains pass by small towns and rural areas all but forgotten by the forces of progress. The tracks metaphorically separate the small-town simplicity of Hopper's boyhood from the more complex urban concerns of his adulthood. This motif is repeated often, as in his etching *American Landscape* (1920) or in the watercolor *Lime Rock Railroad* (1926). In *Railroad Crossing*, a drypoint of 1923, Hopper showed a farmer and his cow waiting for the train, emblematic of progress, to pass by. It is this rural–urban dichotomy that suggests Hopper's ambivalence about the trials of modern life.

In *Approaching a City* of 1946, Hopper said he wanted to express "interest, curiosity, fear"—the emotions one has arriving by train into a strange city (figure 129).[20] The compositional structure of tracks passing into a dark tunnel beneath city streets recalls an earlier work, the etching *The Locomotive* (1923). In each of these images the focus is on the black hole under the viaduct, bridge, or tunnel—the locus of the unknown "fear." Another of Hopper's etchings, *Train and Bathers* of 1920 (figure 130), is related compositionally to *Approaching a City* and clarifies the "fear" to which Hopper alluded. The image of the two nude bathers scrambling behind bushes while a train rushes by is a strange one for Hopper. The eroticism here is overt: the women, identified with the "feminine" landscape, are violated by the aggressive, phallic train rumbling by; the large black hole under the viaduct recalls the Freudian analogy of the female to a vessel, cave, or chasm.[21] Linking the black hole of the tunnel to the

129
Edward Hopper, *Approaching a City,* 1946.
Oil on canvas, 27⅛ × 36 in. The Phillips
Collection, Washington, D.C.

130
Edward Hopper, *Train and Bathers,* 1920.
Etching, 11⅝ × 13¾ in. Whitney Museum
of American Art. Josephine N. Hopper Bequest. Acq. 70.1054.

"devouring female" explains the "fear" in *Approaching a City.* Hopper's composition forces the viewer to
notice the absence of the train in that canvas, which
he painted at the age of sixty four, when his own energy was much diminished. Although Hopper indicated his awareness of at least some of the ideas of
Freud and Jung in one of the caricatures he made for
Jo, any sexual symbolism in *Train and Bathers* or
Approaching a City was almost certainly uncon-
scious. Indeed, Hopper saw his art primarily as a re-
flection of his own psyche: "So much of every art is
an expression of the subconscious, that it seems to
me most of all of the important qualities are put
there unconsciously, and little of importance by the
conscious intellect. But these are things for the psy-
chologist to untangle."[22]

Hopper's last painting, *Two Comedians* (1965),
was intended as a personal statement, a farewell of
sorts, for when he portrayed Jo and himself as two
clowns gracefully bowing out, he had been ill and
would die less than two years later.

Chair Car, painted just prior to *Two Comedians*,
also suggests death (figure 131). Here the deliberately introspective mood is expressed with great se-
verity. The setting is a parlor car of the 1930s with a
high ceiling, and glaring sunlight pours through the
window, entirely obscuring the exterior world. The
chairs, like the space itself, seem too large. The curious penetrating gaze of the woman on the left, who
looks across the aisle at the woman reading, creates
an uneasy air. Perhaps, as John Hollander has suggested, Hopper is using the enclosed railcar setting
to announce the last journey, the passage of dead
souls across the River Styx: "With its closed-off back
wall (that of a room, rather than of a railroad carriage), the flag-like light falls, and the strange dispo-
sitions of the figures, this has always seemed to me
to be a version of Charon's ferry."[23]

Through the railroad imagery, Hopper expressed
his relationship to his own surroundings—his youthful thirst for adventure; his fascination with escape
through travel, literature, and the cinema; his dis-
appointments in life and his melancholy longing
for something more, for opportunity lost; his romantic and sensual nature and his nostalgia for his
youth; and, finally, his acceptance of the inevitable,
his own end. These personal concerns, particularly
his alienation, parallel problems in contemporary society. The desire to escape boredom and his anxious
view of death, which resound in his train images,
convey a sense of psychological immediacy undimin-
ished by the passage of time.

178

131
Edward Hopper, *Chair Car*, 1965. Oil on
canvas, 40 × 50 in. Private collection.

Notes

1

Quoted in Lloyd Goodrich, *Edward Hopper* (New York: Harry N. Abrams, 1971), 152. For additional information and for reproductions of works by Hopper referred to in this article but not illustrated, see Gail Levin, *Edward Hopper: The Art and the Artist* (New York: W. W. Norton & Company, 1980); Gail Levin, *Edward Hopper as Illustrator* (New York: W. W. Norton & Company, 1979); and Gail Levin, *Edward Hopper: The Complete Prints* (New York: W. W. Norton & Company, 1979).

2

For a discussion of the relevance of Hopper's childhood work to the art of his maturity, see Gail Levin, "Hopper un gigante del realismo americano: l'american e sola al mondo" *Bolaffi Arte* (October 1980).

3

"Edward Hopper Objects" (letter from Hopper to the editor, Nathaniel Pousette-Dart), *The Art of Today* 6 (February 1935): 11.

4

Quoted in William C. Seitz, *Edward Hopper in Sao Paulo* 9 (Washington, D.C.: Smithsonian Press, 1969), 22.

5

For the influence of French art and culture on Hopper, see Gail Levin, "Edward Hopper, Francophile," *Arts Magazine* 53 (June 1979): 114–21.

6

Thomas Cole's *The Oxbow* was reproduced in the *Bulletin of The Metropolitan Museum of Art* III (December 1908): 227 and discussed on p. 229 in the article "Principal Accessions" as "being one of the most important productions in pure landscape painting." This landscape would have been exhibited in "The Accessions Room," which "changed each month at the time of the publication of the Bulletin."

7

James T. Soby, *Contemporary Painters* (New York: Simon & Schuster, 1948), 179–80: "There is a decided affinity between the two painters as to their conception of the dramatic possibilities of arrested time." Robert M. Coates, "Edward Hopper," *The New Yorker* (February 26, 1950), referring to *Dawn in Pennsylvania*, stated, "Hopper has, in a denser, more compact, and possibly less purely poetic fashion, something of the evocativeness of Chirico."

8

Wolfgang Schivelbusch, *The Railway Journey: Trains and Travel in the 19th Century* (New York: Urizen Books, 1979).

9

Ibid., 65–66.

10

Quoted in ibid., 57.

11

Ibid., 40.

12

Ibid.

13

Ibid., 67–70.

14

Translated by Gertrude Hall, in *Baudelaire, Rimbaud, Verlaine: Selected Verse and Prose Poems* (New York: Citadel Press, 1947). In French, the poem reads:

Le paysage dans le cadre des portières
Court furieusement, et des plaines entières.
Avec de l'eau, des blès, des arbres et du ciel
Vont s'engouffrant parmi le tourbillon cruel
Où tombent les poteaux mines du télégraphe
Dont les fils ont l'allure étrange d'un paraphe.

Hopper owned the volume Paul Verlaine, *Choix de Poésies* (Paris: Bibliotheque-Charpentier, 1922), which was given by Jeanne Chéruy in 1922.

15

See Levin, *Edward Hopper: The Art and the Artist*, 61–63, for a discussion of times of day in Hopper's work, and Gail Levin, "Edward Hopper's Evening," *The Connoisseur* 205 (September 1980): 56–63.

16

Now a tender and vast appeasement seems to descend from the firmament with the irised star . . . Ah, exquisite hour," from *Paul Verlaine, Selected Poems*, translated by C. F. MacIntyre (Berkeley: University of California Press, 1948), 95. Hopper quoted this poem in French in his Christmas card of 1923 for Jo and again in an unpublished letter of August 7, 1955, to Donald Adams, editor of the *New York Times Book Review.* He also quoted it again to Brian O'Doherty for an interview published as "Portrait: Edward Hopper," *Art in America* 52 (December 1964): 80.

17

Translated by C. F. MacIntyre, *Paul Verlaine, Selected Poems*, 113–114:

"Combien, ô voyageur, ce paysage blême
Te mira blême toi-même,
Et que tristes pleuraient dans les hautes feuillées
Tes espérances noyées?"

18

Jo also noted that the painting had an "Emphasis on mood." The record books are in the collection of the Whitney Museum of American Art, New York.

19

Quoted in O'Doherty, 72–73.

20

Quoted in Goodrich, 106.

21

Leo Marx, *The Machine in the Garden: Technology and the Pastoral Ideal in America* (New York: Oxford University Press, 1964), 29, noted with reference to American writers "the sense of the machine as a sudden, shocking intruder upon a fantasy of idyllic satisfaction. It invariably is associated with crude, masculine aggressiveness in contrast with the tender, feminine, and submissive attitudes traditionally attached to the landscape." For a discussion of the feminine symbolism of chasms, caves, etc. as "the earth womb that demands to be fructified," see Erich Neumann, *The Great Mother* (New York: Pantheon Books, 1963), 44–47. Hopper's association of tunnels with fear is also indicated by his painting *Bridle Path* (1939), in which the man's horse rears back before entering a dark tunnel in Central Park.

22

Edward Hopper to Charles H. Sawyer, letter of October 29, 1939. Quoted in Goodrich, 164. Hopper also indicated his awareness of modern psychology in a remark he made about the short stories of Thomas Mann: "Rough going. Well depressing. Freudian. A great writer of fiction" (quoted in O'Doherty, 73).

23

John Hollander, "Hopper and the Figure of Room," presented October 27, 1980, at the Edward Hopper Symposium organized by the Whitney Museum of American Art and published in *Art Journal* 41 (Summer 1981): 155–60.

8 The Railroad-in-the-Landscape: An Iconological Reading of a Theme in American Art

Leo Marx

When we try to understand . . .[a work] as a document of . . .[a] civilization . . . we deal with the work of art as a symptom of something else which expresses itself in a countless variety of other symptoms, and we interpret its compositional and iconographical features as more particularized evidence of this "something else." The discovery and interpretation of these "symbolical" values (which are often unknown to the artist himself and may even emphatically differ from what he consciously intended to express) is the object of what we may call "iconology" as opposed to "iconography."
Erwin Panofsky, "Iconography and Iconology"

Of all the great modern innovations, the railroad is probably the one to which American artists have accorded the most significance. The passenger railroad first appeared on the American scene in the 1830s, and it almost immediately caught the eye of several of the nation's most gifted landscape painters. By the time of the Civil War the new machine had already been incorporated in the work of Thomas Cole, Thomas Doughty, Asher Durand, and John Kensett. The subject attracted their attention because of its newness—its radically innovative character—and because of its compelling visual properties. A steam-powered locomotive moving across the landscape is an arresting sight—so arresting, indeed, that its visual character alone might seem to account for the strong hold it so quickly took on the imagination of artists. Here, after all, was an imposing, mobile, man-made contrivance, a complicated mechanism wrought of dark metal in various shifting geometric forms; the engine's motive power was made visible by the train of cars it pulled, the surging puffs of smoke and steam (black or white or both) that trailed behind it, and the intermittent flashes of red when its fire box was open.

The "iron horse" is a fascinating object, it is true, yet even a brief survey of the American paintings and photographs in which it appears reveals that what artists often have found most interesting is not so much the machine itself—its inherent visual attributes—but its presence *in the countryside:* the evocative juxtaposition of the mechanical artifact with the shapes, lines, colors, and textures of the natural setting, whether wild or rural. What captivated them was the coming together of the locomotive's smooth, metallic efficiency, compact with purpose, and the organic forms of the landscape; it was a set of contrasts between the dark smoking engine and the soft colors—blues, greens, browns, and whites—of the sky, fields, and woods; between the sharp-edged lines of the machine and the irregular (flowing, rounded, or jagged) lines of the clouds, mountains, rivers, trees, and flocks.

But the more we consider the evocative power of this complex image, the more apparent it will be that from the time of its initial appearance in the American landscape the railroad's merely visual or perceptual attributes have been inseparably bound up with its underlying thematic, social, or ideological significance. Perhaps this is only to say that the idea of "merely visual or perceptual attributes," however useful for purposes of analysis, is a fiction. As Rudolf Arnheim and E. H. Gombrich have so persuasively argued, seeing and thinking, perception and cognition, are interactive aspects of a single process.[1] In fact there is one significant group of mid-nineteenth-century American paintings in which the artists apparently set out, quite deliberately and with a manifestly "ideological" purpose, to ignore or render inconspicuous the appealing visual attributes of the railroad-in-the-landscape.

In any event, the significance of the railroad, like that of most technical innovations, was present in the culture before the thing itself was. Long before the first passenger railroad lines began operations, indeed before the steam-powered locomotive was in evidence, the press had begun to inform the public about its unique physical properties and its capacity to effect change. It could pull more weight faster and further than people had thought possible, and it soon became obvious that this method of transportation was to have far-reaching economic and social consequences. For some fifteen or twenty years after the first passenger railroads began operations, about 1830, while the press kept up the excitement with stories about every imaginable aspect of the new technology and practitioners of the popular arts contributed songs and pictures, poems and fictions to the hubbub, the public in England and the United States was in the throes of what was called, even then, "railroad mania." In those days the railroad was as great a source of wonder and excitement as the computer is today.[2]

Neither the railroad's newness nor the "mania" it initially aroused, however, can account for the remarkably enduring interest of serious artists in the subject. Indeed, many of the most distinguished treatments of the subject were not accomplished until long after the initial excitement had subsided. No doubt the novelty of the railroad was still a factor in attracting the attention of mid-nineteenth-century landscape painters like Jasper Cropsey, George Inness, Thomas Moran, and Albert Bierstadt; in several instances, in fact, the work of painters and photographers was commissioned by the railroad companies as part of their effort to promote tourist travel by rail and, probably more important, to improve what now would be called their "public relations" with a view, especially, to winning large grants of free land from the Congress. But the aura of discovery, innovation, and modernity that originally surrounded the new machine surely had dissipated long before the subject caught the attention of such modernist photographers as Alfred Stieglitz, Charles Sheeler, and Walker Evans. In the work of twentieth-century painters like Arthur Dove, Georgia O'Keeffe, John Sloan, George Bellows, Charles Burchfield, and Edward Hopper, the railroad has less to do with a sense of the future than of the past—less with hope or foreboding than with nostalgia. And after World War II, when the documentary impulse embodied in nineteenth-century theories of aesthetic realism had lost most of its vigor, we find that the railroad still figures prominently in the work of such modernists as David Smith, Franz Kline, and John Baeder. All of which is to say that American artists have invested the railroad with a range and depth of significance that transcends the excitement surrounding its initial appearance, or its novelty as a visual object, or its manifest importance as a technological and economic innovation.

How, then, are we to account for the fascination this subject has exercised on the imagination of

American painters and photographers? That their interest in the machine is not attributable to its inherent properties is further confirmed by the fact that the airplane, in many respects a more radical invention and a more arresting, less mundane subject, did not attract anything like the same amount of attention from artists. What larger significance, then, have graphic artists discovered—or invested—in the railroad and, most particularly, in the railroad-in-the-landscape? How shall we get at the cultural significance of their work? An adequate answer to these questions requires that we identify, by means of what Erwin Panofsky called iconological analysis, the "intrinsic" (or implicit) meanings in this body of American art—meanings that may not be immediately apparent on the surface, but whose presence may nonetheless be inferred from the "underlying principles" that the work shares with the rest of the corpus and with the culture to which it belongs. These intrinsic meanings derive, in Panofsky's account, from the largely tacit presuppositions governing "the basic attitude of a nation, a period, a class, a religious or philosophical persuasion—qualified by one personality and condensed into one work."[3]

Perhaps the most commonly expressed response to the appearance of the railroad on the American scene in the 1830s was a heightened sense of change itself—its accelerating pace and its potentially all-encompassing scope. But at that time, it should be said, the unusual mutability of American life already was a familiar idea. It had achieved a certain currency by the time of the revolution, and during the early years of the republic it was a popular literary theme; its most memorable embodiment was no doubt Washington Irving's "Rip Van Winkle" (1819). When Rip returned from his famous twenty-year nap, he ostensibly found his world almost unrecognizable. But from the vantage of American readers twenty or thirty years later, in the hectic railroad era, it must have seemed as if remarkably little had happened during Rip's absence. To be sure, the little Dutch inn's name had been changed from George III to George Washington, but what might well have surprised a mid-nineteenth-century audience was the fact that the old inn was still standing right where it always had been, that it had not been razed to make way for the latest "internal improvement." By that time the acute feeling of impermanence induced by the "age of steam," and accentuated in the United States by the absence of a visible past, had become pervasive. Thus Nathaniel Hawthorne, in *The House of the Seven Gables* (1851), describes the sense of unreality, dislocation, and flux induced by seeing the world through the window of a rapidly moving train:

At one moment, they were rattling through a solitude;—the next a village had grown up around them;—a few breaths more and it had vanished, as if swallowed by an earthquake. The spires of meeting-houses seemed set adrift from their foundations; the broad-based hills glided away. Everything was unfixed from its age-long rest, and moving at whirlwind speed in a direction opposite to their own.[4]

Everything was unfixed! What is most striking about Hawthorne's account is its extravagance: the abrupt and radical transformation of human experience he associates with the arrival of the new mechanized motive power in the landscape. At that time the railroad was also being introduced in Britain and in much of western Europe, but though regarded as a token of change everywhere, it seldom elicited reactions as extreme as that inscribed here: the feeling that *everything*—the location of villages; the base of the hills; the foundations of religion; the very size, shape, and character of the nation—suddenly was unfixed or gliding away or vanishing. If there were distinctively American responses to the onset of the new industrial order, one of them surely was this heightened sense of the sudden, dramatic, and all-encompassing character of the changes it entailed.

To do things, as the popular phrase had it, "railroad fashion," was to do them as rapidly, thoroughly, and efficiently as possible—in the most advanced nineteenth-century spirit. According to a commonplace of the period borrowed from Alexander Pope, the railroad represented those new powers over nature that were effecting a virtual "annihilation of space and time." Today informed scholarly opinion tends to confirm the nineteenth-century sense of the railroad's enormous importance as a vehicle of change. Of all the great modern inventions, indeed, it probably is the one to which today's historians accord the greatest influence. They remind us that the steam-powered locomotive was the first important innovation in overland transportation since before the time of Julius Caesar and that it was one of the chief pivots on which the industrial revolution turned. The more scholarly research has revealed about the changes caused by the railroad, the less manic, the more reasonable or at least understandable that initial mania has come to seem.

The railroad was vital to a young republic bent on the rapid building of a nationwide market economy. Before large-scale production could be profitable, farmers and manufacturers had to gain access to much larger markets. But in the early nineteenth-century, American roads were notoriously bad, and

goods shipped between distant American states were sometimes transported back and forth across the Atlantic. Inadequate transportation was no doubt a constraint upon economic development everywhere, but it was a major obstacle for a relatively underpopulated new nation engaged in the occupation of a vast, largely undeveloped terrain. Earlier, it is true, the new canals and steamboats had begun to enlarge the geographical scope of domestic markets in the United States, but it was not until the advent of the railroad that it became economically feasible to ship goods long distances over land.

The distinctively heightened sense of change that Americans invested in the railroad therefore had a basis in geographical, economic, and social reality. In the long run many of the New World conditions that had seemed to be obstacles to capitalist development proved to be propitious, and although industrialization began later in the United States than in Britain, once it had begun it accelerated more rapidly and cohesively. In Britain, for example, the factory system had been introduced during the 1780s, roughly half a century before the railroad, but in the United States the two were introduced more or less simultaneously. Perhaps even more telling is the fact that the building of the American railroads coincided with the building of a new society and with the final phase of the European occupation of the continent.

Between 1830 and 1860, when the first 30,000 miles of track were laid, the line of permanent white settlements moved further west than it had moved in the previous two centuries. If the significance of the American railroad was different from the European, then, it is partly because the geographical, socioeconomic, and political contexts—not to mention the very character of the terrain—were different. In Europe the tracks usually were laid alongside existing, often ancient, roadways, but in many parts of the United States the land first had to be cleared and leveled.[5] The American railroad, in short, was a vehicle of territorial conquest and nation-building.

Then, too, the unprecedented scale of the railroad companies' operations demanded an entirely new kind of business organization. Running a railroad efficiently called for precise scheduling, a foolproof network of communications, and many workers with a variety of special skills on duty all along the right-of-way twenty-four hours a day. What was needed, by way of planning, training, discipline, and vigilance, had more in common with a military organization than with the traditional family-owned, family-run firm. As Alfred Chandler has shown, railroading, more than any other industry, called forth the new kind of large, impersonal, hierarchical corporation run by specially trained professional managers.[6] No technology, in short, did more to hasten the rationalization and bureaucratization of business, or indeed the overall transition to a highly centralized form of corporate capitalism. Few artists at the time or later were conscious of all of these indirect, often obscure, long-term consequences of railroad-building; but they nonetheless contributed, if only in a piecemeal, inchoate manner, to a pervasive sense of the railroad as a vehicle of radical change.

It is important to acknowledge that much of what I have been saying is the potentially misleading product of hindsight. When we now discuss the emergence of urban industrialism, we invariably rely upon a language derived from insights and judgments that were unavailable to the people living through those changes. Such shorthand terms as "the industrial revolution" or "urban industrialism" are invaluable aids to current discourse, but they may also seem to imply, among other dubious ideas, that the emergence of industrial society was something like a unitary event. Even the most sophisticated historians, who know very well that the change in question was comprised of many changes, that it was an intricate, multifaceted process spanning many decades, are likely to refer to this complex of economic, social, and technological innovations as if it constituted a single, determinate "event." "By any

reckoning," writes E. J. Hobsbawm in a spirited and persuasive defense of the concept of the industrial revolution, "this was probably the most important event in world history, at any rate since the invention of agriculture and cities."[7] It is one thing, however, to insist upon the unique historical significance of industrialization and quite another to suggest, or to allow the supposition, that the process was experienced by people at the time as an "event."

Summary abstractions like "industrial revolution," however useful they may be as a kind of retrospective shorthand, can only be a serious impediment to an understanding of what that radical transformation of life meant to people who actually lived through it. At the time, for one thing, this barely perceptible chain of events had yet to be given a widely recognized name. To say of the railroad when it first appeared that it meant (or represented) the "industrial revolution" is grossly misleading, if only because that term, which had been coined shortly before the beginning of the railroad era, did not gain widespread currency until late in the century. In fact, most of the words and phrases we now use to designate the great transition to social modernity—industrial revolution, the rise of industrial capitalism, industrialization, urbanization, rationalization, mechanization, modernization, Westernization, etc.—had not at the time been coined or had not yet

won currency. What really matters, of course, is not so much the unavailability of the words themselves as of the ideas to which they refer—ideas we now rely upon to designate and, at the same time, to make sense of the great transformation. To read widely in the literature and the public discourse of that critical era, accordingly, is to become aware of an enormous conceptual void and a yearning to fill it—to find some way, if not to explain, at least to represent what was happening.

Of course the existence of a "cultural lag" between events and their naming, or conceptualization, is not in itself unusual. If the lag was particularly large in the case of industrialization, that is partly because the process remained so nearly invisible for such a long time after it had begun. It was invisible in the sense, first, that the early stages of most great historical processes and movements are invisible. In the Year One A.D., as M. I. Finley observes in a telling and witty essay, nobody knew that one of the greatest religious movements in world history was beginning. The fact is that no one alive at the time or for some three centuries afterward had any idea that it *was* the Year One.[8] Much the same may be said about the beginning of the several interacting trends which, taken together, comprise the "event" we now call the "industrial revolution." At the time the Lowell factories began operations, for example, no one knew that the newly recruited work force marked the beginning of what eventually was to become a national labor market for women. Nor could anyone have known how that innovation would contribute to the decline of the family as a self-contained economic unit and to the virtual disappearance of the family-operated subsistence farm.[9] It was only later that historians were able to trace the extensive consequences of such innovations and, even more important, their subtle, endlessly ramifying relatedness—the putative unitary and perhaps even systemic character of the overall transition to an entirely new kind of society.

There is another, perhaps more fundamental if elusive sense in which the transition to economic and social modernity was invisible. It is arguable, following a line of analysis that leads from Adam Smith to Karl Marx and Louis Althusser, that in its deepest inner workings the new industrial capitalist order (as compared with other socioeconomic orders) is uniquely invisible. To Smith the most salient of those hidden inner features, which he so memorably calls "the invisible hand," is the self-regulating operation of the market economy. To Marx the invisibility of capitalism inheres in such of its key features as the highly abstract character of capital (as compared with land) as the basic form of property, in the masked appropriation by the owners of capital of the "surplus value" created by labor, and in the reifying, quasi-mystical form of behavior he names "commodity fetishism." To Althusser, reinterpreting Marx in the idiom of twentieth-century structuralism, the invisibility of the capitalist economy is attributable to the essentially intangible, relational, or conceptual character of its structure; or, put differently, its invisibility follows from the fact that the essence of what Marx meant by capitalism resides in a set of relations apprehensible chiefly by, and largely indistinguishable from, its effects. The effects of those relations, in other words, have no clearly identifiable cause or origin other than the whole: they are not traceable to the system's constituent parts, only to the overall structure or ensemble of those parts. The essential character of an industrial capitalist society therefore inheres nowhere but in the totality of those effects, and to call it invisible, from Althusser's standpoint, is something of a tautology.[10]

Whatever the validity of Althusser's highly speculative theory, it testifies to the persistence of the idea, which arose early in the industrial era, that essential features of the new way of life were hidden from view. This widespread notion had the effect, among other things, of intensifying the preoccupation of nineteenth-century intellectuals, writers, and artists with seeing in general and with the visual symbols of change. When the social forces shaping society are thought to be in large measure imperceptible, then what actually can be seen to be new and different takes on all the more significance. "The artist," wrote Ralph Waldo Emerson in 1841, "must employ the symbols in use in his day and nation to convey his enlarged sense to his fellow-men." Emerson's prescription was something of a radical departure from received aesthetic practice. Most artists of his generation were still committed (as he himself had been not so long before), to the neoclassic doctrine that stressed the necessary reliance of art upon the universal, ostensibly timeless forms and themes inherent in the underlying nature of things. They had little use for the new or original in art. But here Emerson is not merely opening the doors of art to the new; he is saying that artists, in order to make their work meaningful to their contemporaries, *must* seize upon what is most distinctive in the life of the times. He means, quite literally, that they have no choice. Or, put differently, that their only choice, finally, is between deliberately seizing the new or allowing it to manifest itself inadvertently and ineffectually. Emerson's point is that whatever choice artists make, the spirit of the age will unavoidably make itself felt in their work:

No man can quite emancipate himself from his age and country, or produce a model in which the education, the religion, the politics, usages and arts of his times shall have no share. Though he were never so original, never so wilful and fantastic, he cannot wipe out of his work every trace of the thoughts amidst which it grew. *The very avoidance betrays the usage he avoids.*[11]

An artist who incorporates images of the new machinery in his work might well produce the kind of "model" Emerson envisages—one in which the usages and arts of the times have a share. On this theme, he almost certainly had been influenced by Thomas Carlyle, who had proposed in a truly seminal essay, "Signs of the Times" (1829), that the oncoming age was to be "the Age of Machinery in every outward and inward sense of that word; the age which, in its whole undivided might, forwards, teaches and practices the great art of adapting means to ends." Carlyle was also one of the first to recognize that the use of mechanized motive power in production and transportation amounted to a quantum leap in mankind's progressive separation from nature: "Our old modes of exertion are all discredited, and thrown aside. On every hand, the living artisan is driven from his workshop, to make room for a speedier, inanimate one."

Carlyle's most effective argument was devoted to the "inward sense" in which the machine was emblematic of the age. He saw the proliferation of the new technology as the outward sign of what really mattered: the immense power of the "mechanical philosophy," a popular name for the empirical method of Locke and Hume, and its continental equivalent, the scientific rationalism of Descartes. At the center of Carlyle's post-Kantian argument was his clear delineation of a crucial conflict between two modes of consciousness: one, which he called "Mechanical," was scientific and practical rationality, and the other, called "Dynamical," was the poetic or metaphoric imagination that lent expression to pre-cognitive and (though he did not know the word) preconscious sources of thought. He argued in favor of an equilibrium between the two, but he clearly was writing to sound an alarm about the impending triumph of Mechanical, or what we might call technocratic, thinking. This argument was to have an immense influence on American intellectuals, writers, and artists, and it is worth noting that the most explicit and forceful American reply to Carlyle was a lawyer's brief for the progressive world view called "A Defense of the Mechanical Philosophy."[12]

Of all the new machines, none provided a more meaningful or evocative image of the rapidly changing times than the railroad. The "iron horse" embodied virtually all of the prominent sensuous attributes of the new industrial power—iron, fire, steam, smoke, noise. Then, too, the railroad as a system incorporated most of the essential features of the emerging industrial order: the substitution of metal for wood construction; the replacement of age-old sources of locomotive energy—water, wind, animals, human beings—by coal power; the vastly enlarged geographical scale of economic activities; speed, rationality, impersonality, and a spirit of efficiency that included an unprecedented emphasis on precise timing. The railroad figured forth the rapidly accelerating rate of technological innovation that is perhaps the salient feature of modern society. Even more than the "iron horse" itself, however, it was the image of the railroad-in-the-landscape that attracted the attention of American painters and photographers, for it was a "model" that enabled them to convey, in Emerson's language, their enlarged sense to their fellow men.

I began by saying that a characteristic American reaction to the initial appearance of the railroad was a heightened sense of accelerating "change"; but certain vocal and influential Americans soon adopted a less neutral way of putting it—one that was more committed and enthusiastic, not to say celebratory. The manifest dynamism of the new machine technology made it (and images representing it, like that of the railroad) a particularly effective embodiment of the idea that now, in an age of revolution, "change" had taken on an unmistakably forward-moving aspect. Here at last was confirmation of the Enlightenment passion to know, of the assumption that the course of history could be, and to a gratifying extent already was being, determined by human beings—by the steady, cumulative, continuous (perhaps, as some thought, preordained) expansion of their knowledge and power. A corollary of this exhilarating assumption was that the citizens of a democratic republic surely would see to it that the newly acquired knowledge and power were used to enhance the general well-being. In the dominant culture, in other words, the onset of industrialism was greeted as hard evidence that what once had been perceived as "change" had acquired the unmistakable character of continuous, linear, predictable *progress*. Like a railroad moving across the landscape, the course of events itself could now be thought of as advancing, liberating, improving, beneficent, or, in a word, progressive.

An unusual aspect of the progressive world view is the extent to which it was disseminated, without benefit of words or ideas, by the mere appearance of the new instruments of power. Their physical presence alone enabled the new machines, in John Stuart Mill's words, to inculcate "a feeling of admiration for

modern, and disrespect for ancient times" in the entire population, "down even to the wholly uneducated classes." (It is worth noting, incidentally, that the occasion for this insight was Mill's review of Tocqueville's *Democracy in America*.[13]) To contemplate a modern invention, Mill is saying, an invaluable machine unknown to one's parents' generation, is to summon the thought that the present is an improvement on the past, and that the future will be superior to both. To be sure, this pervasive attitude was also nurtured by such advances of theoretical science as nineteenth-century models of biological evolution and by the compelling notion of the progressive "ascent of man" they fostered. Unlike abstruse scientific theories, however, the revolution in technology made its significance felt wordlessly, without the help of any expressive or mediating intelligence. Mill's point is that the import of the railroad—its bearing on conceptions of past, present, and future—was immediately accessible to almost everybody. The mere sensuous presence of the new power encouraged each successive generation to think of its situation, as well as that of its own successor, as superior to the situation of all previous generations.

The image of the railroad was made into a potent symbol of progress, but the image of the railroad-in-

the-landscape was to be even more powerful, particularly in the United States, where from the beginning the native landscape had been invested with a special set of meanings, values, and purposes. To account for the powerful grip that this complex image was to have on the imagination of American painters and photographers, it is necessary to emphasize its bipolarity: the fact that the symbolic efficacy of the railroad-in-the-landscape arises from the bringing together of two powerful cultural images. When Europeans first contemplated the New World, they perceived it not as a society, but as a place, a terrain, a landscape. Topographical images were the most obvious, evocative tokens of the redemptive possibilities held forth by a new society in the unspoiled New World. By the nineteenth century they already had served for some four hundred years as visual embodiments of the myth of a new beginning for European civilization. It had been an enormously hopeful myth to begin with, but now, with the onset of the new machine power in America, that hope was immeasurably enhanced.

Depicted in an American setting, the new railroad was often made into a virtual allegory of the Enlightenment belief in the impending liberation of humanity from the age-old constraints of nature. Daniel

Webster, Senator from Massachusetts, recognized spokesman for the industrialists of New England, and one of the foremost orators of his day, said as much at the dedication of a New Hampshire railroad in 1847:

It is an extraordinary age in which we live. It is altogether new. The world has seen nothing like it before. I will not pretend, no one can pretend, to discern the end; but everybody knows that the age is remarkable for scientific research into the heavens, the earth, and what is beneath the earth; and perhaps more remarkable still for the application of this scientific research to the pursuits of life. The ancients saw nothing like it. The moderns have seen nothing like it till the present generation. . . . We see the ocean navigated and the solid land traversed by steam power, and intelligence communicated by electricity. Truly this is almost a miraculous era. What is before us no one can say, what is upon us no one can hardly realize. The progress of the age has almost outstripped human belief; the future is known only to Omniscience.[14]

The railroad in the American landscape is for Webster a figural embodiment of the progressive world view. Although the modern idea of science-based progress, as formulated by such writers as Bacon and Condorcet, Franklin and Jefferson, had been couched in largely secular language, Webster's bow to "Omniscience" brings in that touch of divine providence characteristic of the nineteenth-century "rhetoric of the technological sublime." As depicted in this popular rhetorical style, the great new works mentioned by Webster—the telegraph, steamboats, and railroads—are figurations of the human capacity to approximate the unsurpassable, never wholly expressible, power and immensity and majesty—in short, sublimity—of the Creation itself. The new machines thus become objects of awe, reverence, and exaltation comparable only to that invested in Nature by rhetoricians of the metaphysical sublime.[15] No event invited a greater outpouring of this enthusiastic rhetoric than the appearance of the railroad on the national scene at just the right—the providential—moment, when the white settlers were poised for their final push to the Pacific. This wonder-inspiring conjunction of events, like the working out of a grand historical design, comported with the belief in the imminence of the Christian millennium that pervaded evangelical Protestantism (especially the fundamentalist sects), the most popular American religious dispensation at the time.

Of the great nineteenth-century American writers, Walt Whitman probably was the most sympathetically attuned to the the spirit of the technological sublime. (Hawthorne used it satirically in his sharp attack on glib progressivism, "The Celestial Railroad," and Melville, by putting it into the mouth of mad Captain Ahab, picked up the pathologically obsessive will to power, the sublimated sexuality, it sometimes betrayed.) As Whitman describes the locomotive in his Emersonian apostrophe "To a Locomotive in Winter," it is in effect a transcendental, a sublime machine that embodies forces, meanings, and purposes common to nature and to man (or history); it is as much a manifestation of "the continent" as of thrusting, hard, practical, unsentimental, male power and modernity. It is indeed the very "Type of the modern—emblem of motion and power—pulse of the continent."

Law of thyself complete, thine own track firmly
   holding,
(No sweetness debonair of tearful harp or glib piano
   thine,)
Thy trills of shrieks by rocks and hills return'd,
Launch'd o'er the prairies wide, across the lakes,
To the free skies unpent and glad and strong.[16]

The "iron horse," as depicted in the more nationalistic celebrations of the technological sublime, became a divinely ordained instrument for penetrating the wilderness, driving out the Native Americans, subduing the earth, and taking dominion over the vast trans-Mississippi West. It thus enabled Americans to fulfill the famous injunction of Genesis. Countless sermons and speeches of the period caught the exhilarating mood in stock images of trains hurtling across the rivers, plains, and mountains of the West. These images, widely disseminated by popular prints like the Currier & Ives *Westward the Course of Empire Takes Its Way*, figured forth the quasi-religious, expansionary, and patriotic fervor contained in slogans like "the triumph of civilization over savagery," "the conquest of nature," and "Manifest Destiny." The secular belief in history as a record of progress and the religious faith in the imminence of God's earthly kingdom thus converged. They seemed to chart much the same route into the future and to represent the essence of what was emerging as the prevailing American world view.

That Webster's celebration of progress exemplifies the dominant American response to the onset of industrialism is not open to serious question. (By "dominant" I mean the response characteristic of the most powerful and influential social groups, and hence the most widely disseminated. It was not necessarily the most representative of the majority viewpoint.) Until twenty or thirty years ago, the received judgment among historians was that during the nineteenth century the vast majority of Americans were untroubled, fervent believers in technological progress. That judgment was amply supported, or so it seemed, by the available evidence. The fact is that Americans did not mount any opposition to the new

machinery comparable in militancy to that of the English Luddites, nor any opposition to capitalism comparable in political efficacy to that of the socialist movements of the European working class. Indeed, save for adherents of the Southern slavery system, no powerful social group in the United States offered any sustained, overt resistance to industrialization. The only other overt expression of dissent came from a few outspoken individuals, most of them eccentric intellectuals, churchmen, writers, and artists. Until the 1960s, however, the views of such intelligent and articulate people as Orestes Brownson, George Perkins Marsh, Thomas Cole, Henry Thoreau, or Herman Melville had been dismissed by most cultural historians as the relatively insignificant expression of a tiny, unrepresentative minority.

As recently as 1961, Perry Miller, perhaps the most highly regarded American intellectual historian of this century, argued that the significance of that eccentric minority's unorganized, seemingly ineffectual, and almost exclusively moral, aesthetic, and intellectual dissent had been blown out of all proportion. He saw no reason to take its criticism of the new industrial order seriously, and he charged modern scholars who have expressed interest in those

nineteenth-century deviants with a snobbish or elitist bias, with an anti-democratic tendency to "emphasize the minorities who have protested here and there against the majority's infatuation with the machine." Miller admitted that there may have been rural backwaters where the people clung to a simpler preindustrial economy, and that there also may have been a certain amount of what he called "folk resistance to the temptations of the machine." But all of these deviations, taken together, were of negligible significance compared to the attitude of most Americans. As for what that prevailing attitude was, Miller had no doubt whatever:

On the whole, the story is that the mind of the nation flung itself into the mighty prospect, dreamed for decades of comforts that we now take for granted, and positively lusted for the chance to yield itself to the gratifications of technology. The machine has not conquered us in some imperial manner against our will. On the contrary, we have wantonly prostrated ourselves before the machine.[17]

Since Miller made that polemical statement, the views he expounded have been questioned by a number of skeptical scholars. It is now apparent that, like many historians, he assumed that spokesmen for the dominant culture were expressing the viewpoint of virtually the entire population; that is partly because they mistook the relative absence in America of overt European-style class struggle for unqualified approval of the new order, and because they were excessively reliant upon the public record, which tends to be biased in favor of views held by the most powerful and articulate social groups. The result, in any case, is that they awarded too much of the contentious past to the victors—to those who held an uncritical view of the dawning industrial era as a boon to humanity. In the light of subsequent research, Miller's description of the vast majority of Americans "lusting" to be ravished by the machine has come to seem grossly misleading.

Following E. P. Thompson's exemplary work on the early responses to industrialization of the English working class, historians have been looking more carefully at the attitudes of nineteenth-century Americans. Apart from such obvious symptoms of discontent as union organizing, protests, and strikes, they have discovered evidence of widespread, if often inarticulate or masked, dislike of the new industrial workplace. Many workers resorted to indirect forms of resistance or sabotage: they impeded the introduction of new technologies by slowdowns, absenteeism, a calculated inability to master new methods, and, perhaps most often, simply by quitting their jobs and moving on. The unusual mobility (geographic and social) enjoyed by Americans lent a somewhat less militant cast to their dissidence. Yet

even the internationally famous mill girls of Lowell—those apple-cheeked, ostensibly virtuous and happy recruits from New England farms—soon became disenchanted with conditions in the showplace of America's idyllic factory system.[18]

But discontented industrial workers and adherents of the slavery system were by no means the only Americans who did not share the quasi-official enthusiasm for technological progress. Social and cultural historians recently have learned a good deal about a variety of inchoate, semi-articulate, obliquely manifested or symbolic forms of dissent in nineteenth-century America. These include such difficult to assess, often merely tacit (and sometimes inadvertent) forms of "resistance" to the new order as the deep ambivalence about the direction of society that is central to the work of the classic American writers and the behavior of entire rural communities, where local merchants, farmers, and artisans stubbornly tried to hold on to the old ways. (The statistical record of the mass movement into the cities may not mean that people preferred urban life, but merely that they needed jobs.) To gauge accurately the full range and extent of such covert dissidence, it is also necessary to take account, as cultural historians have barely begun to do, of the apprehension,

anxiety, and guilt aroused in many people by the expulsion and mass murder of the "Indians"; by the heedless destruction of forests and soil, wild birds and animals; by such early warnings of ecological devastation as that set forth by George Perkins Marsh and the initial impulses toward conservation they provoked; and, most important for our purposes, by the impending and irremediable destruction of the unspoiled American wilderness.

It has long been a commonplace of cultural history that the modern belief in Nature as the ultimate repository of meaning, value, and purpose was one of the chief forms in which Western intellectuals reacted to the rationalistic mentality of modern science and technology and to the coincident transformation of Western societies. This "romantic reaction," an alienation first given expression in the late eighteenth century, is associated with the viewpoint of European and British writers like Rousseau, Schelling, Goethe, Blake, Coleridge, and Wordsworth. The philosophic core of their critical attitude to these forces of change, as cogently defined by Alfred North Whitehead, was "a protest on behalf of the organic view of nature, and also a protest against the exclusion of value from the essence of matter of fact." What requires emphasis here is the peculiar susceptibility of certain Americans to variants of this "romantic reaction" and to the idea of nature as (in

Emerson's resonant phrase) "the present expositor of the divine mind." If industrialization activated a desire to "recover the natural" in European intellectuals, it is not surprising that it provoked even stronger pastoral impulses in their American counterparts. The point is that the anomalous New World situation, notably the onset of the new power in a vast, rich, magnificent, still largely undeveloped and seemingly unclaimed continent, brought into sharp relief much of what was most problematic, morally and aesthetically, about the emergence of the new urban-industrial order. The character of the half-wild terrain, hence the sharpness of the contrast between the forces of society and nature, lent the ambiguous import of what was happening a sensuous clarity and intensity—a visibility—it had possessed nowhere else.[19]

Thomas Cole (1801–48) was not the most gifted American painter of his time, but he was the nation's best-known and most influential landscapist. His arrival in New York in 1825 marked the beginning of a major shift, like the one that had already begun in Europe, in the character of serious painting. It was a shift away from the earlier generation's preoccupation with historic events and personages as subject matter—the "history painting" associated in America with Copley, West, and Allston—to the native landscape. But as Barbara Novak compellingly argues, this was a less radical change than it seems, for in taking the landscape as their subject, Cole and the other members of the Hudson River school in effect transferred the aims of history painting to another idiom.[20] Their predecessors of the post-revolutionary era had wanted to endow the young republic's story with imperial grandeur and monumentality, but their depictions of historical subjects—American battle scenes and political assemblies, generals and statesmen—tended to be indistinguishable from familiar European models. Most of this work was so derivative in form, so conventional, indeed, as to be devoid of fresh, identifiably American feeling. Although born in England, Cole probably was the first painter to see the striking topography of the new nation as a possible source of what its artists had failed to get from its meager history: a truly distinctive native idiom in which to figure forth intimations of New World beauty and sublimity.

Novak's point is that in the early nineteenth century, when many Americans had begun to look upon the landscape as a "repository of national pride," Cole saw that it also might provide the nation's artists with "an effective substitute for a missing national tradition." He was thinking about painting in the pastoral manner by such accomplished European landscapists as Poussin, Claude, and Salvator Rosa. But the changing American terrain proved to be a substitute for the nation's history in a more subtle and important sense than Cole had realized. What he and other landscapists inadvertently discovered in the next few decades was a new, distinctively nineteenth-century historical iconography. Whereas the traditional images invoked by the earlier generation of "history painters" had about them an essentially static, ineradicable *pastness*, images of the landscape and its increasingly rapid transformation by the hand of man directed attention to the future. In place of trite military and political subjects, this new iconography represented what was not even thought of as "history," but would come to be recognized as a continuing process of social change that was likely to be carried forward more or less indefinitely. Whether it counted as history or not, the imagery of industrialism, especially when set against the natural landscape, was widely taken as a portent of things to come. It enabled an artist or writer to convey that rapidly growing awareness, so memorably set forth by Carlyle, of life transformed by irresistible and impersonal forces—of a future infused with the emergent spirit of the times. A sense of historical fatality, paradoxically enough, clung to these images of new and unprecedented human power. "We have constructed a fate, an *Atropos*, that never turns aside," wrote Henry Thoreau of the railroad whose whistle penetrated the woods at Walden Pond. "(Let that be the name of your engine.)"[21]

The accelerating transformation of the national terrain soon brought Cole and his fellow landscapists up against a well-nigh insuperable problem. As the art of landscape painting had developed since the seventeenth century, its tacit aim had been to disclose the inherent beauty, order, and harmony of the natural environment. It was closely akin to the pastoral mode in literature, whose central motive was a quasi-religious ideal of harmony, or reconciliation, between man and nature. As Kenneth Clark observes, the inception of landscape painting as a distinct form was closely bound up with the image of an enchanted, paradisiacal garden or, as he says, "a flowery meadow cut off from the world of fierce accidents, where love . . . could find fulfillment." (Clark also notes that "paradise" is the Persian for "a walled enclosure.") But if artists took to painting the visible surface of nature, and if society was inflicting terrible wounds upon that surface, how then would landscapists define their aims?[22]

Since the beginning of settlement in North America, Europeans had treated the land as anything but a sacred place. They behaved as if its resources were undamageable and inexhaustible, and indeed one scholar who has made a comparative study of the treatment accorded the environment by various nations describes the record of Americans as "the most violent and the most destructive in the long history of civilization." As early as 1864 the Vermont ecologist George Perkins Marsh had warned that unless Americans changed their ways, the land would be reduced to "such a condition of impoverished productiveness, of shattered surface, of climatic excess, as to threaten the depravation, barbarism, and perhaps even extinction of the species."[23] It is not surprising, under the circumstances, that accelerating economic development was making the fundamental aim of the landscapists problematic—a fact that was borne in on Cole, it seems, just as he reached the conclusion of his disturbed and disturbing 1836 "Essay on American Scenery."

Although most of the essay is devoted to praise of the rare beauty, picturesqueness, and sublimity of American "scenery," Cole acknowledges early on that this distinctive aesthetic resource is insufficiently appreciated by a people in the sway of a "meager utilitarianism." Cole's praise of America's natural beauty is offset by disquieting thoughts about "what is sometimes called improvement." The inexorable march of improvement is disturbing, he explains, because it "makes us fear that the bright and tender flowers of the imagination shall be crushed beneath its iron tramp." Having set up this received set of oppositions—the beautiful and the practical, imagination and reality, art and progress—Cole concludes with what can only be described as a distraught and vain effort at resolution. It begins on a note of "sorrow":

. . . sorrow that the beauty of such landscapes are [sic] quickly passing away—the ravages of the axe are daily increasing—the most noble scenes are made desolate, and oftentimes with a wantonness and barbarism scarcely credible in a civilized nation. The wayside is becoming shadeless, and another generation will behold spots, now rife with beauty, desecrated by what is called improvement; which, as yet, generally destroys Nature's beauty without substituting that of Art.

Cole follows this unequivocal, reasonably coherent statement with a spasmodic sequence of brief, seemingly inconsecutive thoughts. First, he apologizes "this is a regret rather than a complaint"; and then, in quick succession, he follows this virtual retraction of his gloomy assessment with a gesture of resigned acquiescence ("such is the road that society has to travel"); a rueful guess ("it may lead to a refinement in the end"); and then a wistful hope, which he admits is "feebly urged," that with the triumph of improvement "the importance of cultivating a taste for scenery will not be forgotten." And yet, after having indulged in all this rhetorical twisting and turning, he finally manages to produce a firm if disconsolate moral exhortation: "Nature has spread for us a rich and delightful banquet. Shall we turn from it? We are still in Eden; the wall that shuts us out of the garden is our own ignorance and folly."[24]

In spite of his unease and his circumlocutions, Cole comes close to defining the dilemma "progress" presented to the artists of his time. Granted that the aim of the Hudson River painters, as of the Luminists a few years later, was to celebrate the beauty and sublimity of the native landscape, it was not merely for the sake of art or beauty; the painterly product was not an end in itself, but rather was a way of paying tribute to the national terrain as the outward manifestation of Nature. Like their literary contemporaries, the transcendentalists, they saw the physical entity "nature" (or what is now called, partly in an effort to rid the idea of nature of its ancient metaphysical trappings, "the environment") as "Nature," a source of ultimate meaning and value. Nature, as Emerson explained, was for the nineteenth century what the biblical prophets had been for their times, the "present expositor of the divine mind," and the unspoiled terrain of the United States, the advanced

society where Nature was most accessible, held forth a unique if evanescent possibility: the hope, not so easily credited in retrospect, of achieving harmony between the natural and the social orders.[25]

But what if, as Cole admitted, the iron tramp of improvement already was making "desolate" those "noble scenes"? What if the American people, for all the piety with which they so often invoked the beauty of the national terrain, were in fact engaged in its heedless destruction? How then should Cole and his fellow artists conceive of their work? Should they continue to paint in the spirit of Poussin and Claude, taking as their subject an ideal landscape of order and harmony? Was it possible for them to sustain their commitment to that pastoral ideal and still depict the most striking particularities of the visible *American* landscape? Latent in Cole's 1836 essay, these questions point to underlying connections between the work of American landscapists, to the problems and principles by which it was informed, and to the society's impending transformation. Hence the many paintings and photographs of the railroad, and of the railroad-in-the-landscape, may be said to incorporate "symbolical values" symptomatic, as Panofsky put it, of "something else"—a theme or themes, or a set of concerns, of which the

artists themselves often were not fully aware. To discover and interpret those symbolical values, and the "something else" they represent, it is necessary to approach the compositional and iconographical features of these paintings as the object of "iconology," a version of cultural history in the broadest sense.

Let us suppose that we recruit a disinterested witness, someone who knows nothing about the United States and its cultural history—an intelligent art critic, say, from another planet. We invite her to attend one of the many exhibits of mid-nineteenth-century landscape painting and photography mounted by American museums in recent years. (An iconological analysis of this body of work, incidentally, may cast some light on the remarkable vogue it currently enjoys—remarkable if only because of the low opinion of its aesthetic merit that prevailed in art criticism until recently.) Afterward, we carefully question our visitor. What does she infer from these representative landscapes about the character of relations between society and nature in the United States at the time? What awareness do they give her of the changes being wrought upon the environment?

The interplanetary critic, who assumes that art "reflects" the prevailing beliefs of the time and place, describes a society that cherishes the natural environment. Unfamiliar with the actual terrain, she

196

is chiefly struck by the luminosity and beauty of these painted landscapes, and the reverential feeling for nature they evoke. As for the "scarcely credible" barbarity with which Cole saw the American countryside being devastated, our witness has almost nothing to say. She has picked up a clue here and there—a few tree stumps and ugly clearings in the woods—but no sense of widespread devastation. We then tell her about what was actually happening, using Cole's language (but not identifying the author as one of the artists whose work she has seen), and ask her to comment on this blatant discrepancy between art and social reality. Perhaps, she suggests, most of the artists lived in a secluded place or were shielded, somehow, from what was going on; whatever the explanation, she concludes, most of these landscapists must have been oblivious to the situation described by Cole. When, finally, we point out the presence in several paintings of the railroad and explain that it was generally recognized as the very embodiment of change or improvement, she exclaims, in the very words used recently by Barbara Novak: "Yet how remote and insignificant are the trains that discreetly populate the American landscape paintings of the mid-century!"[26]

But our observer from outer space is of course wrong about the obliviousness of the American landscapists to what their countrymen were doing. Years before Cole's essay appeared many articulate and influential Americans had begun to express concern about the damage being inflicted upon the native environment. As early as 1823 James Fenimore Cooper had made the reckless leveling of the virgin forest and the slaughter of wildlife a major theme of *The Pioneers*, the first of the enormously popular Leatherstocking Tales. By the 1830s lamentation for the forests, mountains, rivers, and plains—even for the noble if benighted "red man"—had become a pervasive though minor theme of popular culture; practitioners of all the popular arts took it up, and though it often comes through the full-throated celebration of progress as a merely touching, exculpatory undertone of pathos, it made what we now call the "environmental issue" difficult to ignore. It would be astonishing, then, if in that milieu any artist, let alone a landscapist, could have remained wholly oblivious to the "wantonness" and "barbarism" with which Americans, in Cole's view, were ravishing the land. Whatever the explanation for the artists' failure to register these harsh facts in their work, ignorance can hardly have been one of the more important reasons. How then shall we understand their viewpoint?

What requires emphasis, to begin with, is how nearly impossible it would have been for Cole, or any other mid-nineteenth-century American artist, to have forthrightly depicted such a panorama of heedless destruction. To have done so would have been to set oneself directly against the overwhelming current of optimistic nation-building, expansionism, and progress. Like everyone else, the artists themselves were vulnerable to the enticing idea of history as continuous amelioration. Quite apart from the compelling influence of the progressive ideology, however, it was the landscapists' own presuppositions, moral and aesthetic, that made it almost unthinkable for them to have taken the devastation of the land as their subject. That would have subverted much of what they—what the dominant culture—took for granted about the intimate relations between their work and the meaning, value, and purpose inherent in the natural world. If visible nature is an "expositor" of the divine mind, then landscape painting is a quasi-religious exercise. (To a considerable degree, no doubt, the preeminence of this transcendental aesthetic was itself a reaction to the accelerating transformation of the face of nature.) Images of the native landscape not only carried a heavy burden of popular religious and nationalistic piety, but, according to the reigning aesthetic doctrine, were also a primary embodiment of the universal order and unity presumed to inhere in Nature. The artists' mission, therefore, was to reveal the presence of a universal and timeless order behind, and made manifest

197

by, the beauty and sublimity of the landscape. It is not surprising, given the conception of their vocation held by Cole and most of his fellow landscapists, that it rarely occurred to them to make the assault on the land their manifest subject.

At first sight it may be tempting to think of the characteristic work of these artists as palpably avoiding, perhaps even denying, social reality. But in fact their reactions were not that simple. Thus Cole himself, having been brought to the verge of despair by the desecration of the landscape, hit upon at least one indirect and, from his standpoint, artistically unobjectionable way to render his response. In some of his more popular work, notably the famous *Course of Empire* series of 1836 (the year he published the essay on American scenery), he resorted to allegory to express his foreboding and, at the same time, to dissociate those feelings from the actual situation that had provoked them. Each of the five paintings represents a stage of the ostensibly universal cycle followed in the rise and fall of empires. The course of empire, as Cole paints it, is fated to be downward (its idyllic or pastoral stage, executed in an undisguisedly reverent Claudian idiom, is only the second stage), but though the consummation of empire (stage three) leads to a final state of desolation not unlike the situation presaged in his essay by the iron tramp of nineteenth-century progress, he leaves all possible contemporary applications to the viewers' imagination. The monumental, neoclassic ruins in the final painting of the series reassuringly belong to some other, presumably ancient, time and place. Although *The Course of Empire* is charged with Cole's displaced social despair, it accords with his conviction that in art truth is conveyed by imitations of ideal, not real, forms.

Allegory was not the only way American painters responded to the "iron tramp" of improvement. Another way, endorsed by Emerson, might be called the style of pastoral accommodation. In his linked essays "Art" and "The Poet" (1841 and 1844), Emerson propounded an idealist philosopher's program for coping with the changes so alarming to Cole. In keeping with his transcendentalist philosophy, Emerson believed that the ability of artists to resolve conflicts of value and meaning in their work could help society resolve the same, or analogous, conflicts in reality. To his injunction that artists employ symbols (like the railroad) in use in their own day and nation, Emerson therefore would add this: employ them in a manner calculated to help overcome any destructive consequences they might have, whether in fact or in mind, including of course any sense of danger, anxiety, or dislocation they might arouse.

For, as it is dislocation and detachment from the life of God that makes things ugly, the poet, who reattaches things to nature and the Whole—reattaching even artificial things, and violations of nature, to nature, by a deeper insight—disposes very easily of the most disagreeable facts. Readers of poetry see the factory-village and the railway, and fancy that the poetry of the landscape is broken up by these; for these works of art are not yet consecrated in their reading; but the poet sees them fall within the great Order not less than the bee-hive, or the spider's geometrical web. Nature adopts them very fast into her vital circles, and the gliding train of cars she loves like her own.[27]

Emerson calls upon artists to depict typical scenes of the era, such as the new factories, steamboats, or railroads in the landscape, but to depict them from an ideal viewpoint, affirmatively, as a farsighted, aspiring citizen of a young republic would want and expect them to look. To assimilate the new railroad to the purposes of landscape painting, he assumes, is to achieve in art a virtual resolution of the problems or conflicts to which the new power gives rise in reality. The aesthetic order represented by such a landscape of reconciliation can show others the way—if only as a kind of optimistic forecast, a testimonial to the possible—to achieve the equivalent order in society. The strongest and most hopeful Emersonian position (he did not always hold it) is that a genuine work of art is a model, or imitation, of the way to create social order. The Emersonian artist's aim, in other words, is to exemplify the assimilability—the naturalness and benignity—of the new machine power and, by implication, of the oncoming social order. His is a virtual achievement of what society must achieve in fact.

With Emerson's program in view, it is easier to make sense of a curious group of paintings that seem to belie my initial claim that the railroad-in-the-landscape was an imposing, universally recognized, and all but impossible to ignore thematic image, or symbol, of social transformation. The group includes Cole's *River in the Catskills* (figure 2), Doughty's *A View of Swampscott, Massachusetts* (figure 3), John Frederick Kensett's *Hudson River Scene* (1857) and George Inness's *Delaware Water Gap* (figure 61). The railroad is present in each of these paintings, but so far from calling attention to itself, to its portentous presence and power or to the contrast it makes with the preindustrial setting, it is barely visible. It is as if these artists were bent on making the new machine blend as inconspicuously as possible into its natural surroundings. In *River in the Catskills* Cole admits as much, for he makes the railroad a central but a distant, gentle, small, unobtrusive feature of what had

been one of his favorite scenes before the projected building of the railroad.[28] These are precisely the sort of paintings, of course, that misled our interplanetary critic, or led Barbara Novak to remark on the curious remoteness and insignificance of the railroad in the work of mid-century American landscapists. And as she suggests, they manifest the artists' desire to preserve "the transcendental whole" (a synonym for Emerson's "Nature") by harmoniously painting the railroad into it. What requires further emphasis, though, is the extent to which the same paintings testify to the importance of the new power. An iconological analysis suggests that their "symbolical" significance may differ from what the artists consciously intended to express.

In a painting like Doughty's *A View of Swampscott, Massachusetts*, for example, the locomotive is so nearly lost to view among the trees that its presence, were it not for the central place it occupies in the composition, might be considered of negligible significance. But its centrality indicates that it is of paramount importance. The more one looks at the painting, the more evident are the subtle means by which Doughty draws our attention to the well-nigh hidden machine. The space among the trees where he locates the train is at the apex of flat, inverted triangle formed by the line of the horizon and the tree lines, and the focal point of these converging

lines is accentuated by the brighter light that Doughty casts on the diminutive locomotive, thereby setting it off from the dark foliage through which it is moving. Although the engine is at the center of the design, it is so harmoniously blended into the ostensibly seamless fabric of nature that it might be a rabbit or deer scurrying across the open space. Doughty could hardly have done much more to exemplify Emerson's conviction that "the poetry of the landscape" need not be broken up by the instruments of technological progress. Yet the central place he gives the railroad in the composition, when considered in the larger cultural context, suggests that he may well have shared Cole's anxiety.

Other painters of the landscape of reconciliation used different compositional devices for achieving a sense of harmony between the new technology and nature. In *Delaware Water Gap*, Inness uses the elongated *S* curve of the river to evoke an initial sense of meandering ease, of water quietly flowing through a land without evident conflict, disorder, or anxiety. The river dominates the painting, filling its lower left quadrant. The water is so nearly still as to reflect clear images of the trees along the bank, and as we follow the curve back into the distance it intersects with the gap in the hills that lends the region its name. Then, too, the pastoral feeling evoked by the

199

meandering river is intensified by the answering curve of the darker wooded slope that fills the right center of the canvas. And there, also following the curve, close to the tree line, is the minuscule engine and its train of cars, unobtrusive, unthreatening, and, at this great distance, almost certainly inaudible. The ideal figured forth by the tranquil atmosphere and by the composition, with its topographical congruities, has manifest transcendental overtones: it implies the existence of an underlying correspondence between the order of nature and the man-made order of the arts, both fine and practical. As Inness would have us see the new technology, it is perfectly attuned to the basic flow and rhythm of the natural world.

But it would be wrong to imply that landscapists were able to evoke this pastoral feeling only by making the railroad inconspicuous. In Jasper Cropsey's *Starrucca Viaduct* (figure 10), the smoking locomotive and its cars are in plain view at the center of the painting, and the gaze of the highly accentuated figure in the foreground guides our eyes directly to the railroad. It is unquestionably the focal point, yet Cropsey manages to bathe it in an atmosphere no less serene, orderly, and harmonious than that created by Doughty or Inness. To do so he adapts some of the stock devices of the pastoral mode in landscape painting: the placid reflecting surface of the river; the conformity of the curving railroad right-of-way with the matching curves of the river and the hills; the location of the machine at a great distance, its small scale making it seem, for all its prominence, toylike and wholly in accord with the sublime, panoramic landscape that surrounds it. The most novel feature here is the handsome masonry viaduct with its preindustrial, archaic air, like the Roman viaducts of southern France; this railroad, far from portending a sudden, disruptive, revolutionary change, seems only to mark the most recent phase in a long, continuous history of innovation stretching back to remote antiquity. Like the paintings in which the railroad's presence is deliberately played down, *Starrucca Viaduct* reinforces the Emersonian faith, or hope, that the new power falls "within the great Order no less than the bee-hive or the spider's geometrical web."

These are landscapes of reconciliation in the sense, finally, that they divest the new machine power of its chief attributes as a stock emblem of progress. So far from representing a novel kind of power—the noisy, disruptive, fire-breathing, smoke-belching iron horse of popular journalistic illustration—artists like Cropsey, Inness, and Doughty depict a neutralized technology, one that is easily harmonized with the natural environment. A telling clue to the impulse behind these paintings is the frequent presence in them of a herdsman. In the Doughty, for example, he and his animals appear in a small clearing in the lower left foreground. In some cases this pastoral figure is not accompanied by animals, but often, as in Inness's *The Lackawanna Valley* (figure 58), he can be identified by his staff or crook and, perhaps even more important, by the relaxed, ruminative air with which he contemplates the appearance of the new machine power in the American landscape. Like the shepherd in literary pastoral, he performs a tutelary role in these paintings, gently suggesting an appropriate response to the scene. This is, in short, painting in the pastoral mode, conceived in obedience to the desire, in the face of the growing complexity and power of organized, industrializing society, to recover and reaffirm the ideal of a simpler, more harmonious way of life "closer" to nature.

So far we have considered two styles of landscape depiction that enabled nineteenth-century artists to express their feelings (or some part of them) about the accelerating transformation of life in their time. One is the landscape of allegory, the other the idyllic landscape of reconciliation. The latter evokes a sense of almost perfect harmony like that which had long been the aim and the hallmark of a conflict-free, or sentimental, pastoralism. Both are ideal landscapes, and the conventions on which they rest exclude any direct pictorial reference to the conflicts, tensions, or destructiveness that attended the appearance of the new machine power.

But mid-century artists did find a way to represent some of the harsher, less easily harmonized features of the national scene without betraying their commitment to the ideal landscape. This style, a more complex version of pastoral, is exemplified by Asher Durand's *Progress* (figure 43) and Inness's *The Lackawanna Valley.* Most of the iconographical elements characteristic of work done in this style are the same as those we find in the landscapes of pastoral accommodation. Except for the human figure, which is of secondary interest, these constituent images belong either to the realm of external nature (sky, trees, meadows, animals, mountains, rivers, etc.), or to the realm of art (locomotives, cars, tracks, bridges, viaducts, houses, roads, smoke, etc.). But complex pastoralism, as a landscape style, is distinguished by the presence of a quite different and less easily assimilated set of images: patches of unruly, wild vegetation; the jagged stumps of recently felled trees; unsightly clearings in the forest; the dark smoke of locomotives filling the sky, or the glare of their headlights penetrating the dark; fleeing, frightened animals; Native Americans, sometimes in defiant or menacing postures, sometimes in melancholy retreat before the forward march of white European civilization. It is one thing to discover these discordant images, however, and quite another to know what their presence signifies.

Consider, for example, Durand's *Progress*, and in particular the three Native Americans in the left foreground who are contemplating the industrious society in the valley below them. Their postures, their semi-nudity, the wild, unimproved bit of nature they occupy—all of these convey a strong impression of their powerlessness. It is as if they are about to be backed right out of the picture by the oncoming march of progress. But what are we to make of their impending expulsion? In itself the image might be taken either as a justification or—it is less likely but by no means inconceivable—a condemnation of what was meant, in the dominant culture, by "progress." Durand's treatment of the industrializing society in the right foreground (with its smoking locomotive and train) makes it probable that he intends his title as an unironic affirmation of material improvement and the progressive world view. But that still does not tell us what the presence of the Native Americans signifies, or how their fate is connected to the painting's larger affirmation.

To fully elucidate the significance of the discordant elements in works of complex pastoralism, it is not enough merely to identify and categorize images. It is necessary to look beyond the works themselves to the part played by those images in the enveloping culture; or, as Panofsky asserts in the statement quoted at the outset, it is necessary to employ an iconological rather than a merely iconographical method. The distinction is between an analytic and a synthetic procedure or, as he describes it, between a primary focus on the content of art as against a far-reaching concern with the interplay between art and the larger culture.[29] To answer the questions raised by Durand's *Progress*, in other words, it is necessary to clarify both the relationship, as it has been conceived by Americans up to that time, between wild and cultivated nature, and how that dual conception of nature was incorporated in the prevailing response to the great social transformation of the nineteenth century.

When colonization began, the dominant images of the New World landscape were as radically divergent as a hellish, savage, hideous wilderness and a lovely, benign, Edenic (or Arcadian) garden. Each image comported with a quite different conception of the relations between humankind and nature. To emphasize the wild, untrammeled, threatening aspect of the natural (as the New England Puritans had done) was to justify a policy of domination, conquest, and (as it came to be known in the nineteenth century) "progress"; to emphasize the nurturing, orderly, beautiful aspects of the natural (as certain "romantic" intellectuals, writers and artists did) was to lend credence to the ancient pastoral vision of harmony with nature. By the time the railroad appeared on the scene, however, a way had been found to reconcile those opposed ideals and to incorporate them in a vision of history that was particularly compelling to mid-century America.

The special conditions of life in North America helped disguise the latent contradiction between the progressive and pastoral ideals. What evidently made the most difference was the raw state of the seemingly boundless, seemingly unclaimed continental terrain. This meant Americans might enact the ambitious expansionary project of democratic capitalism, driving the native population from the land, leveling the forests, building roads and factories and cities in the wilderness, and yet, at the same time, they might with some plausibility see themselves as engaged in the recovery of a simpler, more natural and harmonious way of life, at least as compared with the prototypical industrializing societies of western Europe. In other words, the aggressive conquest of wild nature, or "progress," was

widely regarded by Americans as a means to an ideal end: the achievement, in a new kind of society, of a *via media* between the oppressive over-civilization of the Old World and the menacing wildness of the Western frontier. The visual emblem of this Jeffersonian ideal was neither the city nor the wilderness, but a partly developed or "middle landscape" blending the best of art with the best of nature.

Seen from this historical perspective, the significance of the discordant imagery in landscapes like Durand's *Progress* is clear. The bemused helplessness of the Native Americans, which might otherwise give pause to sentimental pastoralists or other susceptible viewers, is explained and, as it were, condoned by the setting in which Durand places them. The unpleasing disarray that surrounds the red men—the unsightly rocks and the ugly, jagged, dead trees—is a vestige of that untrammeled, menacing, wild nature whose conquest had long been seen as a prerequisite for the very existence of American society. By setting this rude, slack, unimproved state of nature against a highlighted vision of the industrious, ordered, advancing society that is about to replace it, Durand leaves little doubt about how we are to see the plight of the pathetic "savages." (To make the point even more emphatic, Durand locates this social *via media* midway between the wilderness and a blaze of supernal light—locus of an even more

perfect state of being?—that suffuses the background.) The Native Americans belong to the doomed hideous wilderness. If their suffering evokes feelings of guilt in Durand's audience, they may be assuaged by contemplating the other side of the canvas; the bustling scene reminds us of the benefits industrial progress holds in store for a people so busily engaged in building a society of the middle landscape.

Of the well-known mid-century American landscape paintings, Durand's *Progress* probably is the most successful in reconciling the pastoral ideal with a sense, however rationalized, of the discord, pain, and ugliness coincident with the iron march of improvement. In spite of the facile, not to say banal, character of Durand's unambiguous solution, and if only because most of his fellow artists succeeded in ignoring the problem, the painting is something of an achievement. Except for George Inness, most of the landscapists who dared to acknowledge the unpretty face of progress either had never been drawn to or had simply abandoned the pastoral aesthetic and its ideal landscape of reconciliation. I am thinking of works like Thomas Rossiter's *Opening of the Wilderness* (figure 7), Andrew Melrose's *Westward the Star of Empire Takes Its Way* (figure 16), or Theodore Kaufmann's *Railway Train Attacked by Indians* (figure 17).

Each of these paintings of the railroad-in-the-landscape takes account of some unhappy implication of the subject. The Rossiter, with its stark foreground of rocks, half-bare trees, and sharp stumps, could hardly be less Arcadian in spirit. The little frontier settlement, crowded between the hillside and the river, is wholly dominated by the roundhouse and the four smoking locomotives, and indeed it looks less like a rural village than a military outpost on the eve of battle. In the Melrose and the Kaufmann, the battle has been joined, and the manifest imbalance of the contending forces evokes that familiar sense of the pathos attendant upon progress: the frightened deer scattering in the glare of the train's headlight or the Indians' pitiful gesture of resistance to the oncoming train. All three of these landscapes in effect literalize the popular rhetoric of the era, depicting the railroad as a weapon in a cruel but inescapable "conquest of nature."

According to a standard version of art history, the abandonment of the pastoral aesthetic ideal by nineteenth-century American landscapists is an aspect of the transition from "romanticism" to "realism." The trouble with such a simple reductionist formula, whatever its ultimate validity, is that it may well cause us to miss, or to slight, what happened in the interval: the discovery, by some artists, of the rich

expressive possibilities inherent in the effort to adapt established aesthetic doctrines, forms, and conventions to the new social facts. In American writing of the period, we have the example of Hawthorne and Melville, whose adaptation—a virtual inversion—of the pastoral romance to the new materials proved to be much more interesting and successful, finally, than most writing done under the banners of the new realism or naturalism. In American painting the conspicuous example, deservedly considered the masterwork of this sub-genre, is George Inness's *The Lackawanna Valley.*

Judging by the rest of Inness's landscapes, especially the other versions of the railroad-in-the-landscape he painted after *The Lackawanna Valley*, it is clear that he was by inclination a conventional pastoralist. When left to his own devices, as in the two *Delaware Water Gap* paintings of 1857 (figures 61, 62), he was inclined to paint relatively bland variants of the landscape of reconciliation. In 1854, however, he had accepted a commission from the president of the Delaware, Lackawanna, and Western Railroad to paint the scene of the company's operations, the railroad yards in Scranton, Pennsylvania. It was a large, bare, treeless site whose conspicuous features were a roundhouse, several machine shops, smoking locomotives, and at least two lines of track leading off into the countryside.

How was a landscapist to treat such unpromising material? Inness's problem was not only to represent those particulars in a landscape painting, but to represent them accurately enough to satisfy a patron who, after all, was buying verisimilitude. The problem was to adapt the pastoral mode to the rendering of those massive industrial artifacts. The pastoral mode is not inherently inflexible, and many interesting, enduring expressions of the pastoral impulse in art do succeed (in contrast to some of the sentimental pastoral landscapes we have considered) in conveying a lively sense of the conflict between the complex and the simple, the world of art and of nature. *The Lackawanna Valley* is such a complex work; the conflict it sets forth is so pervasive, so deeply felt, and the contending forces so evenly matched, that viewers have found themselves torn between two compelling but antithetical ways of interpreting the painting.

One way is to see *The Lackawanna Valley* as a fulfillment of Emerson's prescription for achieving harmony between the new technology and nature. On this view, the forces of nature dominate the painting, and the railroad contributes to the sense of underlying order and unity. Moving toward us from the roundhouse, the conspicuous train in the foreground (three other locomotives are barely discernible in the distant yard) threads its way into the surrounding countryside. The hills in the background and the trees in the middle distance gently envelop the bare industrial terrain adjacent to the roundhouse; no sharp lines set off the man-made from the natural world. Nor does the smoke seem an ugly pollutant. The cottony puffs that rise from the engines and the shops seem to duplicate the puff that rises from behind the church—an ingenious touch! Instead of separating the terrain into sharp, rectilinear segments, as railroad tracks often do, the right-of-way curves gracefully across the center of the canvas, and there it divides in two, forming the delicately touching ovals that dominate the middle plane. It is noteworthy, also, that the animals in the pasture continue to graze or rest peacefully as the engine approaches. But finally it is the solitary shepherd-like figure reclining beneath the impressive tree in the left foreground (the strongest vertical element in the painting) who most directly conveys the calm, relaxed, contemplative frame of mind that we ordinarily expect a pastoral landscape to evoke.

Seen from a somewhat different perspective, however, these new industrial artifacts have an unremittingly discordant effect, and *The Lackawanna Valley* becomes, as Barbara Novak puts it, "a shocking picture." We see at once that this is not one of those dreamy Hudson River style landscapes that succeed in harmoniously accommodating a single innocuous machine within a preindustrial setting. As all the charmless buildings and engines attest, the subject of *The Lackawanna Valley* is not the appearance in the landscape of a mere "machine," but rather the presence (or emergence) of what now would be called a "technological system." To be sure, neither Inness nor his audience could have said that the railroad was the prototype of a whole new mode of complex economic organization and, indeed, a new urban industrial way of life. But the point is that Inness's faithful treatment of visual detail anticipates that retrospective formulation: the picture is the first to convey a sense of the new machine technology as a determinant and a visible emblem of a new kind of large-scale, expansionary, corporate enterprise. The very size of the space already cleared for the railroad's operations, the field of telltale stumps reaching toward us in the foreground, the smoky haze that hovers over the yard and reaches back toward the hills, the two lines of track that seem to envelope (as much as they are enveloped by) a large part of the terrain—all of these, taken together and reinforced by the affecting contrast between the surrounding green vegetation and the arid yellow-brownishness of the cleared industrial space, convey a sense of enormous power and energy emanating from the squat, fortress-like roundhouse (as if, again, from a base of military operations) into the vulnerable countryside. It is a "shocking picture," in Barbara Novak's judgment, because "the pastoral idea has been so rudely treated."[30]

The Lackawanna Valley transcends the limits of the conventionally bland landscape of reconciliation. It catches the poignant dissonance, a distinctive note of foreboding intermixed with the idyllic, that characterizes many of the most effective expressions of complex pastoralism.[31] It enables us to grasp, as no other American railroad-in-the-landscape painting does, that underlying "something else" of which the artists may not be fully aware, but of which the paintings may be said to be (Panofsky's word) "symptomatic." In this case the "something else" proves to be nothing less than the deep moral ambiguity of material progress, the ineluctable mix of the constructive and destructive (what some would call good and evil) at its core, hence the unresolvable ambivalence evoked by the bipolar image of the new machine power in the landscape. By figuring forth the hauntingly equivocal meaning of that image of technological, masculine, rational power, Inness brought the expression of American pastoralism in landscape painting close to perfection while, at the same time, he transcended the limits of its conventions.

It is ironic that Inness did so perforce, which is to say because the terms of his commission in effect compelled him to attend, more scrupulously than most artists working in the mode, to the actual details of his obdurate subject. In his effort to overcome the seeming incompatibility between form and content, he arrived at a uniquely forthright, unillusioned result; in *The Lackawanna Valley* the ideal of a pastoral America is still present, but in the face of the industrial reality he was obliged to recognize, Inness invests the ideal with an appropriately fragile, almost evanescent, quality. On this view, *The Lackawanna Valley* is the counterpart in painting to such works of the classic American writers as *Walden*, *Moby-Dick*, and *Huckleberry Finn*, all of which achieve comparable effects by comparable means.

Inness's *Lackawanna Valley* is the only American version of the railroad-in-the-landscape that bears comparison with J. M. W. Turner's unsurpassable *Rain, Steam and Speed* (1844). In this astonishing picture, the Great Western locomotive comes out of the mist heading toward us across a bridge. The indistinctness of the surrounding details is a function of the suddenness, the speed, with which the train approaches. At first sight the two bridges (the one that the train is on and another in the distance), and perhaps a small boat on the river below, are the only other identifiable objects. Here Turner has inverted the landscape of pastoral accommodation, for the new machine dominates the scene, and it is the other (nonindustrial) details—the festive crowd waving on one side, the plough on the other, and the hare fleeing from the oncoming train—that are almost imperceptible. Whereas Inness was able to hold in quiet suspension the received dualities of nature and art, the simple and the complex, Turner's bold expressionistic technique enabled him to pass beyond them and to set forth an apocalyptic commingling of the powers represented by the countryside and the railroad in a sunlit swirl of rain, metal, fire, and steam.[32]

In retrospect, the previsionary character of these paintings by Turner and Inness is obvious. Indeed, as John Gage has shown, the Turner was to influence Pissarro's and Monet's treatment of the railroad, and by the early twentieth century, American painters had domesticated the evocative post-impressionist way of blending the machine into a blurry, smoke-filled, urban-industrial landscape. Works by Bellows, Luks, Marsh, and Sloan might also be described as inversions of the railroad-in-the-landscape theme. In Bellow's *Rain on the River* (figure 33), the railroad forms a diagonal boundary between the deserted park, a protected remnant of the old landscape, and the rest of the misty, grimy, workaday harbor setting. The verticals formed by the towering columns of smoke in Luks's *Roundhouses at Highbridge* (figure 34) completely dominate the picture, a formal embodiment of the industrial society's imperial domination of nature. In his 1930 watercolor *Chicago* or his etching of the same year, *Erie Railroad and Factories*, Marsh depicts the structures we are used to seeing out of train windows in that distinctive environment, the corridor formed by the railroad's right-of-way.[33] In Sloan's *The City from Greenwich Village* (figure 35), where the elevated train winds through a sparkling, brilliantly lit New York night scene, the city has become an F. Scott Fitzgerald fairyland, a magical embodiment of the promise once held forth by the fresh, green breast of the new world.

None of these cityscapes gives us reason to doubt that the social order they represent, an order in large measure shaped by industrial power, is alien to the idealized "nature" of mid-nineteenth-century painting. They exhibit few vestiges of the natural landscape, yet it seems evident that they derive a good deal of their power from its conspicuous absence.

(But it also should be said, incidentally, that there is no literal absence of "pastoral" scenery in the United States today, and that the decision to paint a "city-" as against a "land-" scape is an interpretative judgment.) In looking at these paintings, it often seems that we are as deeply affected by what is missing— or, put differently, by our memory of the earlier mode of landscape painting—as by the urban-industrial setting itself. Indeed, when we consider the enormous importance that nineteenth-century artists invested in the visible, preindustrial landscape as the locus of beauty, order, and meaning, it becomes evident that we need to know a lot more about the exact relationship between the transformation of the visible world (and its consequent loss of exemplary value for artists) and the emergence of various abstract modernist styles.

And when, finally, we turn to the unillusioned treatment of the railroad-in-the-landscape by photographers like A. J. Russell, Walker Evans, or Alfred Stieglitz, it becomes obvious that photography played an important part in the transition. Nowadays, to be sure, it is fashionable to dismiss the easy identification of photography with "realism" in the arts or a "realistic" view of the world, but in this context that too facile equation does gain a certain brute plausibility.

With the lovely paintings by our mid-century landscapists in view, especially the primitives with their cute, toylike trains and Disneyesque iron horses, Russell's uncompromising camera work is like a "worst case" of the harsh, unadorned truth. There is no trace of pastoralism in his railroad pictures. In *Granite Cañon, Black Hills* (1869) we see no vegetation whatever. The right-of-way is an arid, rocky, rubble-strewn waste where nothing could possibly grow, and the camera's openness to sharp detail banishes all notions of the railroad as an exemplar of linear order and beauty. The line of the track wavers, the sleepers are uneven, rude, unshapely, and all in all the scene is one of gray, oppressive, deadly ugliness. As Susan Danly shows us, Russell's photographs of the building of the transcontinental railroad evoke the endless blasting, the backbreaking labor, the dirt and noise and discomfort and danger suffered by the workers. Nor is there any vestige of pastoral feeling in Walker Evans's picture of the depot and its surroundings in *Edwards, Mississippi* (figure 37). Here again the camera picks up telling details (the litter around the tracks), as well as the dreary plainness of the nearby station houses and, above all, the melancholy emptiness (as in Edward Hopper's forlorn railway hotels and stations) that envelopes the small-town depot in the depths of the Great Depression. When Stieglitz called his

nightmare vision of the industrial dark age *The Hand of Man* (figure 30), the irony seems to have been directed at the Emersonian faith that the railroad would fall naturally into the quasi-divine Order of Nature.

Yet it makes no sense, as Charles Sheeler's work reminds us, to cast the railroad—or "the machine" or the abstract noun "technology"—as a villain of modern history. In both the 1939 photograph (figure 116) and the painting called *Rolling Power* (figure 109), he offers us futuristic visions of a locomotive as an embodiment of order, beauty, and purpose. There is no trace of the landscape in either. Indeed, Sheeler's photo-like mode of composition lends both the painting and the photograph on which it is based an exemplary futuristic quality, as if they were tokens (in form as well as content) of the possibilities offered by advanced technology in the service of imaginative artists. By compelling us to focus our attention on this intricate work of engineering intelligence—precise, efficient, and (in its cool way) beautiful—these Sheelers serve as a check against easy antitechnological solutions. How foolish it is, they remind us, to hold any machines or implements of power responsible for the damage people have done, or may yet do, with their help.

Notes

1

Rudolf Arnheim, *Visual Thinking* (Berkeley: University of California Press, 1969); "A Plea for Visual Thinking," *Critical Inquiry* 6 (Spring 1980): 489–497; E. H. Gombrich, *Art and Illusion* (New York: Bollingen Foundation, 1960).

2

George Rogers Taylor, *The Transportation Revolution, 1815–1860* (New York: Rinehart & Co., 1951).

3

Erwin Panofsky, "Iconography and Iconology: An Introduction to the Study of Renaissance Art," from *Studies in Iconology* (New York: Oxford University Press, 1939); reprinted in *Meaning in the Visual Arts* (New York: Doubleday Anchor, 1957), 26–54.

4

Nathaniel Hawthorne, *The House of the Seven Gables* (New York: W. W. Norton, 1967), 256.

5

Wolfgang Schivelbusch, *The Railway Journey, Trains and Travel in the Nineteenth Century* (New York: Urizen Books, 1979). The first chapter is a useful summary of the argument for the importance of the railroad and the mechanization of motive power as originally set forth by Werner Sombart.

6

Alfred Chandler, *The Visible Hand: The Managerial Revolution in American Business* (Cambridge, MA: Harvard University Press, 1977).

7

E. J. Hobsbawm, *The Age of Revolution, 1789–1848* (New York: New American Library, 1962), 46.

8

M. I. Finley, "The Year One," in *Aspects of Antiquity* (New York: Pelican Books, 1977), 185–199.

9

Thomas Dublin, *Women at Work* (New York: Columbia University Press, 1979).

10

Louis Althusser and Etienne Balibar, *Reading Capital* (New York: Pantheon Books, 1970), chapter IX.

11

Ralph Waldo Emerson, *The Complete Essays and Other Writings* (New York: The Modern Library, 1950), 306; the emphasis is mine.

12

Thomas Carlyle, *Critical and Miscellaneous Essays* (New York: Bedford, Clarke & Co., n.d.), III, 5–30; Timothy Walker, "Defense of Mechanical Philosophy," *North American Review*, 33 (July 1831): 122–136. I discuss the argument between Carlyle and Walker in *The Machine in the Garden: Technology and the Pastoral Ideal in America* (New York: Oxford University Press, 1964), 170–190.

13

J. S. Mill, "M. de Tocqueville on Democracy in America," *Edinburgh Review* (October 1840), reprinted in *Dissertations and Discussions: Political, Philosophical, and Historical* (Boston: W. V. Spenser, 1865), 2, 148.

14

"Opening of the Northern Railroad," remarks made at Grafton and Lebanon, New Hampshire, *The Writings of Daniel Webster* (Boston: Little, Brown, 1903), 4, 105–117.

15

For the rhetoric of the technological sublime, see Marx, *The Machine in the Garden*, 190–209.

16

Walt Whitman, *Leaves of Grass* (New York, W. W. Norton, 1973), 471–472.

17

Perry Miller, *The Responsibility of Mind in a Civilization of Machines* (Amherst: University of Massachusetts Press, 1979), 198.

18

Dublin, *Women at Work*; David Montgomery, *Workers' Control in America* (Cambridge: Cambridge University Press, 1979).

19

Alfred North Whitehead, *Science and the Modern World* (New York: Macmillan, 1947), 138. For the indirect resistance to industrialization on the part of entire communities, see Merritt Roe Smith, *Harpers Ferry Armory and the New Technology* (Ithaca: Cornell University Press, 1977); Anthony F. C. Wallace, *Rockdale* (New York: Alfred A. Knopf, 1978). For the disquiet aroused by the expulsion of the Native Americans, see Richard Slotkin, *Regeneration Through Violence* (Middletown: Wesleyan University Press, 1973). For the indirect moral and aesthetic expression of anxiety aroused by industrialization, see Thomas

Bender, *Toward an Urban Vision* (Lexington: University Press of Kentucky, 1975), and Lee Clark Mitchell, *Witnesses to a Vanishing America* (Princeton: Princeton University Press, 1981).

20

Barbara Novak, *Nature and Culture; American Landscape and Painting, 1825–1875* (New York: Oxford University Press, 1980), 18–33.

21

Henry David Thoreau, *Walden and Other Writings* (New York: The Modern Library, 1950), 107.

22

Kenneth Clark, *Landscape into Art* (New York: Harper & Row, 1976), 6–8.

23

Fairfield Osborn, *Our Plundered Planet* (Boston: Little, Brown, 1948); George Perkins Marsh, *Man and Nature*, ed. David Lowenthal (Cambridge, MA: Harvard University Press, 1965), 43.

24

Thomas Cole, "Essay on American Scenery," in *The American Landscape: A Critical Anthology of Prose and Poetry*, ed. John Conron (New York: Oxford University Press, 1973), 568–578.

25

Emerson, 36.

26

Novak, *Nature and Culture*, 172.

27

Emerson, 328.

28

The case is complicated, as Kenneth Maddox has shown, by the fact that the locomotive depicted in Cole's *River in the Catskills* is imaginary. The rail line through Cole's cherished Catskill oasis had been chartered in 1830, and by 1839 twenty-six miles of track had been laid, but the locomotive the company had ordered was defective, and it never functioned. The line was forced to use horses for power, and in 1842, the year before Cole included the locomotive in this painting, the line had been abandoned. One can only conjecture that Cole's motives, like his conception of the Ideal in art generally, comported with the idealistic Emersonian aesthetic described above. See Kenneth W. Maddox, "The Railroad in the Eastern Landscape: 1850–1900," in *The Railroad in the American Landscape*, ed. Susan Danly Walther (Wellesley, MA: The Wellesley College Museum, 1981), 17–33.

29

Panofsky, "Iconography and Iconology," in *Meaning in the Visual Arts*. In reprinting the introduction to his 1939 *Studies in Iconology*, Panofsky revised it and amplified the distinction between iconography and iconology. See especially p. 32.

30

Novak, *Nature and Culture*, 172; for the continuing discussion of *The Lackawanna Valley*, see Marx, *The Machine in the Garden*, 220–222; Nicolai Cikovsky Jr., "George Inness and the Hudson River School: *The Lackawanna Valley*," *American Art Journal* 2, no. 2 (Fall 1970): 52;

Maddox, "The Railroad in the Eastern Landscape" and Marx, "Introduction," both in *The Railroad in the American Landscape*.

31

Panofsky, "Et in Arcadia Ego: Poussin and the Elegiac Tradition," in *Meaning in the Visual Arts*, 295–320.

32

The apocalyptic implications of *Rain, Steam and Speed* were recognized by Théophile Gautier, who describes the painting in his *History of Romanticism* as "a real cataclysm. Flashes of lightning, wings like great fire-birds, towering columns of cloud collapsing under the thunderbolts, rain whipped into vapour by the wind. You would have said it was the setting for the end of the world. Through all this writhed the engine, like the Beast of the Apocalypse, opening its red glass eyes in the shadows, and dragging after it, in a huge tail, its vertebrae of carriages." Cited by John Gage, *Turner: Rain, Steam and Speed* (New York: The Viking Press, 1972), 33.

33

John R. Stilgoe, *Metropolitan Corridor; Railroads and the American Scene* (New Haven: Yale University Press, 1983).

Contributors

Susan Danly is Associate Curator of American Art at the Henry E. Huntington Library and Art Gallery. She is the co-author of several publications, including *The Railroad in the American Landscape: 1850–1950*, the catalogue of an exhibition she curated at the Wellesley College Museum (1981).

Leo Marx is the William R. Kenan Professor of American Cultural History in the Program in Science, Technology, and Society at Massachusetts Institute of Technology. Among his many publications in the field of American cultural history is *The Machine in the Garden: Technology and the Pastoral Ideal in America* (1964).

Kenneth W. Maddox is a Ph.D. candidate at Columbia University whose dissertation concerns the iconographic significance of the train in nineteenth-century American landscapes. He has lectured and published widely on the subject.

Nicolai Cikovsky, Jr., is Curator of American Art at the National Gallery in Washington and a former professor at the University of New Mexico. A scholar of nineteenth-century American painting, his publications include books and articles about George Inness, Sanford Robinson Gifford, William Merritt Chase, Samuel F. B. Morse, Winslow Homer, and others.

James F. O'Gorman is the Grace Slack McNeil Professor of American Art at Wellesley College. He is the author of several books on American architecture, including *H. H. Richardson: Architectural Forms for an American Society* (1987).

Dominic Ricciotti is an Associate Professor at Winona State University in Minnesota. He is the author of several articles on urban imagery in American art and culture of the twentieth century, which was the subject of his dissertation (1977) at Indiana University.

Susan Fillin-Yeh is Assistant Professor of Art at Yale University. She has published widely on twentieth-century American painting, especially on Charles Sheeler and the Machine Age, the subject of her dissertation (1981) at CUNY.

Gail Levin is a member of the faculty of Baruch College, CUNY. She was curator of the Hopper Collection at the Whitney Museum, has published a number of books and articles on his work, and has in preparation *Edward Hopper: A Catalogue Raisonné*.

Index